VISUAL QUICKSTART GUIDE

Excel 5

FOR MACINTOSH

Maria Langer

Peachpit Press

Excel 5 For Macintosh
Visual QuickStart Guide
Maria Langer

Peachpit Press
2414 Sixth Street
Berkeley, CA 94710
510/548-4393
510/548-5991 (fax)

Find us on the World Wide Web at:
http://www.peachpit.com

Peachpit Press is a division of Addison-Wesley Publishing Company.

Copyright © 1995 by Maria Langer

Editor: Jeremy Judson
Cover design: The Visual Group

Notice of Rights
All rights reserved. No part of this book may be reproduced or transmitted in any form by any means, electronic, mechanical, photocopying, recording, or otherwise, without the prior written permission of the publisher. For information on getting permission for reprints and excerpts, contact Peachpit Press.

Notice of Liability
The information in this book is distributed on an "As Is" basis, without warranty. While every precaution has been taken in the preparation of the book, neither the author nor Peachpit Press, shall have any liability to any person or entity with respect to any loss or damage caused or alleged to be caused directly or indirectly by the instructions contained in this book or by the computer software and hardware products described in it.

ISBN 0-201-88358-9

9 8 7 6 5 4 3 2 1

Printed and bound in the United States of America

Printed on recycled paper

Dedication

To my grandmother, Maria Soricelli, who continues to work harder at the age of 83 than most of the people I know.

Thanks!

To Jeremy Judson, Ted Nace, and the rest of the folks at Peachpit Press, for letting me write another book for them. (Can you believe they're actually going to let me write a third?)

To Terry Wilson and Mark Budzyn, for being such sharp-eyed (especially Terry) and nit-picky (especially Mark) editors.

To Paul Yager (wherever you are), for getting me started with Excel when I was a mere Lotus jockey.

To Microsoft Corporation, for continuing to refine and expand Excel.

To Mike, for understanding.

TABLE OF CONTENTS

Chapter 1: **The Excel Workplace**
Introduction..1
The Excel Screen...2
Key to the Excel Screen 2
To use the mouse..4
About Menus..4
To use a menu 5
To use shortcut menus 5
To use a shortcut key 6
To use toolbar buttons...6
About Toolbars 7
About Dialog Boxes..8
To use a dialog box...8
To browse Excel Help 10
To search Excel Help...11
To get context-sensitive help................................12
To use Balloon Help 12

Chapter 2: **Worksheet Basics**
How Worksheets Work 13
To launch Excel 14
To create a new workbook file.............................14
To open a workbook file 15
About Cells 16
To move the cell pointer and make a cell active..16
About Selecting Ranges 17
To select a range of cells.......................................17
To select an entire column...................................18
To select an entire row 18
To select multiple columns or rows..................18
To select the entire worksheet 18
To select multiple ranges 19
To deselect cells 19
About Entering Values and Formulas............20
About Values 21
To enter a value...21
About Formulas..22
How Excel Calculates Complex Formulas......22

v

Table of Contents

	To enter a formula by typing	23
	To enter a formula by clicking	24
Chapter 3:	**Editing Worksheets**	
	About Editing	25
	To change an entry as you type it	25
	To change a completed entry	25
	To clear cell contents	26
	About Inserting and Deleting Cells	27
	To insert a column or row	27
	To delete a column or row	28
	To insert cells	29
	To delete cells	29
	About Copying Cells	30
	To copy with Copy and Paste	31
	About the Fill Handle	32
	To copy with the fill handle	32
	About the Fill Command	33
	To use the Fill command	33
	About AutoFill	34
	To create a series with the fill handle	34
	To create a series with the Series command	34
	About Copying Formulas	35
	Relative vs. Absolute Cell References	36
	To include an absolute reference in a formula	37
	About Mixed References	37
	About Moving Cells	38
	To move with Cut and Paste	38
	To move with drag and drop	39
	About Undoing Commands	40
	To undo a command	40
	About Repeating Commands	40
	To repeat a command	40
Chapter 4:	**Working with Files**	
	About Workbook Files	41
	To switch between sheets in a workbook	42
	To select multiple sheets	42
	To insert a worksheet	43
	To insert a chart sheet	43
	To insert a Visual Basic module	43
	To delete a sheet	44

Table of Contents

To rename a sheet 44
To hide a sheet 45
To unhide a sheet 45
To move or copy a sheet 46
About Worksheet Windows 47
To make another window active 47
To create a new window 47
To arrange windows 48
To hide a window 49
To unhide a window 49
To zoom a window's view 50
About Splitting Windows 51
To split a window 51
To adjust the size of panes 51
To remove a window split 51
About Saving Workbooks 52
To save a workbook file 52
About Summary Information 53
To provide summary information 53
About File Formats 54
To save a file in another format 54
Save vs. Save As 55
To close a file 55
About the Find File Command 56
To find a file 56

Chapter 5: Using Functions in Formulas
About Functions 57
Anatomy of a Function 57
About Arguments 58
About Entering Functions 59
To enter a function by typing 59
To enter a function by typing and clicking .. 60
To enter a function with the Function
   Wizard 61
About Math and Trigonometry Functions 63
About the SUM Function 63
To use the AutoSum button 63
To use the AutoSum button on multiple
   cells 64
About the PRODUCT Function 65
About the ROUND Function 65
About the EVEN and ODD Functions 66
About the INT Function 66

vii

Table of Contents

About the ABS Function 66
About the SQRT Function 67
About the PI Function 67
ABout the RAND Function 67
About the RADIANS and DEGREES
    Functions 68
About the SIN Function 68
About the COS Function 68
About the TAN Function 68
About Statistical Functions 69
About the AVERAGE Function 69
About the MEDIAN Function 69
About the MODE Function 69
About the MIN and MAX Functions 69
About the COUNT and COUNTA
    Functions 70
About the STDEV and STDEVP Functions 70
About Financial Functions 71
About the SLN Function 71
About the DB Function 71
About the DDB Function 71
About the SYD Function 71
About the PMT Function 72
To calculate loan payments 72
To create an amortization table 73
To calculate contributions to reach a
    savings goal 74
About the FV Function 75
About the PV Function 75
About the IRR Function 75
About Logical Functions 76
About the IF Function 76
To use the IF Function 76
About Lookup and Reference Functions 77
About the VLOOKUP and HLOOKUP
    Functions 77
To use the VLOOKUP function 78
About Information Functions 79
About the IS Functions 79
About the COUNTBLANK Function 79
About Date and Time Functions 80
About the DATE Function 80
To calculate the number of days between
    two dates 81

viii

Table of Contents

About the NOW and TODAY Functions.........81
About the DAY, WEEKDAY, MONTH, and YEAR Functions................81
About TEXT Functions........................82
About the LOWER, UPPER, and PROPER Functions 82
About the LEFT, RIGHT, and MID Functions 82
About the CONCATENATE Function and Operator 83
To get more information about a function...............84

Chapter 6: **Formatting Worksheet Cells**
About Formatting................85
About Number Formatting 86
To format numbers with toolbar buttons......86
To format numbers with the Format Cells dialog box................87
About Number Format Codes................88
About Alignment................89
To align cell contents with toolbar buttons................89
To align cell contents with the Format Cells dialog box................90
To center cells across columns................90
To word wrap cell contents 91
To change the orientation of cell contents ..91
About Font Formatting................92
To change a font with the Formatting toolbar................92
To change font size with the Formatting toolbar................93
To change font style with the Formatting toolbar or shortcut keys................93
To change font formatting with the Format Cells dialog box................94
About Borders 95
To add borders with the Borders button........95
To add borders with the Format Cells dialog box 96
About Colors, Patterns, and Shading.............97
To add color with the Color button................97
To add color, pattern, and shading with the Format Cells dialog box................98
About the Format Painter................99

ix

Table of Contents

To copy formatting with the Format Painter 99
To copy formatting with the Copy and Paste Special commands 100
To remove only formatting from cells..........100
About Styles...100
About Column Width and Row Height........101
To change column width or row height with the mouse 102
To change column width or row height with menu commands 103
To hide columns or rows 103
To unhide columns or rows.............................103
About AutoFit...104
To use AutoFit..104
About AutoFormat 105
To use AutoFormat 105
About Cell Notes..106
To add a cell note 106
To view cell notes..106

Chapter 7: **Drawing and Formatting Objects**

About Drawing Objects 107
To display the Drawing toolbar.....................107
To hide the Drawing toolbar..........................107
About Objects...108
To draw a line or arrow 108
To draw a rectangle, square, ellipse, or circle 109
To draw a freeform shape...............................110
About Filled Shapes..111
About Modifying Objects 112
To select an object...112
To deselect an object 112
To select multiple objects 113
To group objects 113
To ungroup objects 113
To move an object 114
To copy an object with the Copy and Paste commands.....................................114
To copy an object by dragging.......................114
To delete an object...115
To resize an object...115
To reshape an object 116

Table of Contents

To change the style, color, and weight of lines 117
To change or add arrowheads 118
To change the style, color, and weight of shape borders 119
To change or add fill colors and patterns to shapes 120
About Stacking Order 121
To change stacking order 121
About Text Boxes 122
To add a text box 122
About External Graphics 123
To paste in graphic objects 123
To insert Microsoft ClipArt 124

Chapter 8: Creating Charts
About Charts 125
About the ChartWizard 125
To embed a chart on a worksheet 126
To insert a chart as a separate sheet 126
To use the ChartWizard 127
About Worksheet and Chart Links 130
To add or remove chart data with the ChartWizard 131
To add chart data with the Copy and Paste commands 132
To add chart data with drag and drop 133
To remove a data series 134

Chapter 9: Editing and Formatting Charts
About Editing and Formatting Charts 135
About the Chart Toolbar 135
About Activating Charts and Selecting Chart Items 136
To activate a chart 136
To deactivate a chart 136
To select a chart item 136
To add titles 137
To edit titles 137
To remove titles 137
About Data Labels 138
To add data labels 138
To add a legend 139
To remove a legend 139
About Axes 139

xi

Table of Contents

To add or remove axes 139
About Gridlines 140
To add or remove gridlines 140
About Formatting Titles 141
To format titles 141
About Formatting Data Labels 142
To format data labels 142
About Formatting Legends 143
To format a legend 143
About Formatting Axes 144
To format an axis 144
To change the appearance of an axis and
   its tick marks 145
To change the axis scale 146
About Formatting Gridlines 147
To format gridlines 147
About Formatting the Chart Area 148
To format the chart area 148
About Formatting the Plot Area and
   Chart Walls 149
To format the plot area or chart walls 149
About Formatting a Data Series or Data
   Point 150
To change the appearance of lines and
   markers 150
To change the appearance of bars,
   columns, or pie slices 151
To "explode" a pie chart 151
To rotate a 3-D chart 152
To move a chart item 152
To change the chart type 153
To use AutoFormat 154

Chapter 10: Printing

About Printing 155
About QuickDraw GX 155
About Apple's Chooser 156
To choose a printer 156
To choose a printer with QuickDraw GX 157
About the Page Setup dialog box 158
To set the paper size 159
To set the page orientation 159
To reduce or enlarge a worksheet report 160
To reduce or enlarge a chart 160

Table of Contents

To set margins in the Page Setup dialog box 161
About Page Breaks 162
To insert a page break 162
To remove a page break 163
About Headers and Footers 164
To set header and footer locations 164
To use built-in headers and footers 165
To create custom headers and footers 166
About the Print Area 167
To set the print area for a worksheet 167
About Print Titles 168
To set print titles 168
About other Print Options 169
About Print Preview 170
To preview a report 170
To change margins, header and footer locations, and column widths in Print Preview 171
To print a report 172
To print a report with QuickDraw GX 173

Chapter 11: Working with Databases

About Databases 175
To create a list 176
About the Data Form 176
To browse records with the data form 177
To enter, edit, and delete data with the data form 177
To find records with the data form 178
About AutoFilter 179
To find records with AutoFilter 179
To set a custom AutoFilter 180
To use multiple AutoFilters 180
About Advanced Filters 181
To use advanced filters 181
About Sorting 182
To sort a list 182
About Subtotal and the SUBTOTAL Function 184
To subtotal a list 184
About Outlines 185
About Database Functions 186

xiii

Table of Contents

Chapter 12: Advanced Formula Techniques
About Excel's Advanced Formula
  Techniques 187
About Names 188
To define a name 188
To create a name 189
To delete a name 189
To enter a name in a formula 190
To apply names to existing formulas 191
To select named cells 192
About 3-D References 193
To reference a named cell or range in
  another worksheet 194
To reference a cell or range in another
  worksheet by clicking 194
To reference a cell or range in another
  worksheet by typing 195
To reference a cell with the Paste Special
  command 195
To write a formula with 3-D references 196
To write a formula that sums the same cell
  on multiple, adjacent cells 196
About Opening Worksheet with Links 197
About Consolidations 198
To consolidate based on the arrangement
  of data 198
To consolidate based on labels 200

Chapter 13: Add-ins and Macros
About Add-ins 201
To add add-in files with Setup 202
To install add-ins 203
To remove add-ins 203
About AutoSave 204
To use AutoSave 204
About View Manager 205
To add a view with View Manager 205
To switch to a view with View Manager 206
To delete a view 206
About Report Manager 207
To add a report with Report Manager 207
To print a report with Report Manager 208
To delete a report 208
About Macros 209

		To record a macro with the Macro Recorder 209
		To run a macro 210
Chapter 14:	**Customizing Excel**	
		About Customization..........................211
		About General Options......................212
		To change General Options...............212
		About Editing Options 213
		To change Editing Options 213
		About View Options...........................214
		To change View options 215
		About Calculation Options.................216
		To change Calculation options.........216
		About Custom Lists 217
		To create a custom list......................217
		About Toolbars...................................218
		To show or hide toolbars...................218
		Docked vs. Floating Toolbars...........219
		To move a toolbar 219
		To resize a floating toolbar...............219
		To customize a toolbar 220
		To reset a toolbar 221
		To create a toolbar 221
		To delete a toolbar 222
Appendix A:	**Shortcut Keys**	
		About Shortcut Keys 223
		Modifier Keys.....................................223
		File Menu Commands 223
		Edit Menu Commands 224
		View Menu Commands 224
		Insert Menu Commands.....................224
		Format Menu Commands...................225
		Tools Menu Commands 226
		Data Menu Commands 226
		Window Menu Commands..................226
		Help Commands 226
		Application Menu Commands...........226
		Movement Keys..................................227
		Selection Keys....................................227
		Data Entry & Editing Keys 228
		Dialog Box Keys.................................228
		Edit Box Keys.....................................228

Table of Contents

Appendix B: **Toolbars**
About Toolbars 229
The Standard Toolbar 229
The Formatting Toolbar....................................229
The Drawing Toolbar..230
The Chart Toolbar...230

Appendix C: **Functions**
About Functions..231
Math & Trig Functions......................................231
Statistical Functions..233
Financial Functions...236
Logical Functions 236
Lookup & Reference Functions.......................237
Information Functions 237
Date & Time Functions 238
Text Functions...238
Database Functions...239

THE EXCEL WORKPLACE 1

Introduction

Excel is a powerful and often complex spreadsheet software package. With it, you can create picture-perfect worksheets, charts, and lists based on just about any data you can enter into a Macintosh.

This Visual QuickStart Guide will help you take control of Excel's feature-rich work environment by providing step-by-step instructions and plenty of illustrations. A generous helping of tips show you how you can be more productive and avoid the "traps" that new, uninformed Excel users may encounter.

This book is designed for page-flipping. Use the thumb tabs, index, or table of contents to find the topics for which you need help. But if you're brand new to Excel, I recommend that you begin by reading at least the first two chapters. These chapters contain important information you'll need to fully understand the instructions presented in the rest of the book.

One last word of advice before you start: don't let Excel intimidate you! Sure, it's big, and yes, it has lots and lots of commands. But as you work with Excel, you'll quickly learn the techniques and commands you need to get your work done. That's when you'll be on your way to harnessing the real power of Excel.

Start Here

Chapter 1

The Excel screen

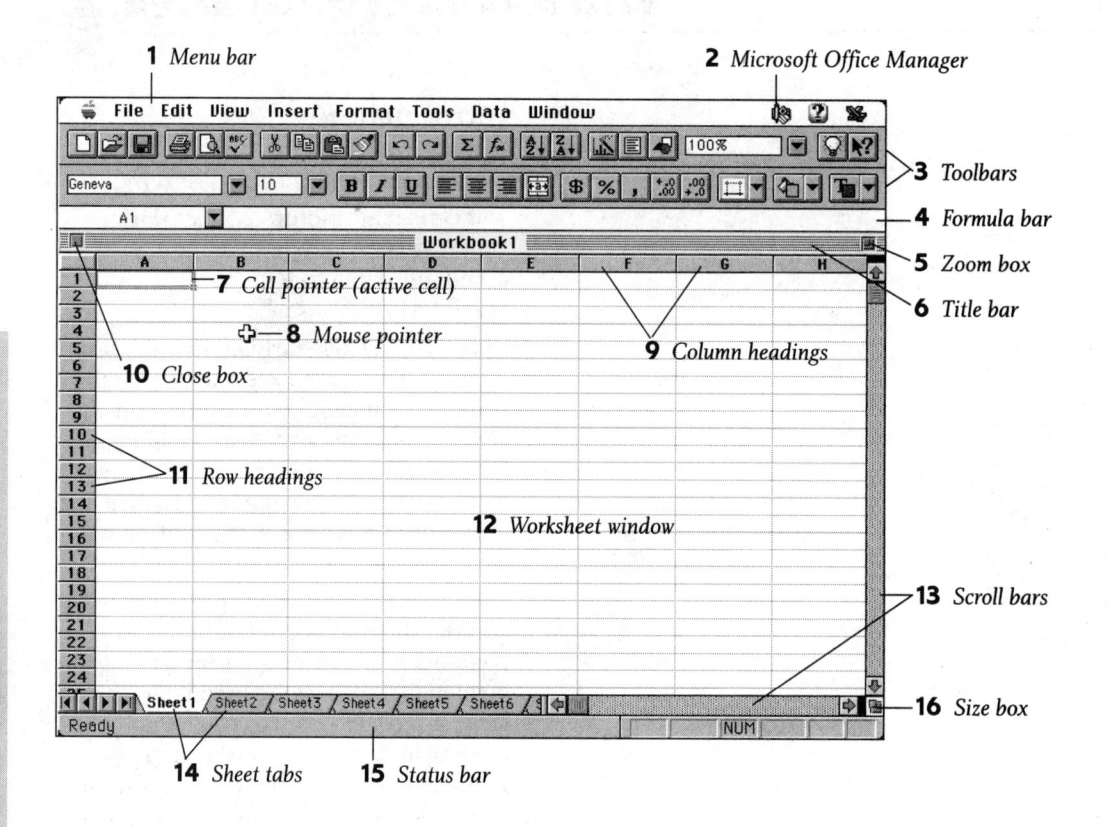

Figure 1. *The Excel workplace.*

Labels in figure:
1. Menu bar
2. Microsoft Office Manager
3. Toolbars
4. Formula bar
5. Zoom box
6. Title bar
7. Cell pointer (active cell)
8. Mouse pointer
9. Column headings
10. Close box
11. Row headings
12. Worksheet window
13. Scroll bars
14. Sheet tabs
15. Status bar
16. Size box

Key to the Excel Screen

1 *Menu bar*

The menu bar gives you access to all of Excel's commands, as well as the Apple menu, Microsoft Office Manager, online help (including Balloon Help), and other applications.

2 *Microsoft Office Manager*

If Excel is installed as part of Microsoft Office, you may have the Microsoft Office Manager control panel installed. If so, this icon appears in your menu bar and gives you access to all of the Microsoft Office products installed on your Macintosh.

3 *Toolbars*

Excel's toolbars put a wide variety of menu commands within easy reach of your mouse pointer. You can show, hide, or customize any of Excel's toolbars.

Key to the Excel Screen (continued)

4 *Formula bar*
The formula bar displays the contents of the active cell, as well as that cell's address or reference.

5 *Zoom box*
The zoom box lets you toggle the window from full size (shown in **Figure 1**) to a custom size you specify with the size box. To use the zoom box, just click it.

6 *Title bar*
The title bar displays the name of the current document. You can move a window by dragging it by its title bar.

7 *Cell pointer (active cell)*
The cell pointer is a heavy border surrounding the active cell. The active cell is the cell in which text and numbers appear when you type.

8 *Mouse pointer*
When positioned within the worksheet window, the mouse pointer appears as a hollow plus sign. You can use the mouse pointer to select cells, enter data, choose menu commands, and click buttons.

9 *Column headings*
Each worksheet column is labeled with one or two letters of the alphabet. These are column headings.

10 *Close box*
The close box offers one way to close the active window. To use the close box, just click it.

11 *Row headings*
Each worksheet row is labeled with a number. These are row headings.

12 *Worksheet window*
The worksheet window is where you'll be doing most of your work with Excel. This window has a series of columns and rows which intersect at cells. You enter data and formulas in the cells to build your spreadsheet.

13 *Scroll bars*
Scroll bars let you shift the contents of the window so you can see information that does not fit in the window. To use a scroll bar, click an arrow at one end, click in the gray area between the arrows, or drag the square tab.

14 *Sheet tabs*
Each Excel document has one or more sheets combined together in a *workbook*. The sheet tabs let you move from one sheet to another within the workbook. To use the sheet tabs, just click on the tab for the sheet you want to view.

15 *Status bar*
The status bar provides information about your work and any commands you have selected.

16 *Size box*
The size box lets you resize the window. To use the size box, drag it to move the right and bottom sides of the window. When you release it, the window changes its size.

Chapter 1

To use the mouse

There are four basic mouse techniques:

- Pointing means to position the mouse pointer so that its tip is on the item on which you are pointing (see **Figure 2**).

Figure 2.
Pointing to the File menu.

- Clicking means to press the mouse button once and release it. You click to make a cell active, position the insertion point, or choose a toolbar button.

- Double-clicking means to press the mouse button twice in rapid succession. You double-click to open an item or select text for editing.

- Dragging means to press the mouse button down and hold it down while moving the mouse. You drag to resize or reposition a window, select multiple cells, or choose menu commands.

About Menus

All of Excel's menu commands are accessible through its menus. **Figures 3**, **4**, and **5** show examples of Excel's menus.

- A menu command that appears in gray cannot currently be selected.

- A menu command followed by an elipsis (…) displays a dialog box. I discuss dialog boxes later in this chapter.

- A menu command followed by a triangle has a submenu. The submenu displays additional commands when the main command is highlighted.

- A menu command followed by the ⌘ (Command key) symbol and a letter or number can be chosen with a shortcut key.

- A menu command preceded by a check mark has been "turned on." To toggle the command from on to off or off to on, choose it from the menu.

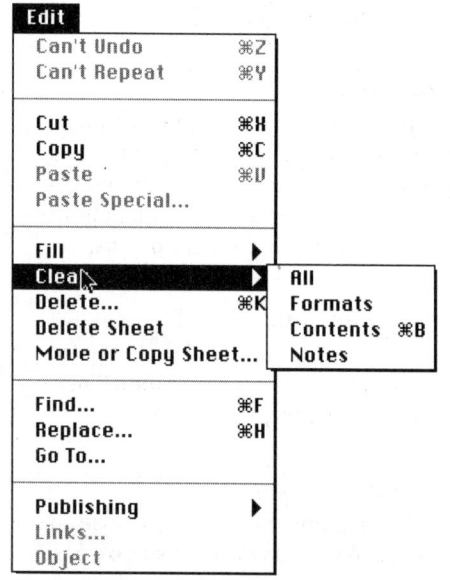

Figure 3. *An Excel menu with submenus.*

Using the Mouse

4

To use a menu

1. Point to the menu from which you want to choose a command.
2. Press the mouse button down and hold it down to display the menu.
3. Drag the mouse pointer down until the command you want is highlighted (see **Figure 4**). If the command is on a submenu, display the submenu and then drag the mouse pointer to the right and down until the submenu command is highlighted (see **Figure 5**).
4. Release the mouse button. The command may blink before the menu disappears, confirming that it has been successfully selected.

Figure 4. Selecting a command from a menu.

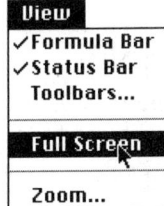

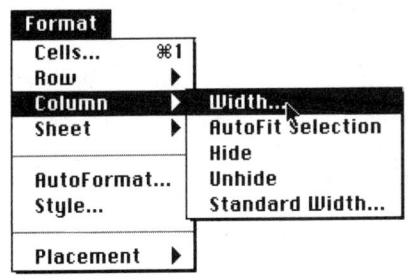

Figure 5. Selecting a command from a submenu.

To use shortcut menus

Excel's shortcut menus are hidden until you display them. Once displayed, they offer only those commands applicable to the current selection.

1. Hold down the Control key

   or

   Hold down the Command (⌘) and Option keys together.
2. Click on the current selection. A menu appears at the mouse pointer (see **Figure 6**).
3. Drag down to highlight the command you want.
4. Release the mouse button to complete the selection.

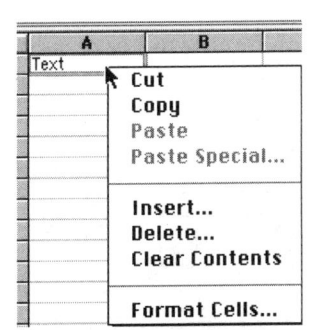

Figure 6. *Hold down the Control key and click on the selection to display a shortcut menu of applicable commands.*

To use a shortcut key

1. Hold down the modifier key for the shortcut (normally the Command key, which is represented on menus with the ⌘ symbol).
2. Press the shortcut key.

For example, the shortcut key for the Save command (under the File menu; see **Figure 7**) is ⌘S. To use this shortcut key, hold down the Command key and press the S key.

Figure 7. *The Save command and its shortcut key.*

✔ Tip

- Many shortcut keys are standardized from one application to another. The Save, Print, and Quit commands are three good examples; they're usually ⌘S, ⌘P, and ⌘Q.

To use toolbar buttons

Excel's toolbars offer another quick way to choose commands.

1. Point to the button for the command you want. A tiny yellow box called a *Tooltip* appears, telling you what the button does (see **Figure 8**).
2. Click once on the toolbar button to activate the command.

Figure 8. *The Bold button and its Tooltip.*

✔ Tips

- Buttons that have triangles on them are really menus. Click the button and hold your mouse button down to display the menu. Then drag to select the option you want (see **Figure 9a**).
- If you keep dragging a button menu away from the toolbar, it'll tear off and become a movable palette (see **Figure 9b**). Then you can just click on buttons to select them.

Figure 9a. *The Borders button is really a menu in disguise.*

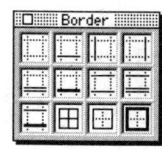

Figure 9b. *If you drag the Borders button menu away from the toolbar, it tears off.*

The Excel Workplace

About Toolbars

By default, two toolbars are automatically displayed by Excel when you launch it:

- The Standard toolbar (see **Figure 10**) offers buttons for a wide range of commonly-used commands.
- The Formatting toolbar (see **Figure 11**) offers buttons for commonly-used formatting commands.

✔ Tip

- Other toolbars may appear automatically depending on the type of sheet or object you are working with. For example, when you work with a chart, the Chart toolbar appears.

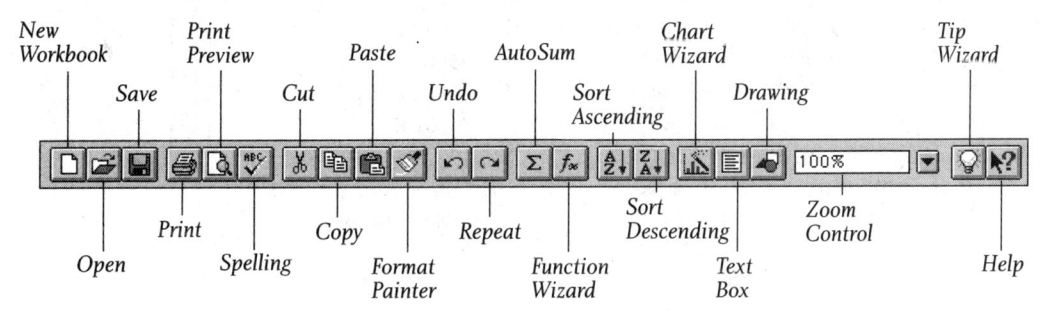

Figure 10. *The Standard toolbar.*

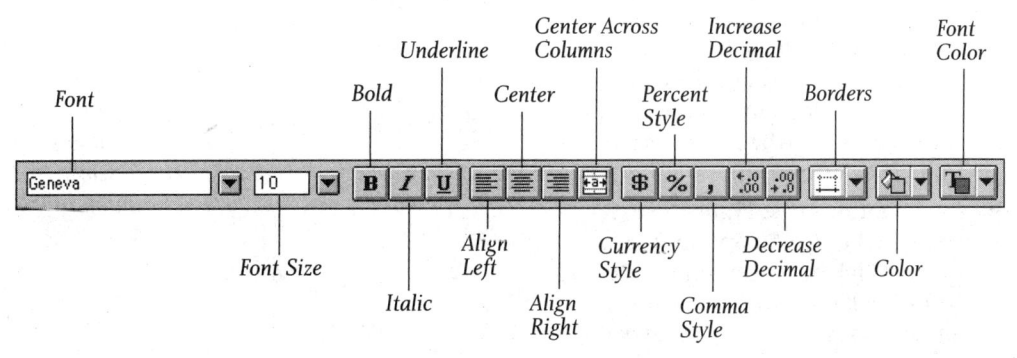

Labels: New Workbook, Save, Print Preview, Cut, Paste, Undo, AutoSum, Sort Ascending, Chart Wizard, Drawing, Tip Wizard, Open, Print, Spelling, Copy, Format Painter, Repeat, Function Wizard, Sort Descending, Text Box, Zoom Control, Help

Figure 11. *The Formatting toolbar.*

Labels: Font, Bold, Underline, Center Across Columns, Increase Decimal, Font Color, Font Size, Italic, Align Left, Center, Align Right, Percent Style, Currency Style, Comma Style, Borders, Decrease Decimal, Color

Using Toolbars

7

About Dialog Boxes

Excel uses dialog boxes to get information from you before it completes the execution of a command. Dialog boxes have many standard parts that work the same way to gather information about your choices.

To use a dialog box

- Tabs (see **Figure 12a**), which appear at the top of some dialog boxes, let you move from one group of dialog box options to another. To switch to another group of options, click its tab.

- Edit boxes (see **Figure 12b**) let you enter information from the keyboard. Press the Tab key to move from one edit box to the next or click in the edit box to position an insertion point within it. Then enter a new value.

- Scrolling lists (see **Figure 12c**) offer a number of options to choose from. Use the scroll bar to view options that don't fit in the list window. Click an option to select it; it becomes highlighted.

- Check boxes (see **Figure 12d**) let you turn options on or off. Click in a check box to toggle it. When an X appears in the check box, its option is turned on. When a check box is gray, part of the selection has the option turned on while the rest of the selection has it turned off.

- Radio buttons (see **Figure 12e**) let you select only one option from a group. Click on an option to select it. If you click on an option that is not already selected, the one that was selected is turned off.

Figure 12a. *Tabs let you switch from one group of options to another within the same dialog box.*

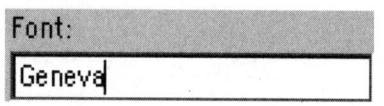

Figure 12b. *Edit boxes let you enter text or numbers.*

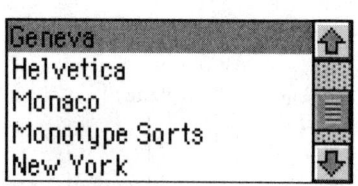

Figure 12c. *Scrolling lists let you choose from a number of available options.*

Figure 12d. *Check boxes let you turn options on or off.*

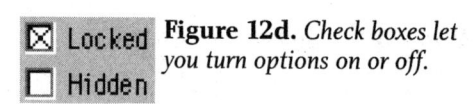

Figure 12e. *Radio buttons let you select one option from a group.*

The Excel Workplace

Figure 12f. *Pop-up menus offer another way to select one option from a group.*

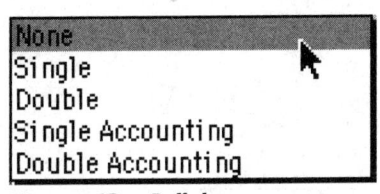

Figure 12g. *Pull down a pop-up menu just like any other menu to select an option.*

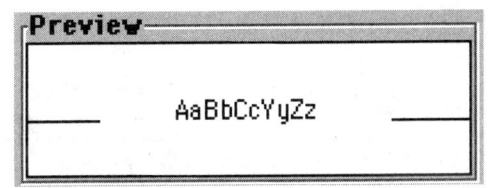

Figure 12h. *A Preview area shows you the effects of any changes you make before you close the dialog box.*

Figure 12i. *Buttons let you accept or cancel changes or open other dialog boxes, like Excel's online help feature.*

- Pop-up menus (see **Figures 12f** and **12g**) also let you select one option from a group. Click the menu and hold down your mouse button to display it. Then choose the option you want just as you would from any other menu.

- Preview areas (see **Figure 12h**), when available, illustrate the effects of your changes before you finalize them by clicking OK.

- Buttons (see **Figure 12i**) let you access other dialog boxes, accept changes and close the dialog box (OK), close the dialog box without making changes (Cancel), or get help about options within the dialog box (Help). To choose a button, click it.

✔ Tips

- When a dialog box appears, you'll have to dismiss it by clicking OK or Cancel before you can continue working with Excel.

- When the contents of an edit box are selected, whatever you type will replace the selection.

- Excel often uses edit boxes and scrolling lists together (see **Figures 12b** and **12c**). You can use either one to make a selection.

- In some scrolling lists (like the Open dialog box), double-clicking an option selects it and closes the dialog box.

- You can turn on any number of check boxes in a group, but you can select only one radio button in a group.

- A dialog box with a title bar can be moved anywhere on screen by dragging it by the title bar.

Chapter 1

Browsing Online Help

To browse Excel Help

1. Choose Microsoft Excel Help from the Macintosh Help menu (see **Figure 13a**), which is also known as the Balloon Help or Guide Help menu.

   or

   Press ⌘/.

   or

   Press the Help key (on extended keyboards only).

   An MS Excel Help window appears (see **Figure 13b**).

2. Click the icon for the topic that interests you. (Your mouse pointer will look like a hand with its forefinger raised; see **Figure 13b**.) The window changes to display a list of subtopics.

3. To zero in on a specific topic, click any green, underlined text related to it.

4. When you are finished browsing help, click the Help window's close box to dismiss it and return to Excel.

✔ Tips

- Click the History button to display a list of all help windows you've viewed during the help session (see **Figure 14**). Double-click on any item in the Help History list to go back to that window.

- Click the Back button to move backwards through all of the help windows you've viewed during the help session.

- To print the contents of a help window, choose Print Topic from the File menu.

   or

   Press ⌘P.

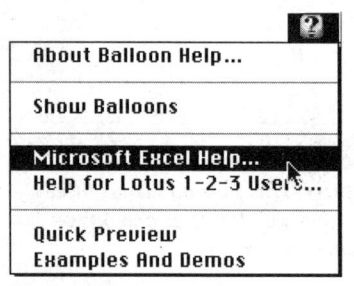

Figure 13a. *Accessing Microsoft Excel Help from the Help menu.*

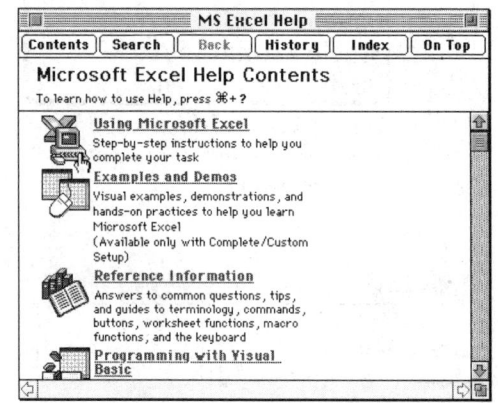

Figure 13b. *The MS Excel Help window's table of contents.*

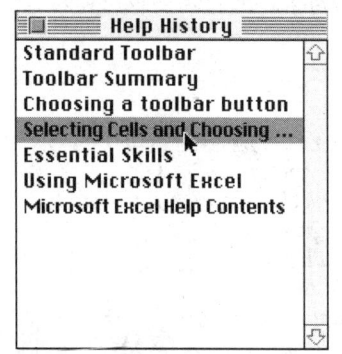

Figure 14. *The Help History window shows all of the help windows you've viewed during the help session.*

10

The Excel Workplace

To search Excel Help

1. Double-click the Help button on the Standard toolbar. The MS Excel Help window appears with a keyword list dialog box on top of it (see **Figure 15a**).

2. In the edit box at the top of this dialog box, type a word for which you want to get help. As you type, the contents of the scrolling list shifts in an attempt to match the word you typed. If there's no exact match, click the closest word or phrase to highlight it.

3. Click the Show Topics button to display a list of specific topics in the bottom part of the dialog box (see **Figure 15b**).

4. Click on the specific topic you want and click Go To or press Return.

   or

   Double-click on the specific topic you want.

   An MS Excel Help window for that topic appears.

5. When you are finished with the Help window, click its close box to dismiss it.

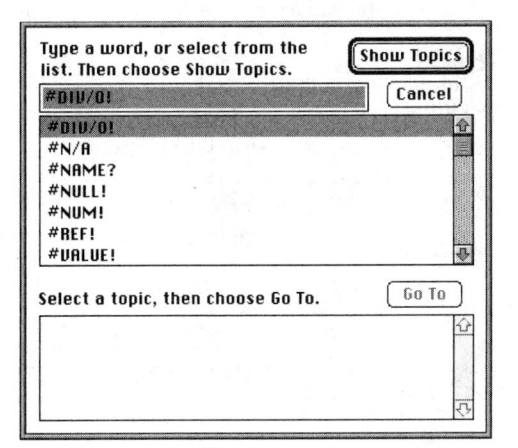

Figure 15a. *Double-clicking the Help button displays a list of keywords for help topics.*

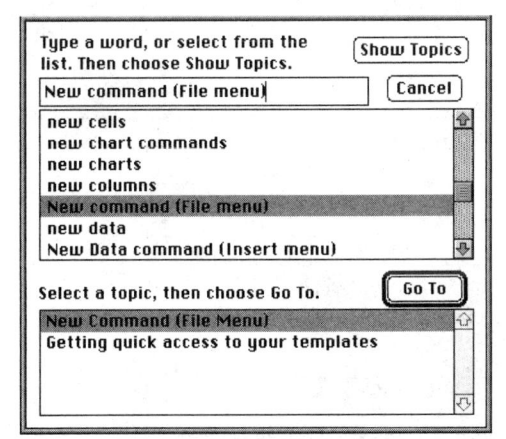

Figure 15b. *The Show Topics button displays a list of specific help topics for the main topic you select.*

✔ Tip

- Use the Contents, Search, and Index buttons at the top of most Help windows (see **Figures 13b** and **16c**) to search for help on specific topics.

Searching Online Help

11

Chapter 1

To get context-sensitive help

1. Click once on the Help button in the Standard toolbar.
2. The mouse pointer turns into an arrow with a question mark beside it (see **Figure 16a**). Use this pointer to choose a menu command or click a window feature for which you want help (see **Figure 16b**). An MS Excel Help window with information about that command or item appears (see **Figure 16c**).
3. When you are finished with the Help window, click its close box to dismiss it.

✔ Tips

- You can also get context-sensitive help by clicking the Help button in any dialog box (see **Figure 12i**).
- A brief description of any button or command you point to is always available in the status bar at the bottom of the screen (see **Figure 17**).

To use Balloon Help

1. Choose Show Balloons from the Macintosh Help menu (see **Figure 18a**).
2. Point to a window element, button, or menu command for which you need help. A cartoon balloon with information about that item pops up (see **Figure 18b**).
3. To turn off Balloon Help, choose Hide Balloons from the Macintosh Help menu.

Figure 16a. *Clicking the Help button once turns the mouse pointer into a help pointer.*

Figure 16b. *Use the help pointer to select a menu command for which you need help.*

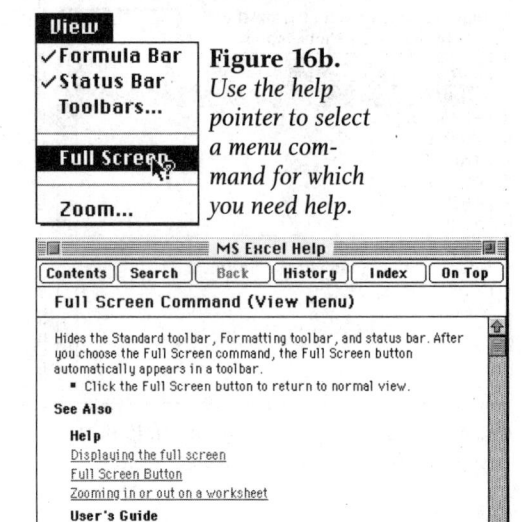

Figure 16c. *Context-sensitive help.*

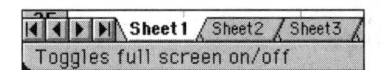

Figure 17. *The status bar displays a brief description of buttons and commands you point to.*

Figure 18a. *Turning on Balloon Help with the Help menu.*

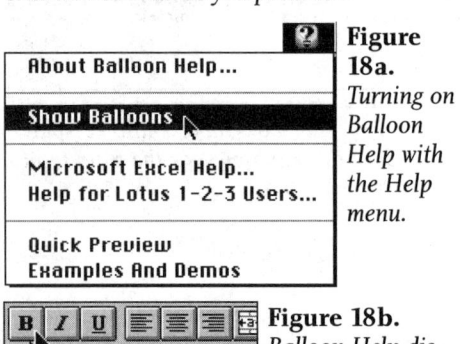

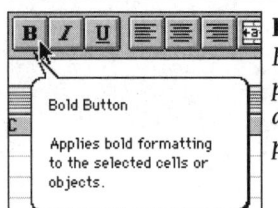

Figure 18b. *Balloon Help displays information about anything you point to.*

Getting Context-Sensitive Help

12

WORKSHEET BASICS 2

How Worksheets Work

Excel is most commonly used to create *worksheets*. A worksheet is a collection of information laid out in columns and rows. As illustrated in **Figure 1a**, each worksheet cell can contain one of two kinds of input:

- A value is a piece of information that does not change. Values can be text, numbers, dates, or times. A cell containing a value usually displays the value.

- A formula is a collection of values, cell references, operators, and predefined functions that, when evaluated by Excel, produces a result. A cell containing a formula usually displays the results of the formula.

Although any information can be presented in a worksheet, spreadsheet programs like Excel are usually used to organize and calculate numerical or financial information. Why? Well, when properly prepared, a worksheet acts like a super calculator. You enter values and formulas and it calculates and displays the results. If you change one of the values, no problem. Excel recalculates the results almost instantaneously without any additional effort on your part. (See **Figure 1b**.)

How does this work? By using cell *references* rather than actual numbers in formulas, Excel knows that it should use the contents of those cells in its calculations. Thus, changing one or more values affects the results of calculations that include references to the changed cells. As you can imagine, this makes worksheets powerful business planning and analysis tools!

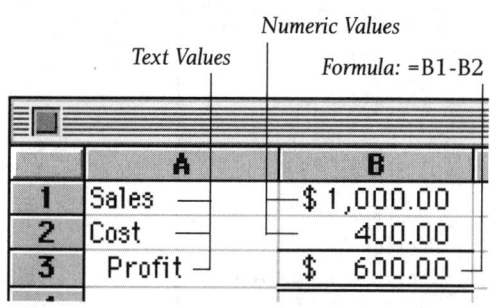

Figure 1a. *This very simple worksheet illustrates how a spreadsheet program like Excel works with values and formulas.*

Figure 1b. *When the value for Sales changes from $1,000 to $1,150, the Profit result changes automatically. Everything else remains the same.*

Chapter 2

To launch Excel

Double-click the Excel application icon (see **Figure 2**).

or

Double-click an icon for an Excel document (see **Figure 3**).

or

If the Microsoft Office Manager control panel is installed, choose Microsoft Excel from the Microsoft Office Manager menu (see **Figure 4**).

✔ Tips

- When you launch Excel by double-clicking its icon or choosing it from the Microsoft Office Manager menu, a blank document window named *Workbook 1* appears. This window is described in Chapter 1.

- When you launch Excel by double-clicking an Excel document icon, the document you double-clicked opens.

- If you click outside an Excel window while Excel is running, you may switch to another running application. See what application is active by pulling down the Application menu on the far right end of the menu bar (see **Figure 5**). The application with the check mark beside it is the active one. Return to Excel by clicking on any Excel window or choosing Excel from the Application menu.

Figure 2. *The Excel application icon.*

Figure 3. *An Excel document icon.*

Figure 4. *The Microsoft Office Manager menu offers another way to launch Excel.*

Figure 5. *The Application menu tells you what application is active and lets you switch from one application to another.*

To create a new workbook file

Choose New from the File menu (see **Figure 6**).

or

Press ⌘N.

or

Click the New Workbook button on the Standard toolbar.

Launching Excel & Creating a New File

14

Worksheet Basics

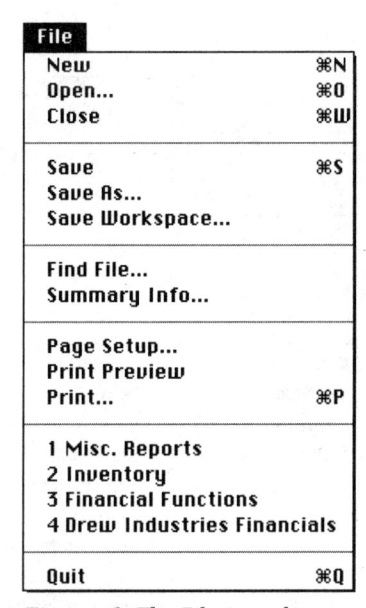

```
File
New              ⌘N
Open...           ⌘O
Close            ⌘W

Save             ⌘S
Save As...
Save Workspace...

Find File...
Summary Info...

Page Setup...
Print Preview
Print...          ⌘P

1 Misc. Reports
2 Inventory
3 Financial Functions
4 Drew Industries Financials

Quit             ⌘Q
```

Figure 6. *The File menu lets you create new files and open existing files.*

To open a workbook file

1. Choose Open from the File menu (see **Figure 6**).

   or

   Press ⌘O.

   or

   Click the Open button on the Standard toolbar.

2. In the Open dialog box that appears (see **Figure 7**), locate the file you want to open.

3. Click the file name to select it and click Open.

   or

   Double-click the file name to select it and open it.

✔ Tip

- If the document you want to open is one of the four most recently opened documents, it may appear in a file list near the bottom of the File menu. If so, simply select it from the File menu to open it quickly.

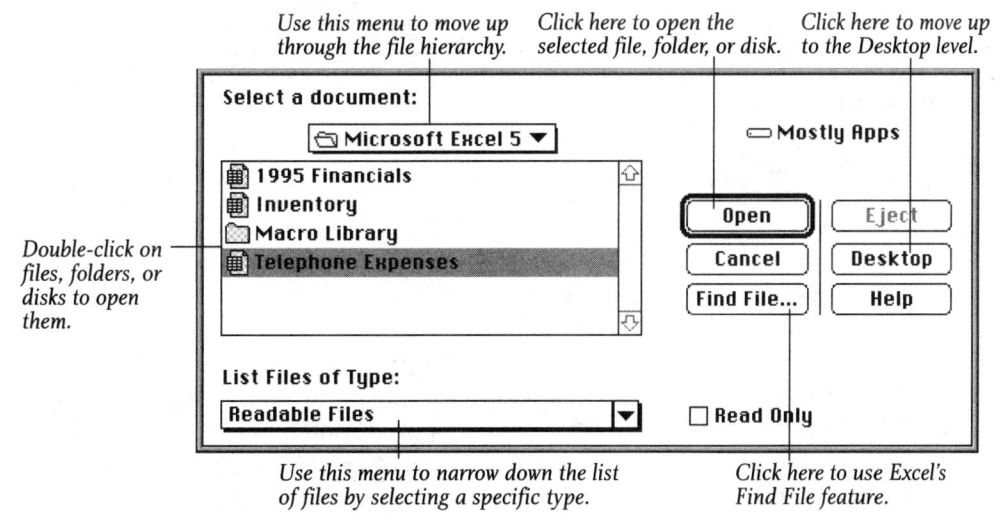

Use this menu to move up through the file hierarchy. *Click here to open the selected file, folder, or disk.* *Click here to move up to the Desktop level.*

```
Select a document:
  📁 Microsoft Excel 5 ▼              ⬜ Mostly Apps
     📄 1995 Financials
     📄 Inventory                      [  Open  ]   [  Eject  ]
     📁 Macro Library
     📄 Telephone Expenses             [ Cancel ]   [ Desktop ]
                                       [Find File...] [ Help  ]

List Files of Type:
  Readable Files              ▼       ☐ Read Only
```

Double-click on files, folders, or disks to open them.

Use this menu to narrow down the list of files by selecting a specific type.

Click here to use Excel's Find File feature.

Figure 7. *Use the Open dialog box to locate and open existing Excel files.*

15

Chapter 2

About Cells

Worksheet information is entered into *cells*. A cell is the intersection of a column and a row. Each little "box" in the worksheet window is a cell.

- Each cell has a unique *address* or *reference*. The reference uses the letter(s) of the column and the number of the row. Thus, cell *B6* would be at the intersection of column *B* and row *6*. The reference for the active cell appears in the formula bar (see **Figure 8**).

- To enter information in a cell, you must make that cell *active*. A cell is active when there is a dark or colored border called the *cell pointer* around it. When a cell is active, anything you type is entered into it.

To move the cell pointer and make a cell active

Use the mouse pointer to click in the cell you want to make active.

or

Use the arrow keys or other movement keys on the keyboard (see **Table 1**) to move the cell pointer to the cell you want to make active.

or

1. Choose Go To from the Edit menu

   or

   Press F5 on an extended keyboard).

2. In the Go To dialog box (see **Figure 9**), enter the cell reference for the cell you want to make active in the Reference edit box.

3. Click OK or press Return or Enter.

   The cell pointer moves to the cell you specified.

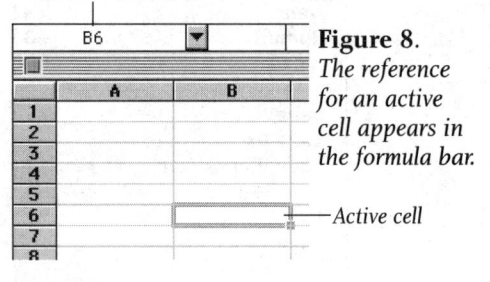

Cell reference in formula bar

Figure 8. *The reference for an active cell appears in the formula bar.*

—Active cell

Key	Movement
Up Arrow	Up one cell
Down Arrow	Down one cell
Right Arrow	Right one cell
Left Arrow	Left one cell
Tab	Right one cell
Home	First cell in row
Page Up	Up one window
Page Down	Down one window
Command-Home or Control-Home	Cell A1
Command-End or Control-End	Cell at intersection of last column and last row containing data

Table 1. *Keys for moving the cell pointer.*

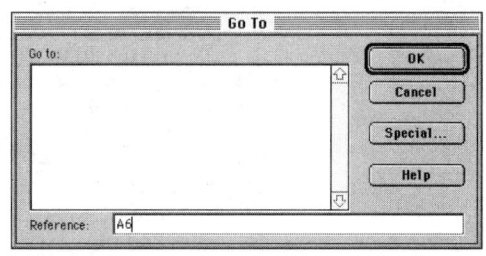

Figure 9. *The Go To dialog box lets you move to any cell quickly.*

✔ Tip

- Using the scroll bars does not move the cell pointer or change the active cell. It merely changes your view of the worksheet's contents.

Working with Cells

16

Worksheet Basics

Figure 10. *In this illustration, the range B1:E4 is selected.*

About Selecting Ranges

By selecting multiple cells or a *range* of cells, you can use commands on all selected cells at once. A range (see **Figure 10**) is a rectangular selection of cells defined by the top left and bottom right cell references.

To select a range of cells

Position the mouse pointer in the first cell you want to select (see **Figure 11a**), press the mouse button down, and drag to highlight all the cells in the selection (see **Figure 11b**).

Figure 11a. *To select these cells, start here...*

Figure 11b. *...press down the mouse button and drag to here.*

or

Click in the first cell of the range you want to select, hold down the Shift key, and click in the last cell of the range. This technique is known as "Shift-Click."

or

Choose Go To from the Edit menu or press F5, enter the reference for the range of cells you want to select in the Reference edit box of the Go To dialog box (see **Figure 12**), and click OK or press Return or Enter.

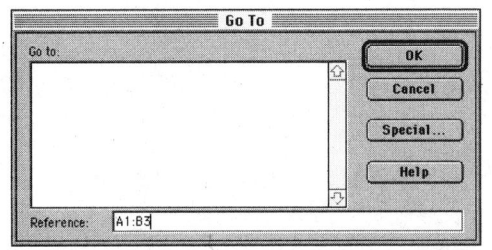

Figure 12. *You can also use the Go To dialog box to select a range of cells.*

✔ Tips

- Although the active cell is always part of a selection of multiple cells, it is never highlighted like the rest of the selection. You should, however, see a dark or colored border (the cell pointer) around it (see **Figure 11b**).

- Although you can select more than one cell at a time, only one cell—the one referenced in the formula bar—is active and can receive information you type in.

- To specify a reference for a range, enter the addresses of the first and last cells of the range with a colon (:) between them.

Selecting a Range of Cells

17

Chapter 2

To select an entire column
Click on the column heading of the column you want to select (see **Figure 13**).

or

Press ⌘Spacebar when the cell pointer is in any cell of the column you want to select.

Figure 13. *Click on a column heading to select that column.*

To select an entire row
Click on the row heading of the row you want to select (see **Figure 14**).

or

Press Shift-Spacebar when the cell pointer is in any cell of the row you want to select.

Figure 14. *Click on a row heading to select that row.*

To select multiple columns or rows
Position the mouse pointer on the first column or row heading, press the mouse button down, and drag along the headings until all the desired columns or rows are selected.

✔ Tip
- When selecting multiple columns or rows, be careful to position the mouse pointer *on* the heading and not *between* two headings! If you drag the border of two columns, you will change a column's width rather than make a selection.

To select the entire worksheet
Press ⌘A.

or

Click the Select All button at the upper left corner of the worksheet window (see **Figure 15**).

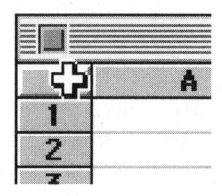

Figure 15. *The Select All button is in the corner of the worksheet where column and row headings meet.*

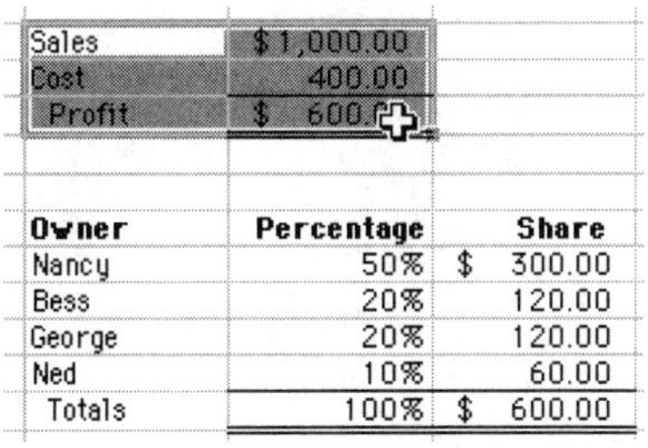

Figure 16a. *To select both ranges of cells, start by selecting this range...*

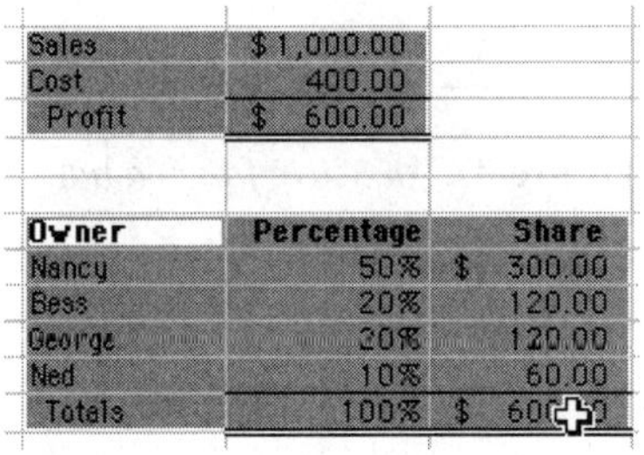

Figure 16b. *...then hold down the Command key and select this range.*

To select multiple ranges

1. Use any selection technique to select the first cell or range of cells (see **Figure 16a**).
2. Hold down the Command (⌘) key and drag to select the second cell or range of cells (see **Figure 16b**).
3. While holding down the Command key, continue to select additional cells or ranges of cells until all ranges are selected.

✔ Tips

- Selecting multiple ranges can be tricky and takes practice. Don't be frustrated if you can't do it on the first few tries!
- To add ranges that are not visible in the worksheet window, be sure to use the scroll bars to view them. Using the keyboard to move to other cells while selecting multiple ranges will remove the selections you've made so far or add undesired selections.
- Do not click in the worksheet window or use the movement keys while multiple ranges are selected unless you are finished working with them. Doing so will deselect all the cells.

To deselect cells

Click anywhere in the worksheet.

or

Press any arrow key, Tab, Page Up, Page Down, or Home.

✔ Tip

- Remember, at least one cell must be selected at all times—that's the active cell.

Chapter 2

About Entering Values and Formulas

To enter a value or formula into a cell, you begin by making the cell active. As you type or click to enter information, the information appears in both the cell and in the formula bar just above the window's title bar. You complete the entry by pressing Return or Enter or clicking the Enter button on the formula bar.

While you are entering information into a cell, the formula bar is *active*. You can tell that it's active because three buttons appear between the cell reference and cell contents areas (see **Figure 17**) and the word *Enter* appears in the status bar at the bottom of the screen.

Figure 17. *An active formula bar.*

There are two important things to remember when the formula bar is active:

- Anything you type or click on may be included in the active cell.

- Many Excel options and menu commands are unavailable (see **Figures 18a** and **18b**).

You deactivate the formula bar by accepting or cancelling the current entry. The three buttons disappear (see **Figures 19b** and **20b**).

✔ Tips

- To cancel an entry before it has been completed, press the Esc key, press ⌘. (Period), or click the Cancel button on the formula bar. This restores the cell to the way it was before you began.

- If you include formatting notation like dollar signs, commas, and percent symbols when you enter numbers, you may apply formatting styles. I tell you more about formatting the contents of cells in Chapter 6.

Figure 18a. *The Edit menu when the formula bar is inactive…*

Figure 18b. *…and when the formula bar is active.*

About Values

As discussed at the beginning of this chapter, a value is any text, number, date, or time you enter into a cell. Values are constant—they don't change unless you change them.

To enter a value

1. Make the cell in which you want to enter the value the active cell.
2. Type in the value. As you type, the information appears in two places: the active cell and the formula bar, which becomes active (see **Figure 19a**).
3. To complete and accept the entry (see **Figure 19b**), press Return or Enter.

   or

   Click the Enter button on the formula bar.

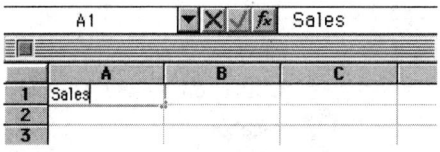

Figure 19a. *As data is entered into a cell, it appears in both the cell and the formula bar.*

Figure 19b. *A completed entry. The insertion point and formula bar buttons are gone.*

✔ Tips

- Pressing Return to complete an entry accepts the entry and moves the cell pointer one cell down. Pressing Enter or clicking the Enter button accepts the entry without moving the cell pointer.
- Although you can often use the arrow keys or other movement keys to complete an entry by moving to another cell, it's a bad habit because it won't always work.
- Excel aligns text against the left side of the cell and aligns numbers against the right side of the cell. I tell you how to change alignment in Chapter 6.
- Don't worry if the data you put into a cell doesn't seem to fit. You can always change the column width to make it fit. I tell you how in Chapter 6.

Chapter 2

About Formulas

Excel makes calculations based on formulas you enter into cells. When you complete the entry of a formula, Excel displays the results of the formula rather than the formula you entered.

- If a formula uses cell references to refer to other cells and the contents of one or more of those cells changes, the result of the formula changes, too.

- All formulas begin with an equal (=) sign. This is how Excel knows that a cell entry is a formula and not a value.

- Formulas can contain any combination of values, references, operators (see **Table 2**), and functions. I tell you about using operators in formulas in this chapter and about using functions in Chapter 5.

- Formulas are not case sensitive. This means that =A1+B10 is the same as =a1+b10. Excel automatically converts characters in cell references and functions to uppercase.

How Excel Calculates Complex Formulas

When calculating the results of expressions with a variety of operators, Excel makes calculations in the following order:

1. Negation.
2. Expressions in parentheses.
3. Percentages.
4. Exponentials.
5. Multiplication or division.
6. Addition or subtraction.

Table 3 shows some examples of formulas and their results to illustrate this. As you can see, the inclusion of parentheses can really make a difference when you write a formula!

Operator	Use	Example
+	Addition	=A1+B10
-	Subtraction	=A1-B10
-	Negation	=-A1
*	Multiplication	=A1*B10
/	Division	=A1/B10
^	Exponential	=A1^3
%	Percentage	=20%

Table 2. *Mathematical operators understood by Excel. Comparison and text operators are discussed in Chapter 5.*

Assumptions:		
A1=5		
B10=7		
C3=4		
Formula	Evaluation	Result
=A1+B10*C3	=5+7*4	33
=C3*B10+A1	=4*7+5	33
=(A1+B10)*C3	=(5+7)*4	48
=A1+10%	=5+10%	5.1
=(A1+10)%	=(5+10)%	0.15
=A1^2-B10/C3	=5^2-7/4	23.25
=(A1^2-B10)/C3	=(5^2-7)/4	4.5
=A1^(2-B10)/C3	=5^(2-7)/4	0.00008

Table 3. *Excel evaluates expressions based on operators, no matter what order the expressions appear in the formula. Adding parentheses can change the order of evaluation and the results.*

Worksheet Basics

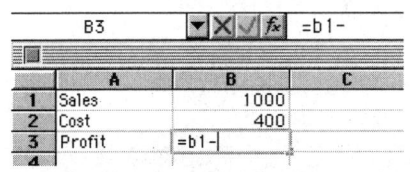

Figure 20a. *As a formula is entered into a cell, it appears in both the cell and the formula bar.*

Figure 20b. *A completed formula entry. The cell shows the results of the formula rather than the formula. But you can still see and edit the formula in the formula bar.*

Figure 21a. *If any of the values change, the formulas will need to be rewritten!*

Figure 21b. *But if the formulas reference cells containing the values, when the values change, the formulas will not need to be rewritten to show correct results.*

To enter a formula by typing

1. Make the cell in which you want to enter the formula the active cell.
2. Type in the formula. As you type, the formula appears in two places: the active cell and the formula bar, which becomes active (see **Figure 20a**).
3. To complete and accept the entry (see **Figure 20b**), press Return or Enter.

    or

    Click the Enter button on the formula bar.

✔ Tips

- Pressing Return to complete an entry accepts the entry and moves the cell pointer one cell down. Pressing Enter or clicking the Enter button accepts the entry without moving the cell pointer.
- Do not use the arrow keys or other movement keys to complete an entry by moving to another cell. Doing so may add cells to the formula!
- Use cell references for values rather than amounts or results of formulas whenever possible. This way, you don't have to rewrite formulas when amounts change. **Figures 21a** and **21b** illustrate this.
- To add a range of cells to a formula, type the first cell in the range followed by a colon (:) and then the last cell in the range. For example: *B1:B10* references the cells from *B1* straight down through *B10*.

Entering Formulas by Typing

23

Chapter 2

To enter a formula by clicking

1. Make the cell in which you want to enter the formula the active cell.
2. Type an equal (=) sign to begin the formula (see **Figure 22a**).
3. To enter a constant value or operator, type it in (see **Figure 22c**).

    or

    To enter a cell reference, click on the cell you want to reference (see **Figures 22b** and **22d**).
4. Repeat step 3 until the entire formula appears in the formula bar.
5. Press Return or Enter (see **Figure 22e**).

    or

    Click the Enter button on the formula bar.

✔ Tips

- If you click a cell reference without typing an operator, Excel assumes you want to add that reference to the formula.
- Be careful where you click when writing a formula! Each click you make will add a reference to the formula you're writing. If you add an incorrect reference, use the Delete key to delete it or click the Cancel button to start the entry from scratch. (I tell you more about editing a cell's contents in Chapter 3.)
- You can add a range of cells to a formula by dragging over the cells.

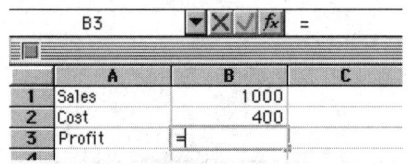

Figure 22a. *To enter the formula =B1–B2, begin by typing = to begin the formula…*

Figure 22b. *…click cell B1 to add its reference to the formula…*

Figure 22c. *…type – to tell Excel to subtract…*

Figure 22d. *…click cell B2 to add its reference to the formula…*

Figure 22e. *…and finally, press Return or Enter to complete the formula.*

Entering Formulas by Clicking

24

EDITING WORKSHEETS 3

About Editing

You can easily make the following edits in an Excel worksheet:

- Change the contents of cells.
- Insert or delete cells, columns, and rows.
- Copy or move cells from one location to another.

This chapter covers all of these techniques as well as the Undo command, which can help you out of a jam when you make an editing mistake.

Figure 1a. *To edit a cell while it is being written, click to reposition the insertion point in the cell…*

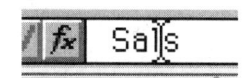

Figure 1b. *…or in the formula bar and make changes as necessary.*

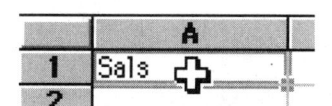

Figure 2. *You can edit a completed entry by making it active again.*

To change an entry as you type it

Use the Delete key to delete incorrect characters and type in new ones.

or

Use the mouse pointer (which turns into an I-beam pointer) to position the insertion point within the cell (see **Figure 1a**) or formula bar (see **Figure 1b**) and insert or delete characters.

To change a completed entry

Click the cell containing the incorrect entry, click in the formula bar to make it active, then insert or delete characters as necessary.

or

Double-click on the cell containing the incorrect entry (see **Figure 2**), then insert or delete characters as necessary right in the cell.

Chapter 3

To clear cell contents

1. Select the cell(s) you want to clear.
2. Choose Contents from the Clear submenu under the Edit menu (see **Figure 3**).

   or

   Press ⌘B.

   or

   Press the Del key (on an extended keyboard only).

Figure 3. *The Edit menu's Clear submenu offers four options to clear selected cells.*

✔ Tips

- To clear the contents of only one cell, make the cell active, press Delete, and then press Return or Enter.
- Do *not* use the Spacebar to clear a cell's contents! Doing so inserts a space character into the cell. Although the contents seem to disappear, they are just replaced by an invisible character.
- Clearing a cell is very different from deleting a cell. When you clear a cell, the cell remains in the worksheet—only its contents are removed. When you delete a cell, the entire cell is removed from the worksheet and other cells shift to fill the gap. I tell you about inserting and deleting cells next.
- The Contents command clears only the values or formulas entered into a cell. To clear everything, including formatting and notes, choose All from the Clear submenu under the Edit menu. To clear only formats or notes, choose Formats or Notes from the Clear submenu. I tell you about formatting cells and adding cell notes in Chapter 6.

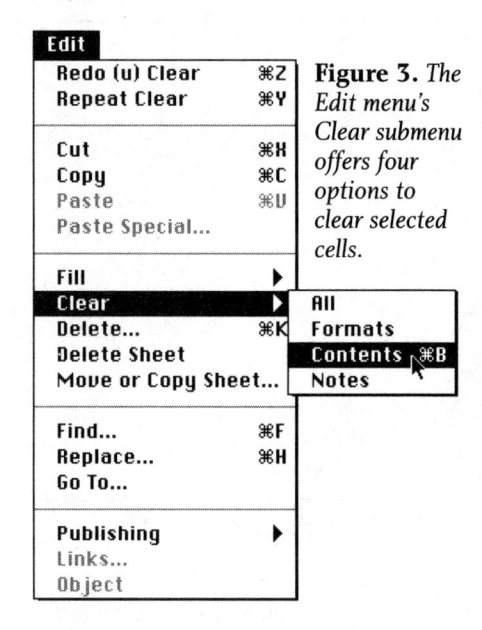

Clearing Cells

26

Editing Worksheets

About Inserting and Deleting Cells

Excel offers an Insert command and a Delete command to insert and delete columns, rows, or cells. When you use the Insert command, Excel shifts cells down or to the right to make room for the new cells. When you use the Delete command, Excel shifts cells up or to the left to fill the gap left by the missing cells.

Figures 4a, **4d**, and **5c** show examples of how inserting a column or deleting a row affects the references of the cells in a worksheet. Fortunately, Excel is smart enough to know how to adjust cell references in formulas so that the formulas you write remain correct.

To insert a column or row

1. Select a column or row (see **Figure 4b**).
2. Choose Columns or Rows from the Insert menu (see **Figure 4c**).

   or

   Choose Cells from the Insert menu.

   or

   Press ⌘I.

✔ Tips

- To insert multiple columns or rows, select the number of columns or rows you want to insert. For example, if you want to insert three columns before column B, select columns B, C, and D.

- If a complete column or row is not selected when you press ⌘I, the Insert dialog box will appear. Just click the appropriate radio button (Entire Row or Entire Column) for what you want to insert, then click OK or press Return.

	A	B	C	D
1		Jan	Feb	Mar
2	Nancy	443	419	841
3	Bess	493	277	45
4	George	301	492	179
5	Ned	67	856	842

Figure 4a. *A simple worksheet.*

	A	B	C	D
1		Jan	Feb	Mar
2	Nancy	443	419	841
3	Bess	493	277	45
4	George	301	492	179
5	Ned	67	856	842

Figure 4b. *To insert a column, begin by selecting the column where you want the new column to go…*

Figure 4c. *…then choose Columns from the Insert menu.*

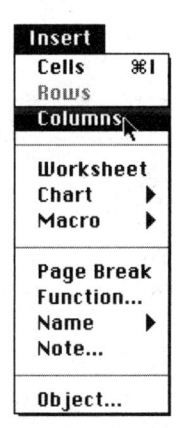

```
Insert
Cells      ⌘I
Rows
Columns
Worksheet
Chart       ▶
Macro       ▶
Page Break
Function…
Name        ▶
Note…
Object…
```

	A	B	C	D	E
1			Jan	Feb	Mar
2	Nancy		443	419	841
3	Bess		493	277	45
4	George		301	492	179
5	Ned		67	856	842

Figure 4d. *Here's what you wind up with when you insert a column.*

Inserting Columns or Rows

27

Chapter 3

To delete a column or row

1. Select a column or row (see **Figure 5a**).
2. Choose Delete from the Edit menu (see **Figure 5b**).

   or

   Press ⌘K.

✔ Tips

- To delete more than one column or row at a time, select all of the columns or rows you want to delete before choosing Delete from the Edit menu.
- If a complete column or row is not selected when you press ⌘K, the Delete dialog box will appear. Just click the appropriate radio button (Entire Row or Entire Column) for what you want to delete, then click OK or press Return.
- If you delete a column or row that contains referenced cells, the formulas that reference the cells may display a #REF! error message. This means that Excel can't find a referenced cell. If this happens, you'll have to rewrite any formulas in cells displaying the error.

	A	B	C	D
1		Jan	Feb	Mar
2	Nancy	443	419	841
3	Bess	493	277	45
4	George	301	492	179
5	Ned	67	856	842

Figure 5a. *To delete a row, begin by selecting the row you want to delete…*

Edit
Undo Delete	⌘Z
Repeat Delete	⌘Y
Cut	⌘X
Copy	⌘C
Paste	⌘V
Paste Special…	
Fill	▶
Clear	▶
Delete	**⌘K**
Delete Sheet	
Move or Copy Sheet…	
Find…	⌘F
Replace…	⌘H
Go To…	
Publishing	▶
Links…	
Object	

Figure 5b. *…then choose Delete from the Edit menu.*

	A	B	C	D
1		Jan	Feb	Mar
2	Nancy	443	419	841
3	Bess	493	277	45
4	Ned	67	856	842

Figure 5c. *Here's what you wind up with when you delete a row.*

Deleting Columns or Rows

28

Editing Worksheets

Figure 6a. *To insert or delete cells, begin by selecting cells.*

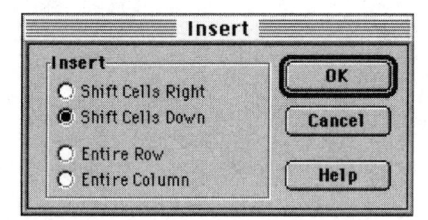

Figure 6b. *Use the Insert dialog box to tell Excel to shift existing cells to the right or down.*

Figure 6c. *Here's what you get if you shift cells down.*

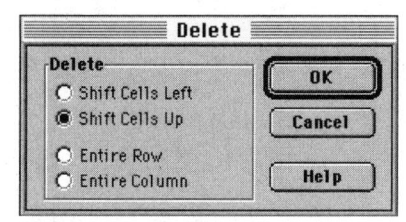

Figure 6d. *Use the Delete dialog box to tell Excel to shift cells around the deleted cells to the left or up.*

Figure 6e. *Here's what you get if you shift cells up.*

To insert cells

1. Select a cell or range of cells (see **Figure 6a**).
2. Choose Cells from the Insert menu.

   or

   Press ⌘I.
3. In the Insert dialog box that appears (see **Figure 6b**), choose the appropriate radio button to tell Excel how to shift the cells—Shift Cells Right or Shift Cells Down.
4. Click OK or press Return or Enter (see **Figure 6c**).

✔ Tip

- Excel always inserts the number of cells that is selected when you use the Insert command. You can see this in **Figures 6a and 6b**.

To delete cells

1. Select a cell or range of cells to delete (see **Figure 6a**).
2. Choose Delete from the Edit menu.

   or

   Press ⌘K.
3. In the Delete dialog box that appears (see **Figure 6d**), choose the appropriate radio button to tell Excel how to shift the cells—Shift Cells Left or Shift Cells Up.
4. Click OK or press Return or Enter (see **Figure 6e**).

✔ Tip

- If you delete a column or row that contains referenced cells, the formulas that reference the cells may display a #REF! error message. If this happens, you'll have to rewrite any formulas in cells displaying the error.

Chapter 3

About Copying Cells

Excel offers several ways to copy the contents of one cell to another: the Copy and Paste commands, the fill handle on the cell pointer, and the Fill command.

How Excel copies depends not only on the method used, but on the contents of the cell(s) being copied.

- When you use the Copy and Paste commands to copy a cell containing a value, Excel makes an exact copy of the cell, including any formatting (see **Figure 7**). I tell you about formatting cells in Chapter 6.

- When you use the fill handle or Fill command to copy a cell containing a value, Excel either makes an exact copy of the cell, including any formatting, or creates a series based on the original cell's contents (see **Figure 8**).

- When you copy a cell containing a formula, Excel copies the formula, changing any relative references in the formula so they're relative to the destination cell(s) (see **Figure 9**).

✔ Tips

- Copy cells that contain formulas whenever possible to save time and ensure consistency.

- The Edit menu's Paste special command offers additional options over the regular paste command. For example, you can use it to paste only the formatting of a copied selection, convert formulas in the selection into values, or add the contents of the selection to the destination cells.

Figure 7. *The Copy and Paste commands make an exact copy.*

Figure 8. *Using the fill handle on a cell containing the word* Monday *generates a list of the days of the week.*

Jan	Feb	Mar
443	419	841
493	277	45
493	277	45
69	856	842
1498	1829	1773

Figure 9. *Copying a formula that totals a column automatically writes correctly referenced formulas to total similar columns.*

Understanding Copying

30

Editing Worksheets

Figure 10a. *Begin by selecting the cell(s) you want to copy...*

Figure 10b. *...choose Copy from the Edit menu...*

Figure 10c. *...a marquee appears around the selection...*

Figure 10d. *...select the destination cell...*

Figure 10e. *...and choose Paste from the Edit menu.*

To copy with Copy and Paste

1. Select the cell(s) you want to copy (see **Figure 10a**).
2. Choose Copy from the Edit menu (see **Figure 10b**).

   or

   Press ⌘C.

   or

   Click the Copy button on the Standard toolbar.

   An animated marquee appears around the selection (see **Figure 10c**).

3. Select the cell(s) to which you want to paste the selection (see **Figure 10d**). If more than one cell has been copied, you can select the first cell of the destination range or the entire range.
4. Choose Paste from the Edit menu.

   or

   Press ⌘V.

   or

   Click the Paste button on the Standard toolbar.

   or

   Press Enter.

   The values are copied to the new location (see **Figure 10e**).

✔ Tips

- If you use the Paste command, ⌘P, or the Paste button, the marquee remains around the copied range, indicating that it is still in the Clipboard and may be pasted elsewhere. The marquee will disappear automatically as you work, but if you want to remove it manually, press Esc.
- Be careful when you paste cells! If the destination cells contain information, Excel will overwrite them without warning you!

Copying with Copy and Paste

31

Chapter 3

About the Fill Handle

The fill handle is a small black or colored box in the lower right corner of the cell pointer (see **Figure 11a**) or selection (see **Figure 11b**). You can use the fill handle to copy the contents of one or more cells to adjacent cells.

To copy with the fill handle

1. Select the cell(s) containing the information you want to copy.
2. Position the mouse pointer on the fill handle. The mouse pointer turns into a crosshairs (see **Figure 12a**).
3. Press the mouse button down and drag to the adjacent cells. A dark border surrounds the destination cells (see **Figure 12b**).
4. When all the destination cells are surrounded by the dark border, release the mouse button. The cells are filled. (see **Figure 12c**).

✔ Tips

- You can use the fill handle to copy any number of cells. The destination cells, however, must be adjacent to the original cells.
- When using the fill handle, you can only copy in one direction (up, down, left, or right) at a time.
- Be careful when you use the fill handle to copy cells! If the destination cells contain information, Excel will overwrite them without warning you!

Figure 11a. *The fill handle on the cell pointer.*

Figure 11b. *The fill handle on a selection.*

Figure 12a. *When the mouse pointer is over the fill handle, it turns into a crosshairs pointer.*

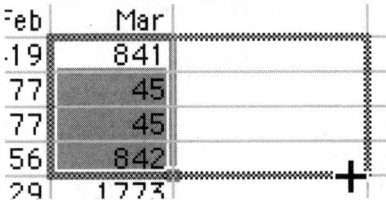

Figure 12b. *As you drag the fill handle, a dark border indicates the destination cells.*

Figure 12c. *When you release the mouse button, the cells in the original selection are copied to the destination cells.*

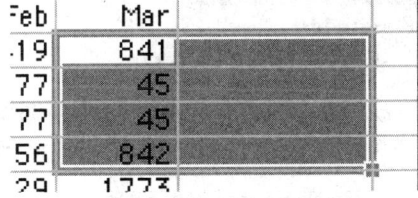

About the Fill Command

The Fill command works a lot like the fill handle in that it copies information to adjacent cells. But rather than drag to copy, you select the source and destination cells at the same time and then use the Fill command to complete the copy. There are several options to copy:

- Down copies the contents of the top cell(s) in the selection to the selected cells beneath it.
- Right copies the contents of the left cell(s) in the selection to the selected cells to the right of it.
- Up copies the contents of the bottom cell(s) in the selection to the selected cells above it.
- Left copies the contents of the right cell(s) in the selection to the selected cells to the left of it.

To use the Fill command

1. Select the cell(s) you want to copy along with the adjacent destination cell(s) (see **Figure 13a**).
2. Choose the appropriate command from the Fill submenu under the Edit menu (see **Figure 13b**): Down, Right, Up, Left.

✔ Tip

- You *must* select both the source and destination cells when using the Fill command. If you only select the destination cells, Excel won't copy the correct cells!

Figure 13a. *To use the Fill command, begin by selecting the source and destination cells...*

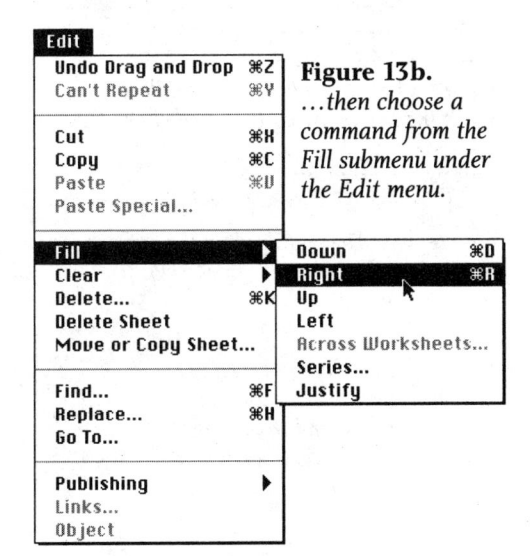

Figure 13b. *...then choose a command from the Fill submenu under the Edit menu.*

Chapter 3

About AutoFill

A *series* is a sequence of cells that form a logical progression. Excel's AutoFill feature can generate a series of numbers, months, days, dates, and quarters.

To create a series with the fill handle

1. Enter the first item of the series in a cell (see **Figure 14a**). Be sure to complete the entry by pressing Return or Enter.
2. Position your mouse pointer on the fill handle and drag. All the cells that will be part of the series are surrounded by a dark border (see **Figure 14b**).
3. Release the mouse button to complete the series (see **Figure 14f**).

To create a series with the Series command

1. Enter the first item in the series in a cell (see **Figure 14a**).
2. Select all cells that will be part of the series, including the first cell (see **Figure 14c**).
3. Choose the Series from the Fill submenu under the Edit menu (see **Figure 14d**).
4. In the Series dialog box that appears (see **Figure 14e**), turn on the AutoFill radio button.
5. Click OK or press Return or Enter to complete the series (see **Figure 14f**).

✔ Tip

- To generate a series that skips values, enter the first two values of the series in adjoining cells, then use the fill handle or Fill command to create the series, including both cells as part of the source (see **Figures 15a** and **15b**).

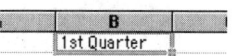

Figure 14a. *Start by entering the first item of the series in a cell...*

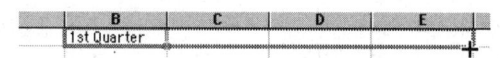

Figure 14b. *...then drag the fill handle to include all cells that will contain the series.*

Figure 14c. *...or select the cells that will contain the series...*

Figure 14d. *...choose Series from the File submenu under the Edit menu...*

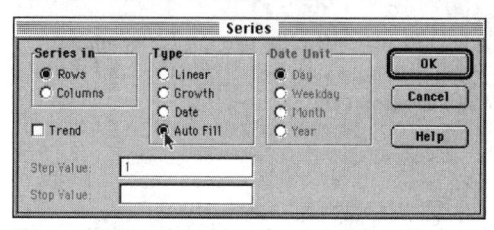

Figure 14e. *...turn on the AutoFill radio button in the Series dialog box, and click OK.*

Figure 14f. *The end result is the same: a series automatically built by Excel.*

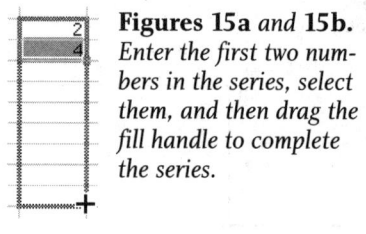

Figures 15a and **15b**. *Enter the first two numbers in the series, select them, and then drag the fill handle to complete the series.*

Editing Worksheets

About Copying Formulas

You copy a cell containing a formula the same way you copy any other cell in Excel: with the Copy and Paste commands, with the fill handle, or with the Fill command. These methods are discussed earlier in this chapter.

Generally speaking, Excel does not make an exact copy of a formula. Instead, it copies the formula based on the kinds of references used within it. Types of references are discussed in detail on the next page.

	A	B	C	D
1	Item	Price	Cost	Markup
2	Product A	24.95	16.73	=(B2-C2)/C2
3	Product B	15.95	5.69	
4	Product C	12.99	4.23	
5	Product D	99.99	62.84	

Figure 16a. *Here's a formula to calculate markup percentage. If the company has 534 products, would you want to write the same basic formula 533 more times?*

✔ Tips

- You'll find it much quicker to copy formulas rather than to write each and every formula from scratch. You can see an example of this in **Figures 16a** and **16b**.

- Not all formulas can be copied with accurate results. For example, you can't copy a formula that sums up a column of numbers to a cell that should represent a sum of cells in a row (see **Figure 17**).

	A	B	C	D
1	Item	Price	Cost	Markup
2	Product A	24.95	16.73	49% — =(B2-C2)/C2
3	Product B	15.95	5.69	180% — =(B3-C3)/C3
4	Product C	12.99	4.23	207% — =(B4-C4)/C4
5	Product D	99.99	62.84	59% — =(B5-C5)/C5

Figure 16b. *Of course not! That's when copying formulas comes in handy. If the original formula is properly written, the results of the copied formulas should also be correct.*

	A	B	C	D	E	F
1			January	February	March	
2		Sales	$1,000.00	$1,250.00	$1,485.00	
3		Cost	400.00	395.00	412.00	
4		Profit	$ 600.00	$ 855.00	$1,073.00	
5						
6						
7	Owner	Pctg	Jan Share	Feb Share	Mar Share	Total
8	Nancy	50%	300.00	427.50	536.50	0
9	Bess	20%	120.00	171.00	214.60	
10	George	20%	120.00	171.00	214.60	=SUM(F4:F7)
11	Ned	10%	60.00	85.50	107.30	
12			$ 600.00	$ 855.00	$1,073.00	

=SUM(C8:C11)

Figure 17. *In this illustration, the formula in cell C12 was copied to cell F8. This doesn't work because the two cells don't add up similar ranges. The formula in cell F8 would have to be rewritten from scratch. It could then be copied to F9 through F11. (I tell you about the SUM function in Chapter 5.)*

Understanding Copying Formulas

35

Chapter 3

Understanding Cell References

Relative vs. Absolute Cell References

There are two main kinds of cell references:

- A *relative cell reference* is the address of a cell relative to the cell the reference is in. For example, a reference to cell *B1* in cell *B3*, tells Excel to look at the cell two cells above *B3*. Most of the references you use in Excel are relative references.

- An *absolute cell reference* is the exact location of a cell. To indicate an absolute reference, enter a dollar sign ($) in front of the column letter(s) and row number of the reference. An absolute reference to cell *B1*, for example, would be written *$B$1*.

As **Figures 18a** and **18b** illustrate, relative cell references change when you copy them to other cells. Although in many cases, you might want the references to change, sometimes you don't. That's when you use absolute references (see **Figures 18c** and **18d**).

✔ Tips

- Here's a trick for remembering the meaning of the notation for absolute cell references: in your mind, replace the dollar sign with the word *always*. Then you'll read *$B$1* as *always B always 1—always B1*!

- If you're having trouble understanding how these two kinds of references work and differ, don't worry. This is one of the most difficult spreadsheet concepts you'll encounter. Try creating a worksheet like the one illustrated on this page and working your way through the figures one at a time. Pay close attention to how Excel copies the formulas you write!

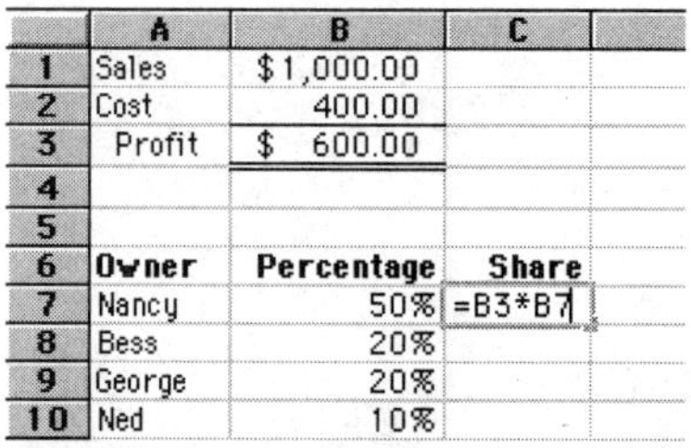

Figure 18a. This formula correctly calculates a partner's share of profit.

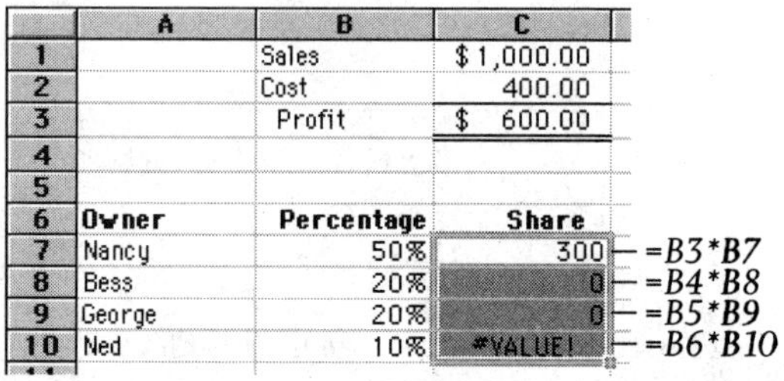

Figure 18b. But when the formula is copied for the other partners, the relative reference to cell B3 is changed, causing incorrect results and an error message!

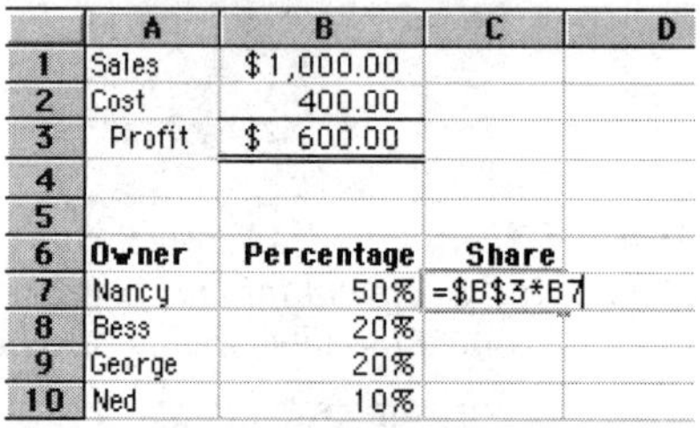

Figure 18c. Rewrite the original formula so it includes an absolute reference to cell B3, which all the formulas must reference.

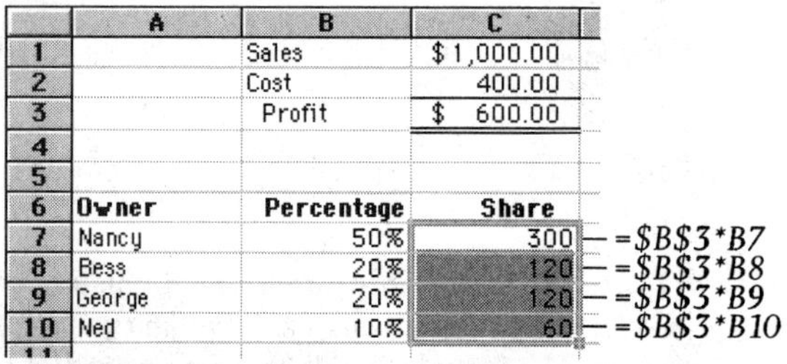

Figure 18d. When the formula is copied for the other partners, only the relative reference (to the percentages) changes. The results are correct.

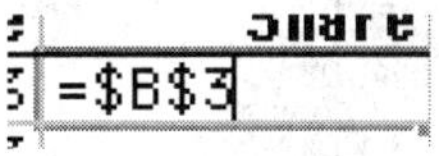

Figure 19. *Either include the dollar signs as you type, or press ⌘T when the insertion point is in a cell reference.*

To include an absolute reference in a formula

1. Enter the formula by typing or clicking as discussed in Chapter 2.
2. Type a dollar sign before the column and row references for the cell reference you want to be absolute (see **Figure 19**).

   or

   With the insertion point on a cell reference, press ⌘T to have Excel insert the dollar signs automatically.
3. Complete the entry by pressing Return or Enter.

✔ Tips

- You can edit an existing formula to include absolute references by inserting dollar signs where needed or using the ⌘T shortcut on a selected reference. I tell you how to edit cell contents earlier in this chapter.
- Do not use a dollar sign in a formula to indicate currency formatting. I tell you how to apply formatting to cell contents, including currency format, in Chapter 6.

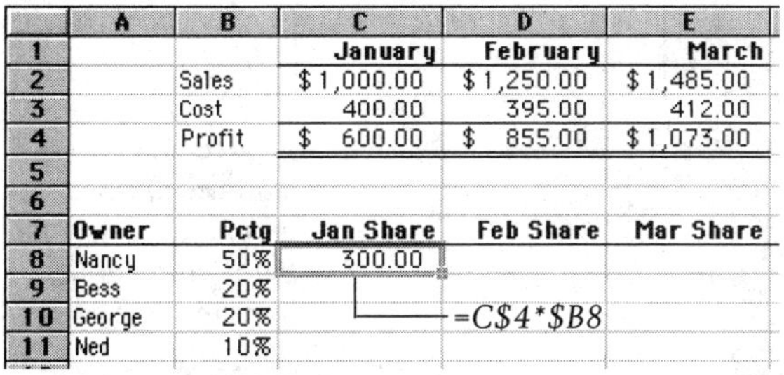

	A	B	C	D	E
1			January	February	March
2		Sales	$ 1,000.00	$ 1,250.00	$ 1,485.00
3		Cost	400.00	395.00	412.00
4		Profit	$ 600.00	$ 855.00	$ 1,073.00
5					
6					
7	Owner	Pctg	Jan Share	Feb Share	Mar Share
8	Nancy	50%	300.00		
9	Bess	20%			
10	George	20%			
11	Ned	10%			

Figure 20. *The formula in cell* C8 *includes two different kinds of mixed references. It can be copied to cells* C9 *through* C11 *and* D8 *through* E11 *for correct results in all cells. Try it for yourself!*

About Mixed References

There's another kind of cell reference. In a mixed cell reference, either the column or row reference is absolute while the other reference remains relative. Thus, you can use cell references like *A$1* or *$A1*. Use this when a column reference must remain constant but a row reference changes or vice versa. **Figure 20** shows a good example.

Chapter 3

About Moving Cells

Excel offers two ways to move the contents of one cell to another: the Cut and Paste commands and dragging the border of a selection. Either way, Excel moves the contents of the cell, including any formatting. I tell you about cell formatting in Chapter 6.

✔ Tip

- When you move a cell, Excel searches the worksheet for any cells that contain references to it and changes the references to reflect the cell's new location (see **Figures 21a** and **21b**).

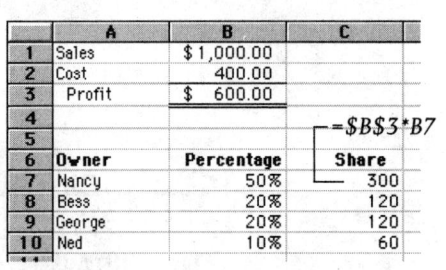

To move with Cut and Paste

1. Select the cell(s) you want to move (see **Figure 22a**).
2. Choose Cut from the Edit menu (see **Figure 22b**).

    or

    Press ⌘X.

    or

    Click the Cut button on the Standard toolbar.

    An animated marquee appears around the selection (see **Figure 22c**).

3. Select the cell(s) to which you want to paste the selection (see **Figure 22d**).
4. Choose Paste from the Edit menu.

    or

    Press ⌘V.

    or

    Click the Paste button on the Standard toolbar.

    or

    Press Enter.

    The cell contents are moved to the new location (see **Figure 22e**).

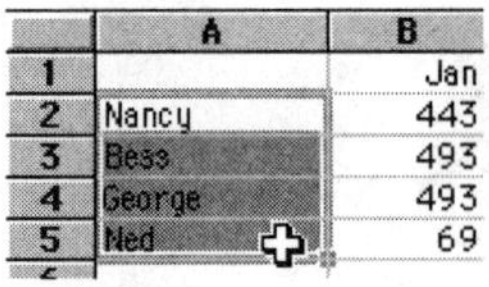

Figure 21a. *Note the formula in cell C7.*

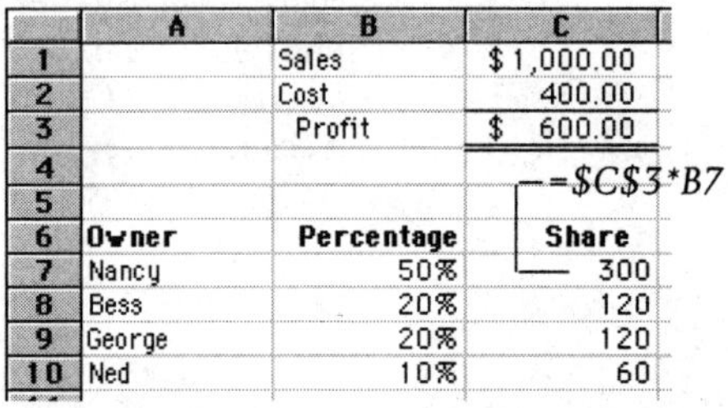

Figure 21b. *See how it changes when one of the cells it references changes?*

Figure 22a. *Begin by selecting the cell(s) you want to move…*

Figure 22b. *…choose Cut from the Edit menu…*

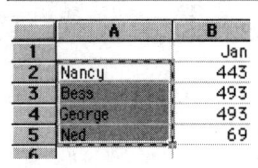

Figure 22c. *…a marquee appears around the selection but it does not disappear…*

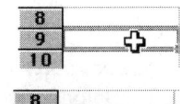

Figure 22d. *…select the destination cell(s)…*

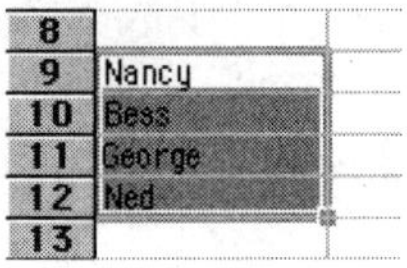

Figure 22e. *…and choose Paste from the Edit menu.*

Editing Worksheets

To move with drag and drop

1. Select the cell(s) you want to move.
2. Position the mouse pointer on the border of the selection. When it is in the proper position, it turns into an arrow pointing up and to the left (see **Figure 23a**).
3. Press the mouse button down and drag toward the new location. As you move the mouse, a dark border the same shape as the selection moves along with it (see **Figure 23b**).
4. Release the mouse button. The selection moves to its new location.

✔ Tips

- If you try to drag a selection to cells already containing information, Excel warns you with a dialog box like the one in **Figure 24**. If you click OK to complete the move, the cells will be overwritten with the contents of the cells you are moving.

- To copy using drag and drop, hold down the Option key as you press the mouse button down. The mouse pointer turns into an arrow with a tiny plus sign (+) beside it (see **Figure 25**). When you release the mouse button, the selection is copied.

- To insert cells using drag and drop, hold down the Shift key as you press the mouse button down. As you drag, a dark bar moves along with the mouse pointer (see **Figure 26**), indicating where the cells will be inserted when you release the mouse button.

Figure 23a. *Position the mouse pointer on the border of the selection.*

Figure 23b. *As you drag, a dark border with the same shape as the selection moves along with your mouse pointer.*

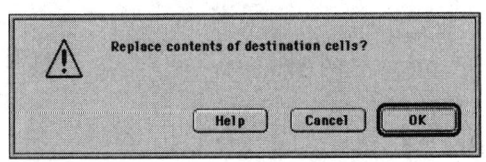

Figure 24. *Excel warns you when you try to drag a selection to occupied cells.*

Figure 25. *Holding the Option key down while dragging a border copies the selection.*

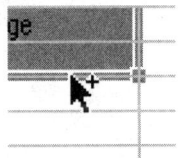

Figure 26. *Holding the Shift key down while dragging a border inserts the cells.*

39

Chapter 3

About Undoing Commands

If you issue a command or change the contents of a cell by mistake, don't panic! Many Excel actions and commands can be reversed with the Undo command.

To undo a command

Choose Undo from the Edit menu (see **Figure 27**). When available, this is the first command on the Edit menu.

or

Press ⌘Z.

or

Click the Undo button on the Standard toolbar.

Figure 27. *The Edit menu's Undo command will reverse the last action taken.*

About Repeating Commands

You can also repeat an action or command. This is especially useful if you've made changes to a cell and want to make the same changes to another cell or group of cells.

To repeat a command

Choose Repeat from the Edit menu (see **Figure 27**). When available, this is the second command on the Edit menu.

or

Press ⌘Y.

or

Click the Repeat button on the Standard toolbar.

✔ Tip

- If the last command or action was to undo the previous action, the Undo command changes to a Redo command (see **Figure 28**). This restores the document to the way it was before the Undo command was used.

Figure 28. *After undoing an action or command, the Undo command turns into a Redo command.*

WORKING WITH FILES 4

Figure 1a. Here's a worksheet to calculate profit and each partner's share.

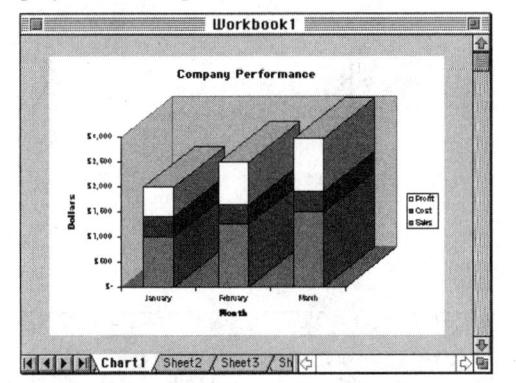

Figure 1b. In the same workbook, here's a sheet to show company sales, cost, and profit.

Figure 1c. Also in the same workbook, here's a Visual Basic macro to project performance using Excel's series feature.

About Workbook Files

In Excel version 5, there's only one kind of file: a *workbook* file. A workbook file can include up to 255 *sheets*, which are like pages in the workbook. Each workbook, by default, includes 16 sheets named *Sheet 1* through *Sheet 16*.

Although there are six kinds of sheets, you'll work most often with only two or three:

- A *worksheet* is for entering information and performing calculations. **Figure 1a** shows an example. You can also embed charts in a worksheet.

- A *chart sheet* is for creating charts that aren't embedded in a worksheet (see **Figure 1b**).

- A *Visual Basic module* is for creating and editing macros with the Microsoft Excel Visual Basic language (see **Figure 1c**). This is an advanced feature of Excel.

The other three kinds of sheets are dialog, Microsoft 4.0 macro sheet, and Microsoft Excel 4.0 international macro sheet.

✔ Tip

- Use the multiple sheet capabilities of Excel 5 workbooks to keep sheets for the same project together. This is an excellent way to organize related work.

Understanding Workbooks

41

To switch between sheets in a workbook

Click the sheet tab at the bottom of the workbook window (see **Figure 2**) for the sheet you want.

or

Press Option-Left Arrow or Option-Right Arrow to scroll through all the sheets in a workbook, one at a time.

Figure 2. *Sheet tabs let you move from sheet to sheet within a workbook.*

✔ Tips

- If the sheet tab for the sheet you want is not displayed, use the tab scrolling buttons (see **Figure 3**) to scroll through the sheet tabs.

- To display more or less sheet tabs, drag the tab split box (see **Figure 4**) to increase or decrease the size of the sheet tab area. As you change the size of the sheet tab area, you'll also change the size of the bottom scroll bar for the workbook window.

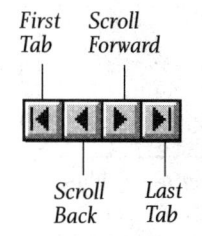

Figure 3. *Use the tab scrolling buttons to view sheet tabs that are not displayed.*

Figure 4. *Drag the tab split box to change the size of the sheet tab area and display more or less sheet tabs.*

To select multiple sheets

1. Click the sheet tab for the first sheet you want to select.

2. Hold down the Command (⌘) key and click the sheet tab(s) for the other sheet(s) you want to select. The sheet tabs for each sheet you include in the selection turn white (see **Figure 5**).

Figure 5. *To select multiple sheets, hold down the Command key while clicking each sheet tab.*

✔ Tips

- To select multiple adjacent sheets, click the sheet tab for the first sheet, then hold down the Shift key and click on the sheet tab for the last sheet you want to select. All sheet tabs in between also become selected.

- Selecting multiple sheets makes it quick and easy to print, delete, edit, format, or perform other tasks with more than one sheet at a time.

To insert a worksheet

1. Click the tab for the sheet you want to insert before (see **Figure 6a**).
2. Choose Worksheet from the Insert menu (see **Figure 6b**)

   or

   Press Shift-F11 (on an extended keyboard).

   A new worksheet is inserted before the one you originally selected (see **Figure 6c**).

To insert a chart sheet

1. Click the tab for the sheet you want to insert before (see **Figure 6a**).
2. Choose As New Sheet from the Chart submenu under the Insert menu (see **Figure 7**).

   The new sheet is inserted and the first dialog box of the ChartWizard appears. I tell you how to create charts with the ChartWizard in Chapter 8.

To insert a Visual Basic module

1. Click the tab for the sheet you want to insert before (see **Figure 6a**).
2. Choose Module from the Macro submenu under the Insert menu (see **Figure 8**).

   The new sheet is inserted and the Visual Basic toolbar appears. I tell you a little more about macros and Visual Basic in Chapter 13.

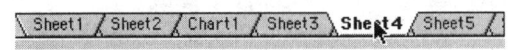

Figure 6a. *Begin by selecting the sheet you want the new sheet to be inserted before…*

Figure 6b. *…then choose Worksheet from the Insert menu.*

Figure 6c. *The new sheet is inserted.*

Figure 7. *Use the Chart submenu under the Insert menu to insert a chart sheet.*

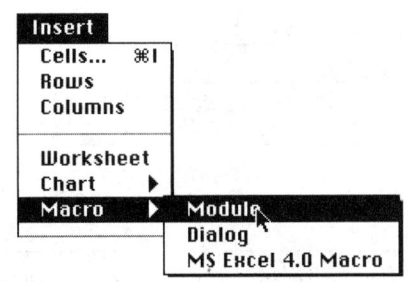

Figure 8. *Use the Macro submenu under the Insert menu to insert a Visual Basic module.*

Chapter 4

To delete a sheet

1. Click on the sheet tab for the sheet you want to delete to make it active.
2. Choose Delete Sheet from the Edit menu (see **Figure 9a**).
3. A warning dialog box appears (see **Figure 9b**). Click OK or press Return or Enter to confirm that you want to delete the sheet.

✔ Tips

- As the dialog box warns, sheets are permanently deleted. That means even the Undo command won't get a deleted sheet back.
- If another cell in the workbook contains a reference to a cell on the sheet you've deleted, that cell will display a #REF! error message. The formulas in that cell will have to be rewritten.

To rename a sheet

1. Click on the sheet tab for the sheet you want to rename to make it active.
2. Choose Rename from the Sheet submenu under the Format menu (see **Figure 10a**).

   or

   Double-click the sheet tab.
3. In the Rename Sheet dialog box that appears (see **Figure 10b**), enter a new name for the sheet.
4. Click OK or press Return or Enter.

The sheet tab for that sheet displays the new name you gave it (see **Figure 10c**).

✔ Tip

- Sheet names can be up to 31 characters long and can contain any character you can type from your keyboard.

Figure 9a. *Choose Delete Sheet from the Edit menu...*

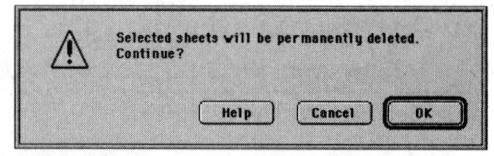

Figure 9b. *...then click OK to confirm that you really do want to delete the sheet.*

Figure 10a. *To rename a sheet, choose Rename from the Sheet submenu...*

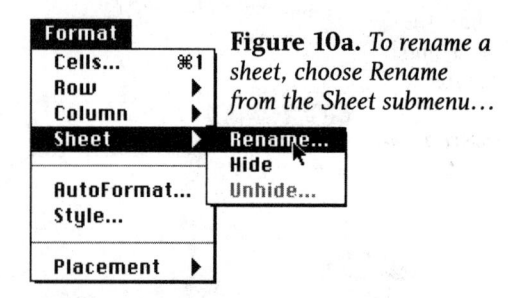

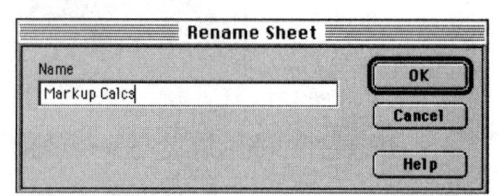

Figure 10b. *...then enter a new name for the sheet and click OK.*

Figure 10c. *The name appears on the sheet tab.*

44

Working with Files

Figure 11. *Use the Hide command under the Sheet submenu to hide selected sheets.*

To hide a sheet

1. Select the sheet(s) you want to hide.
2. Choose Hide from the Sheet submenu under the Format menu (see **Figure 11**).

The sheet and its sheet tab disappear, just as if the sheet were deleted! But don't worry—the sheet still exists in the workbook file.

✔ Tips

- You cannot hide a sheet if it is the only sheet in a workbook.
- Don't confuse this command with the Hide command under the Window menu. These commands do two different things! I tell you about the Window menu's Hide command later in this chapter.

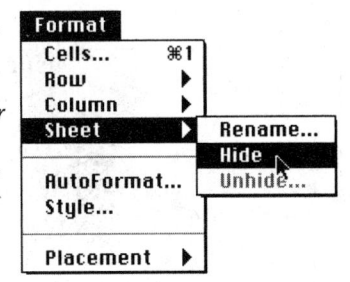

Figure 12. *Use the Unhide command under the Sheet submenu to unhide hidden sheets.*

To unhide a sheet

1. Choose Unhide from the Sheet submenu under the Format menu (see **Figure 12**).
2. In the Unhide Sheet dialog box that appears, select the sheet you want to unhide (see **Figure 13**).
3. Click OK or press Return or Enter.

The sheet and its sheet tab reappear.

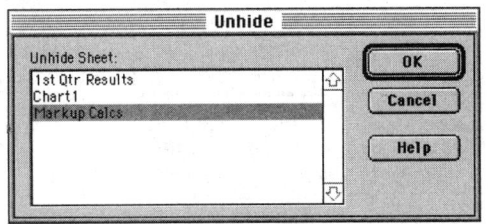

Figure 13. *The Unhide dialog box lets you pick the sheet you want to unhide.*

✔ Tips

- You can only unhide one sheet at a time.
- If the Unhide command is gray, no sheets are hidden (see **Figure 11**).
- Don't confuse this command with the Unhide command under the Window menu. I tell you about the Window menu's Unhide command later in this chapter.

Hiding & Unhiding Sheets

45

To move or copy a sheet

1. Select the sheet(s) you want to move or copy.
2. Choose Move or Copy Sheet from the Edit menu (see **Figure 14a**). The Move or Copy dialog box appears (see **Figure 14b**).
3. Use the To Book pop-up menu (see **Figure 14c**) to choose the workbook you want to move or copy the workbook to.
4. Use the Before Sheet scrolling list to choose the sheet you want the sheet(s) to be copied before.
5. If you want to copy or duplicate the sheet rather than move it, turn on the Create a Copy check box.
6. Click OK or press Return or Enter.

✔ Tips

- To move or copy sheets to another workbook, make sure that workbook is open (but not active) *before* you choose the Move or Copy Sheet command. Otherwise, it will not be listed in the To Book pop-up menu (see **Figure 14c**).
- If you choose (new book) from the To Book pop-up menu (see **Figure 14c**) Excel creates a brand new, empty workbook file and places the selected sheet(s) into it.
- You can use the Move or Copy Sheet command to change the order of sheets in a workbook. Just make sure the current workbook is selected in the To Book pop-up menu (see **Figure 14c**). Then select the appropriate sheet from the Before Sheet scrolling list or choose (move to end), which is the last option in the list.

Figure 14a. *The Move or Copy Sheet command lets you do just that.*

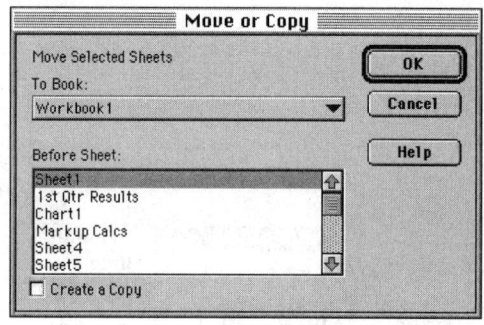

Figure 14b. *Use the Move or Copy dialog box to pick a destination for the sheet(s) and tell Excel that you want to copy them rather than move them.*

Figure 14c. *The To Book pop-up menu lists all the workbooks that are currently open.*

- You can also move or copy a sheet within a workbook by dragging. To move the sheet, simply drag the sheet tab to the new position. To copy the sheet, hold down the Option key while dragging the sheet tab.

About Workbook Windows

Like most Macintosh programs, Excel lets you have more than one document open at a time. (I tell you how to create a new workbook and open an existing workbook in Chapter 2.) But Excel goes a step further by enabling you to open multiple windows for the same workbook. Then, by arranging the windows on screen, you can see and work with more than one of them.

To make another window active

Choose the name of the window you want to make active from the list of open windows at the bottom of the Window menu (see **Figure 15**).

or

Press ⌘M or Control-Tab to go to the next window.

or

Press ⌘Shift-M or Control-Shift-Tab to go to the previous window.

To create a new window

1. Make the workbook you want to create another window for the active window.
2. Choose New Window from the Window menu (see **Figure 15**).

A new window for that workbook appears. It has the same name as the workbook, but the name is followed by the window number, as shown in **Figure 16a**. In addition, a separate item appears at the bottom of the Window menu for the new window (see **Figure 16b**).

✔ Tip
■ If more than one window is open for a workbook and you close one of them, the workbook does not close—just that window.

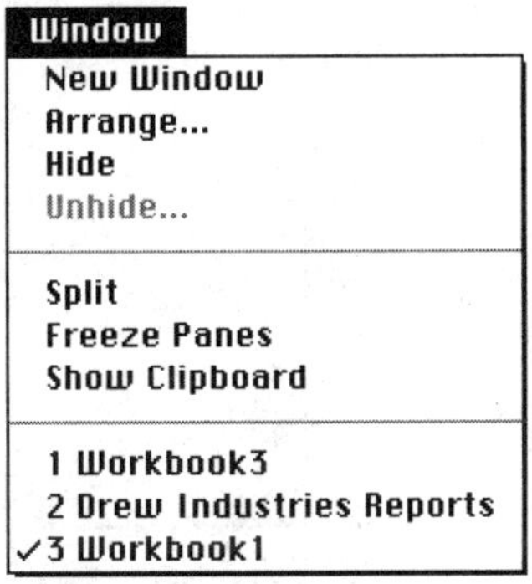

Figure 15. *The Window menu offers commands for working with workbook windows.*

Figure 16a. *The title bar for a new window displays the workbook file name as well as the window number.*

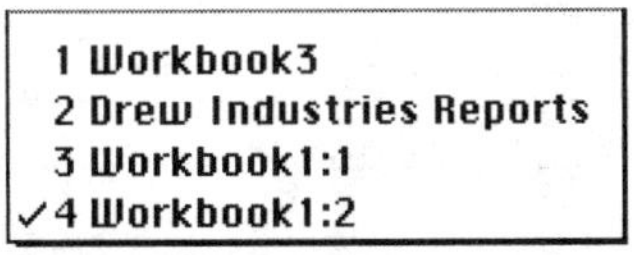

Figure 16b. *The new window is added to the Window menu.*

Chapter 4

To arrange windows

1. Choose Arrange from the Window menu (see **Figure 15**).
2. In the Arrange Windows dialog box that appears (see **Figure 17a**), choose an arrange option. **Figures 17b** through **17e** illustrate all of them.
3. If you want to arrange only the windows of the active workbook, turn on the Windows of Active Workbook check box.
4. Click OK or press Return or Enter.

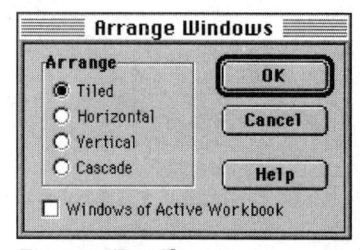

Figure 17a. *The Arrange Windows dialog box offers four arrangement options.*

✔ Tips

- To work with one of the arranged windows, click in it to make it active.
- The window with the striped title bar is the active window.
- To make one of the arranged windows full size again, click on it to make it active and then click the window's zoom box (see **Figure 18**). The window fills the screen while the other windows remain arranged behind it. Click the zoom box again to shrink it back down to its arranged size.

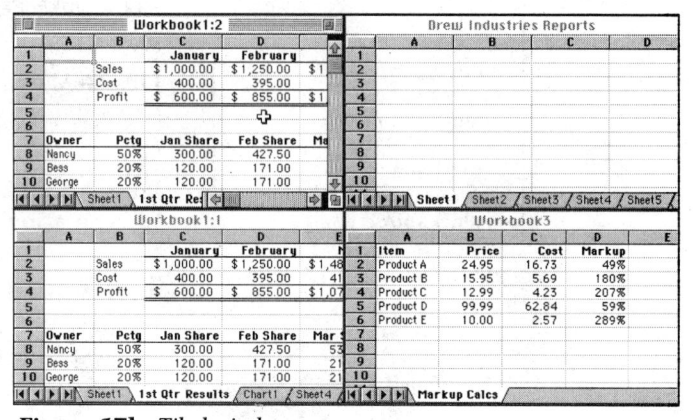

Figure 17b. *Tiled windows.*

Figure 18. *Click a window's Zoom box to toggle the window between full size and a smaller size.*

Figure 17c. *Horizontally arranged windows.*

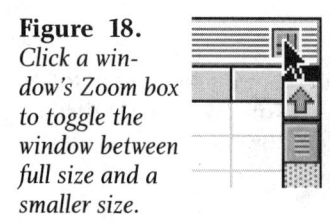

48

Working with Files

To hide a window

1. Make the window you want to hide the active window.
2. Choose Hide from the Window menu (see **Figure 15**).

✔ Tip

- Hiding a window is not the same as closing it. A hidden window remains open, even though it is not listed at the bottom of the Window menu.

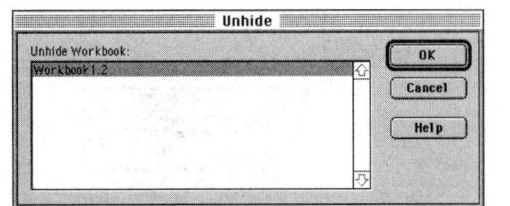

Figure 19. *Use the Unhide dialog box to unhide hidden windows.*

To unhide a window

1. Choose Unhide from the Window menu.
2. In the Unhide dialog box that appears (see **Figure 19**), choose the window you want to unhide.
3. Click OK or press Return or Enter.

✔ Tips

- If the Unhide command is gray, no windows are hidden.
- You can only unhide one window at a time.

Figure 17d. *Vertically arranged windows.*

Figure 17e. *Cascading windows.*

Hiding & Unhiding Windows

49

Chapter 4

To zoom a window's view

1. Choose Zoom from the View menu (see **Figure 20a**).
2. In the Zoom dialog box that appears (see **Figure 20b**), select the radio button for the magnification you want.
3. Click OK or press Return or Enter.

or

1. Click the arrow beside the Zoom control on the Standard toolbar to display a menu of magnifications (see **Figure 21**).
2. Choose the magnification you want from the menu.

Figure 20a. *The Zoom command...*

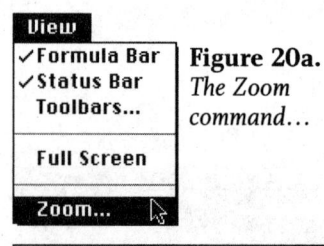

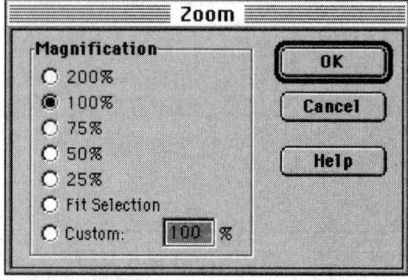

Figure 20b. *...displays the Zoom dialog box, which you can use to change the active window's magnification.*

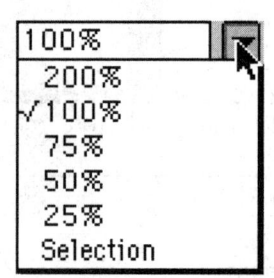

Figure 21. *Or use the Zoom control on the Standard toolbar to set the magnification.*

✔ Tips

- Zoom selected cells so they fill the window by selecting the Fit Selection radio button in the Zoom dialog box (see **Figure 20b**).
- Enter a custom magnification in the Zoom dialog box (see **Figure 20b**) by selecting the Custom radio button and entering a value of your choice.
- Enter a custom magnification in the Zoom control on the Standard toolbar (see **Figure 21**) by clicking the value in the box to select it, typing in a new value, and pressing Return or Enter.
- Custom zoom percentages must be between 10% and 400%.
- Changing the magnification with the Zoom dialog box or Zoom control on the Standard toolbar does not affect the way a worksheet will print.
- A "zoomed" window's sheet works just like any other worksheet.
- When you save a workbook, the magnification settings of its sheets are saved. When you reopen the workbook, the saved magnifications are used.

Working with Files

Figure 22a. *Position the cell pointer where you want the split to occur...*

Figure 22b. *...then choose Split from the Window menu.*

Figure 22c. *The window splits at the cell pointer.*

Figure 23a. *Position the mouse pointer on a split bar...*

Figure 23b. *...then press down the mouse button and drag to split the window.*

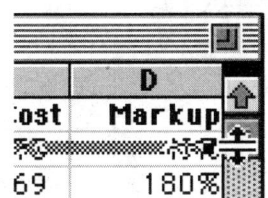

Figure 24. *When the window has a split in it, the Split command turns into a Remove Split command.*

About Splitting Windows

Splitting a window is useful when you need to see and work with two or more parts of a sheet at a time. When you split a window, you separate it into two or four *panes* (see **Figure 22c**). Each pane has its own scroll bars, so you can scroll the view in any pane until it shows exactly what you want it to.

To split a window

1. Position the cell pointer in the cell immediately below and to the right of where you want the split(s) to occur (see **Figure 22a**).
2. Choose Split from the Window menu (see **Figure 22b**).

or

1. Position the mouse pointer on the black split bar at the top or right end of the scroll bar. The mouse pointer turns into a double line with arrows coming out of it (see **Figure 23a**).
2. Press the mouse button down and drag. A dark split bar moves along with the mouse pointer (see **Figure 23b**). When you release the mouse button, the window splits at the bar.

To adjust the size of panes

1. Position the mouse pointer on a split bar.
2. Press the mouse button down and drag until the split bar is in the desired position.

To remove a window split

Choose Remove Split from the Window menu (see **Figure 24**).

or

Double-click a split bar.

Splitting Windows

Chapter 4

About Saving Workbooks

As you work with a file, everything you do is stored in only one place: *random access memory* or *RAM*. The contents of RAM are a lot like the light in a lightbulb—as soon as you turn it off or pull the plug, it's gone. Your hard disk or a floppy disk provides a much more permanent type of storage area. You use the Save command to copy the workbook file in RAM to disk.

To save a workbook file

1. Choose Save or Save As from the File menu (see **Figure 25a**).

   or

   Press ⌘S.

   or

   Click the Save button on the Standard toolbar.

2. Use the Save As dialog box that appears (see **Figure 25b**) to select a directory in which to save the file.

3. Enter a name for the file in the Save As edit box.

4. Click Save or press Return or Enter.

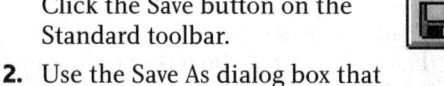

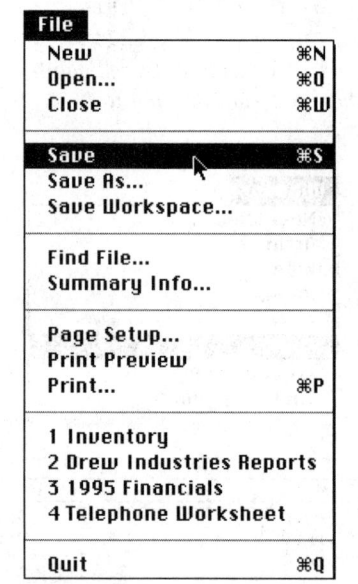

Figure 25a. *Choose Save from the File menu.*

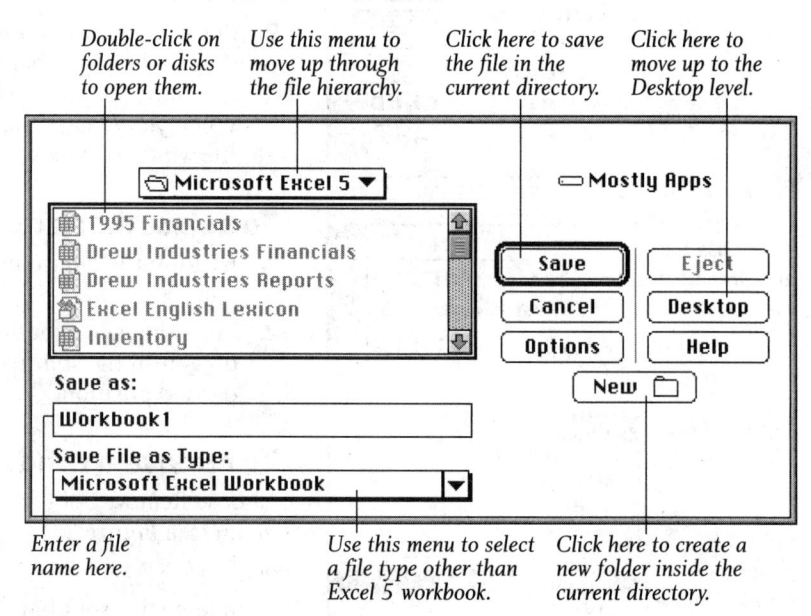

Double-click on folders or disks to open them.

Use this menu to move up through the file hierarchy.

Click here to save the file in the current directory.

Click here to move up to the Desktop level.

Enter a file name here.

Use this menu to select a file type other than Excel 5 workbook.

Click here to create a new folder inside the current directory.

Figure 25b. *Use the Save As dialog box to save a workbook.*

52

Working with Files

Figure 26. *Use the Summary Info dialog box, which is displayed the first time you save a file, to enter information about the file.*

Figure 27. *This check box toggles the automatic appearance of the Summary Info dialog box on or off.*

Figure 28. *Display the Summary Info dialog box for the active file by choosing Summary Info from the File menu.*

About Summary Information

When you save a file for the first time, Excel may automatically display the Summary Info dialog box (see **Figure 26**). You can use this dialog box to enter information about the file you're saving.

✔ Tips

- To turn this feature on or off, choose Options from the Tools menu, click the General tab, and click the check box beside Prompt for Summary Info (see **Figure 27**).

- To manually display the Summary Info dialog box, choose Summary Info from the File menu (see **Figure 28**).

To provide summary information

1. Enter information in the first edit box or *field* of the Summary Info dialog box.

2. Press Tab or click in the next edit box to move to the next field.

3. Repeat steps 1 and 2 until all fields are filled in. You may skip fields if you like. You may also change the contents of any fields automatically filled in by Excel, like the Author field. Standard text editing techniques to select, delete, insert, and replace text apply.

4. Click OK or press Return or Enter to accept your entries and save them with the file.

✔ Tips

- Each Summary Info dialog box field can accept up to 255 characters of information.

- To dismiss the Summary Info dialog box without entering information, click OK or press Return or Enter or click Cancel or press Esc.

Providing Summary Info

53

About File Formats

By default, Excel saves files in Microsoft Excel Workbook file format. This is the format that appears in the Save File As Type pop-up menu in the Save As dialog box (see **Figures 25b** and **29**). If you pull down this menu, you can see the other file types Excel can save. **Table 1** lists some of the more popular file types.

To save a file in another format

1. Choose Save As from the File menu (see **Figure 25a**).
2. Use the Save As dialog box (see **Figure 25b**) to select a directory in which to save the file.
3. Enter a name for the file in the Save As edit box.
4. Choose a file format from the Save File As Type pop-up menu (see **Figure 29**).
5. Click Save or press Return or Enter.

✔ Tips

- If the document has not yet been saved at all, in step 1 above you could also choose the Save command from the File menu, press ⌘S, or click the Save button to display the Save As dialog box.
- If the format you chose in step 4 above saves only the active worksheet, a dialog box like the one in **Figure 30** will appear after you click Save. Click OK or press Return or Enter to complete the save.
- Text (Tab Delimited) is commonly used to save Excel information in a format that can be easily imported into files created with other applications, like Microsoft Word tables or Claris FileMaker Pro databases.

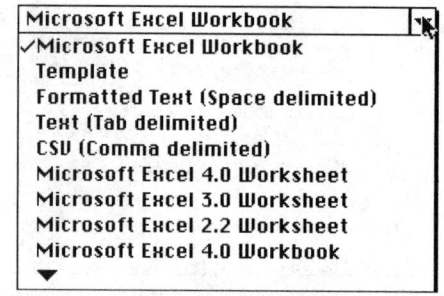

Figure 29. *Pull down the Save File As Type pop-up menu in the Save As dialog box to save a file in a different format.*

Figure 30. *Excel warns you when you're saving only a worksheet rather than an entire workbook.*

Template	Saves the worksheet in a special format that can be used to create similar Excel workbook files.
Text	Saves the active worksheet's contents as plain text, with tab characters between columns and return characters at the end of rows.
Microsoft Excel 4.0, 3.0, or 2.2 Worksheet	Saves the active worksheet in a format that can be read by an earlier version of Excel.
Microsoft Excel 4.0 Workbook	Saves the workbook in a format that can be read by Excel 4.0.
WKS, WK1, or WK3	Saves the active worksheet in a format that can be read by various versions of Lotus 1-2-3.

Table 1. *Here's a list of the more commonly used file formats Excel 5 supports.*

Working with Files

Figure 31. *Once a file has been saved, you must use the Save As command to save it differently.*

Figure 32a. *Click a window's close box to close the window*

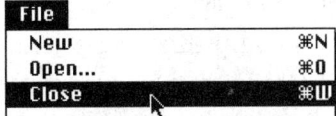

Figure 32b. *The Close command also lets you close the active window or file.*

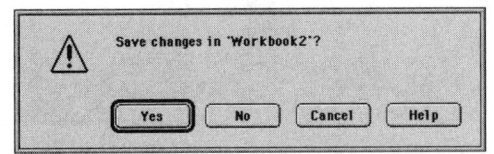

Figure 32c. *If you haven't saved changes, Excel warns you and lets you save them.*

Figure 33. *Hold down the Shift key and pull down the File menu to see the Close All command.*

Save vs. Save As

Once you've saved a file, using the Save command again automatically saves the file with the same name, in the same disk location. If you want to change the name, disk location, or file type of a file, you'll have to use the Save As command (see **Figure 31**). Doing so displays the Save As dialog box (see **Figure 25b**) so you can change the directory or file name or both.

✔ Tip

- Save files often as you work to prevent losing work in the event of a system bomb or power outage. Remember the ⌘S shortcut to access the Save command quickly without reaching for the mouse.

To close a file

Click the close box of the window for the file you want to close (see **Figure 32a**).

or

Choose Close from the File menu (see **Figure 32b**).

or

Press ⌘W.

✔ Tips

- If the file you are closing has not been saved since changes were made to it, Excel displays a dialog box like the one in **Figure 32c**. Click Yes to save changes.

- To close all open windows, hold down the Shift key and pull down the File menu. Choose Close All (see **Figure 33**). Excel offers to save unsaved documents before closing them all, one by one.

Save vs. Save As & Closing Files

55

Chapter 4

About the Find File Command

The Find File command under the File menu gives you access to Excel's powerful file searching utility. You can use this feature to search for any file on any disk that can be read by your Macintosh, including disks accessible via network.

To find a file

1. Choose Find File from the File menu.
2. In the Search dialog box that appears (see **Figure 34a**), enter all or part of the file name in the File Name edit box.
3. If desired, use the File Type and Location pop-up menus to narrow down the search by choosing a specific type of file or specific disk.
4. Click OK or press Return or Enter.
5. After a moment, Excel displays the Find File dialog box (see **Figure 34b**), which includes a list of files that match the search string you provided. Click a file to preview it on the right side of the dialog box. Click the Open button to open a selected file. Use the Commands button/menu to print, copy, delete, or perform other tasks on the selected file.
6. When you are finished with the Find File dialog box, click Close to dismiss it.

✔ Tip

■ The file searching feature of Excel has far more capabilities than I can cover in this book. Explore them on your own the next time you need to find a file. The Advanced Search button in the Search dialog box (see **Figure 34a**) is a good place to start.

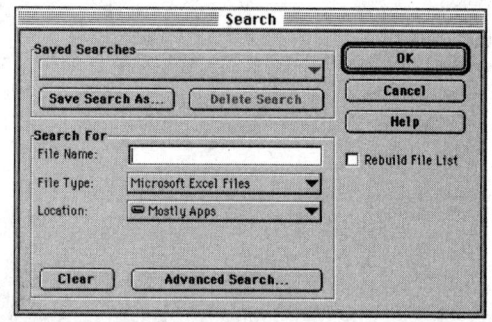

Figure 34a. *The Search dialog box lets you search for files.*

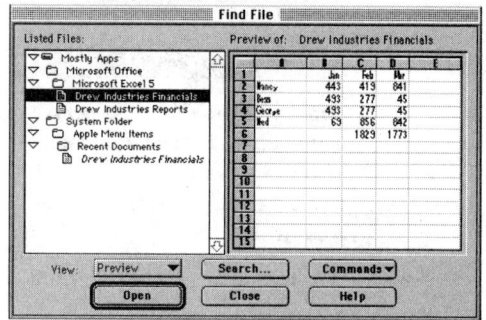

Figure 34b. *Excel displays the results of a search and lets you open, print, copy, or delete files.*

USING FUNCTIONS IN FORMULAS 5

About Functions

A *function* is a predefined formula for making a specific kind of calculation. Functions make it quicker and easier to write formulas.

For example, say you need to add up a column of numbers like the one in **Figure 1**. It's perfectly acceptable to write a formula using cell references separated by the addition operator (+) like this:

=C4+C5+C6+C7+C8+C9+C10+C11

But rather than enter a lengthy formula, you can use the SUM function to add up the same numbers like this:

=SUM(C4:C11)

The SUM function is only one of over 200 functions built into Excel.

	A	B	C
1	Product Inventory		
2			
3	Item Name	Item Number	Qty
4	Blank Tapes	T-00	62
5	Home with Fred	H-236	8
6	Franklin in Paris	F-734	54
7	Deuce Anaheim, Defec	D-154	108
8	Star Wreck	S-48	34
9	David Silvermeadow	D-183	69
10	Pulp Fractions	P-139	75
11	Woodland Gulch	W-87	87
12			

Figure 1. *Using the SUM function makes it easier to add up a column of numbers.*

function name   arguments

SUM(number1,number 2,...)

Figure 2. *The parts of a function.*

Anatomy of a Function

As shown in **Figure 2**, each function has two main parts.

- The *function name* determines what the function does.
- The *arguments* determine what values or cell references the function should use in its calculation. Arguments are enclosed in parentheses and, if there's more than one, separated by commas.

✔ Tips

- If a function comes at the beginning of a formula, it *must* begin with an equal sign (=).
- Some arguments are optional. In the SUM function, for example, you can have only one argument, like the reference to a range of cells used in the example above.

Understanding Functions

57

Chapter 5

About Arguments

Arguments can consist of any of the following:

- **Numbers** (see **Figure 3**). Like any other formula, however, the result of a function that uses values for arguments will not change unless the formula is changed.
- **Text** (see **Figure 4**). Excel has a whole collection of functions just for text. I tell you about them later in this chapter.
- **Cell references** (see **Figures 4** through **8**). This is a practical way to write functions, since when you change cell contents, the results of functions that reference them change automatically.
- **Formulas** (see **Figures 6** and **7**). This lets you create complex formulas that perform a series of calculations at once.
- **Functions** (see **Figures 7** and **8**). When a function includes another function as one of its arguments, it's called *nesting*.
- **Error values** (see **Figure 8**). You may find this useful to "flag" errors or missing information in a worksheet.
- **Logical values.** Some functions arguments require TRUE or FALSE values.

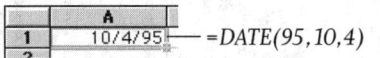

=DATE(95,10,4)

Figure 3. This example uses numbers as arguments for the DATE function.

=IF(B8>400,"Good work!","Try harder")

Figure 4. This example uses cell references, numbers, and text as arguments for the IF function to display a comment.

=SUM(B8:B11)   or
=SUM(B8,B9,B10,B11)

Figure 5. This example shows two different ways to use cell references as arguments for the SUM function to add numbers.

=ROUND(B4*C4,2)

Figure 6. This example uses a formula as an argument for the ROUND function to round calculated commissions.

=ROUND(IF(B8>400,B8*$B$4,B8*$B$5),2)

Figure 7. This example uses the ROUND and IF functions to calculate commissions based on a rate that changes acccording to sales.

=IF(COUNTBLANK(B8:B11)>0,#N/A,SUM(B8:B11))

Figure 8. This example uses three functions (IF, COUNTBLANK, and SUM), cell references, and error values to either indicate missing information or add a column of numbers.

Understanding Arguments

58

About Entering Functions

Excel offers several ways to enter a function:

- by typing
- by typing and clicking
- by using the Function Wizard

There is no "best" way—use the methods that you like most.

To enter a function by typing

1. Begin the formula by typing an equal sign (=).
2. Type in the function name.
3. Type an open parenthesis character.
4. Type in the value or cell reference for the first argument.
5. If entering more than one argument, type each of them in with commas between them.
6. Type a closed parenthesis character (see **Figure 9a**).
7. Press Return or Enter or click the Enter button on the formula bar.

The result of the function is displayed in the cell (see **Figure 9b**).

Figure 9a. *You can type in a function just like you'd type in any other formula.*

Figure 9b. *When you press Return or Enter, the cell containing the function displays the result of the formula.*

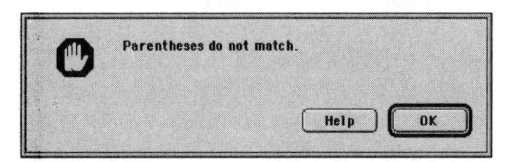

Figure 10. *Excel displays an error message when the parentheses in a function don't match.*

✔ Tips

- Function names are not case sensitive. *Sum* or *sum* is the same as *SUM*. Excel converts all function names to uppercase characters.
- Do *not* include spaces when writing formulas.
- When writing formulas with nested functions, it's vital that you properly match parentheses. Excel helps you by boldfacing parentheses as you type them. If parentheses don't match, Excel may display an error message (see **Figure 10**).

Chapter 5

To enter a function by typing and clicking

1. Begin the formula by typing an equal sign (=).
2. Type in the function name.
3. Type an open parenthesis character.
4. Type in a value or click on the cell whose reference you want to include as the first argument (see **Figure 11a**).
5. If entering more than one argument, type a comma, then type in a value or click on the cell for the next reference (see **Figure 11b**). Repeat this step for each argument in the function.
6. Type a closed parenthesis character (see **Figure 11c**).
7. Press Return or Enter or click the Enter button on the formula bar.

The result of the function is displayed in the cell (see **Figure 9b**).

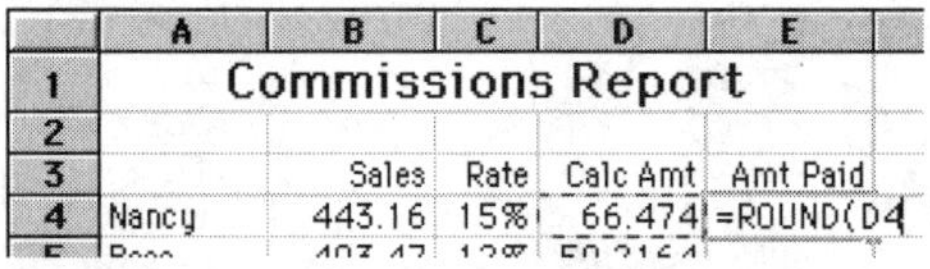

✔ Tips

- To include a range by clicking, in step 4 or 5 above, drag the mouse pointer over the cells you want to include (see **Figure 12**).
- Be careful where you click or drag when entering a function or any formula. Each click or drag may add references to the formula! If you click on a cell by mistake, you can use the Delete key to delete the incorrectly added reference or click the Cancel button on the formula bar to start over from scratch.

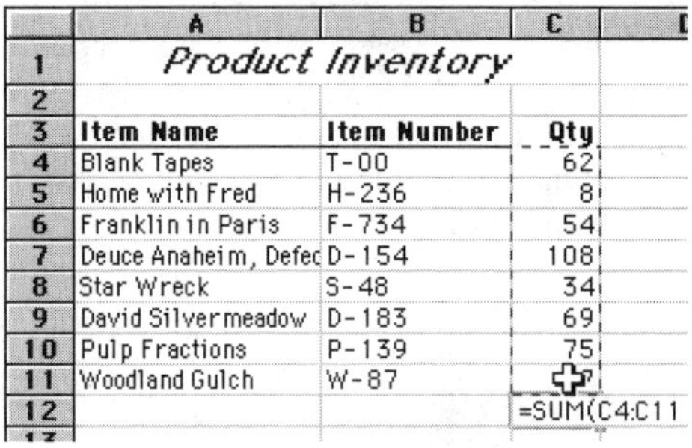

Figure 11a. *After typing the beginning of the function, you can click on cell references for arguments...*

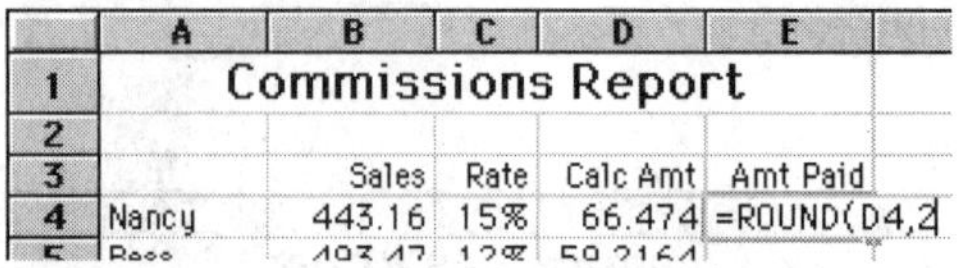

Figure 11b. *...and type in values for arguments...*

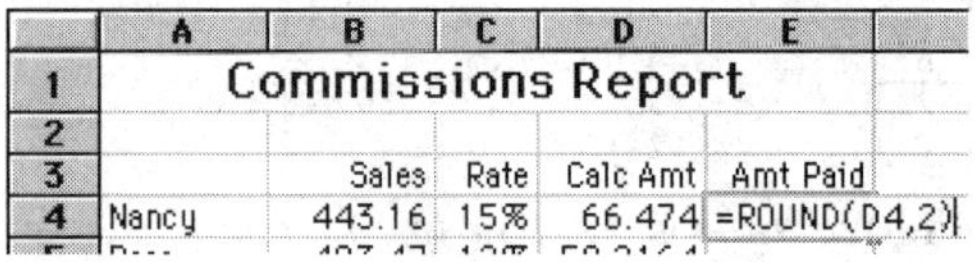

Figure 11c. *...until the function is complete.*

Figure 12. *You can always enter a range in a formula by dragging, even when the range is an argument for a function.*

Using Functions in Formulas

Figure 13a. *Choose Function from the Insert menu...*

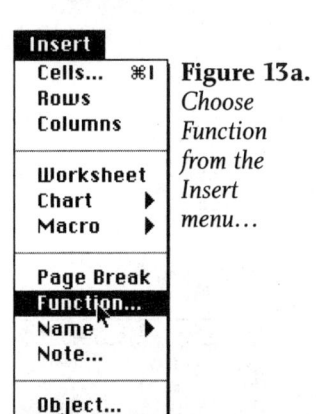

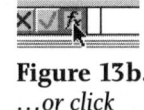

Figure 13b. *...or click the Function button on the formula bar.*

To enter a function with the Function Wizard

1. Choose Function from the Insert menu (see **Figure 13a**).

   or

   Click the Function Wizard button on the Standard toolbar.

   or

   Click the formula bar to make it active, then click on the Function button (see **Figure 13b**).

2. In the Function Wizard – Step 1 dialog box that appears (see **Figure 13c**), choose a category from the Function Category list on the left side of the dialog box.

3. Choose a function from the Function Name scrolling window on the right side of the dialog box. You may have to use the scroll bar to locate the function name you want.

4. Click Next or press Return or Enter.

5. In the Function Wizard – Step 2 dialog box (see **Figure 13d**), enter a value or cell reference for the first argument in its edit box. The value of what you enter appears in the gray box to the right of the edit box.

6. Press Tab or click to move to the next argument's edit box and enter a value or cell reference for it. Repeat this step for each argument. When you're finished, the result of the function appears in the gray Value box in the upper right corner of the Function Wizard window (see **Figure 13e**).

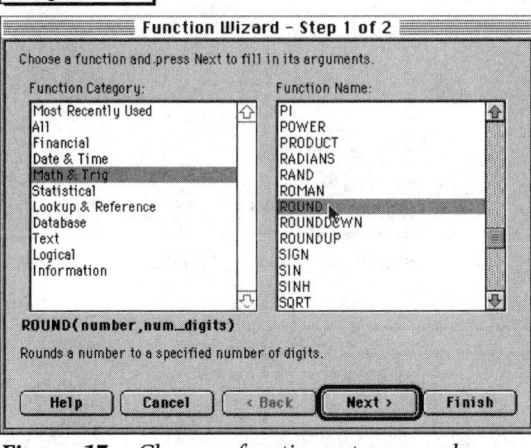

Figure 13c. *Choose a function category and name in Step 1 of the Function Wizard.*

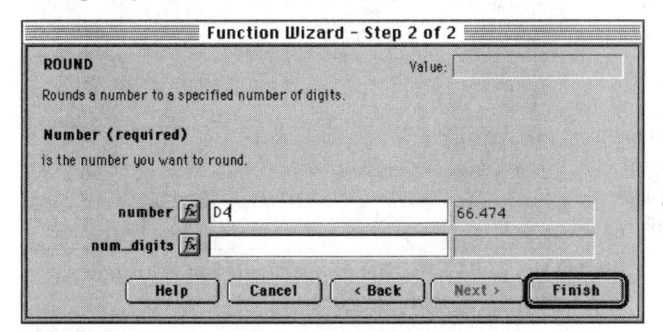

Figure 13d. *Fill in the values or cell references for arguments in Step 2.*

Figure 13e. *The result of the function appears in the Value box.*

Using the Function Wizard

61

Chapter 5

7. Click Finish or press Return or Enter.

8. If you opened the Function Wizard by making the formula bar active and clicking the Function button, press Return or Enter to complete the formula. (If you opened the Function Wizard by using the Function command, this step is not necessary.)

✔ Tips

- While in Step 1 of the Function Wizard dialog box, if you're not sure what category a function is in, choose All. The Function name scrolling list displays all the functions Excel has to offer.

- While in Step 2 of the Function Wizard dialog box, you can click or drag in the worksheet window to enter a cell reference or range.

Figure 14. *If an argument is optional, the Function Wizard tells you.*

- If the Function Wizard dialog box is blocking your view of the worksheet window, you can move it by dragging its title bar.

- If an argument is not required, the Function Wizard tells you so when you click in the argument's edit box (see **Figure 14**).

- You can nest a function as an argument by either typing it into the argument's edit box or using the function button beside the argument to bring up a Function Wizard [Nested] dialog box (see **Figure 15**).

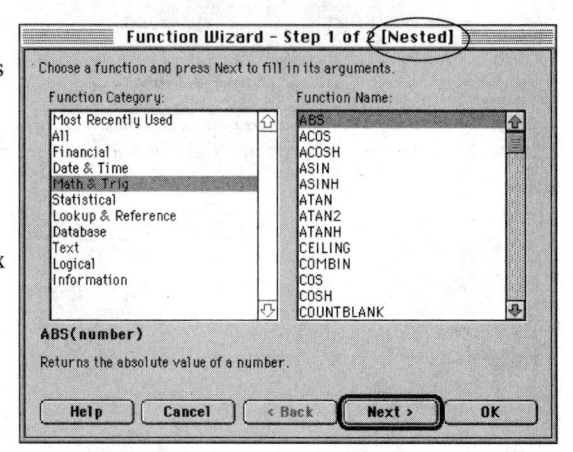

Figure 15. *The Function Wizard can help you write complex nested functions.*

- The Back button available in Step 2 of the Function Wizard lets you go back to Step 1 to choose a different function.

About Math and Trigonometry Functions

Excel has 59 math and trigonometry functions. On the next few pages, I tell you about the most commonly used ones, starting with one so popular it even has its own toolbar button: SUM.

About the SUM Function

The SUM function (see **Figure 16**) adds up numbers. It uses the following syntax:

$$SUM(number1, number2, ...)$$

Although the SUM function can accept up to 30 arguments separated by commas, only one is required.

Figure 16. *Two ways to use the SUM function to add numbers.*   =SUM(B2:D2)   **or**   =SUM(B2,C2,D2)

To use the AutoSum button

1. Select the cell below the column or to the right of the row of numbers you want to add.

2. Click the AutoSum button on the Standard toolbar once.

   Excel examines the worksheet and makes a "guess" about which cells you want to add. It writes the corresponding formula and puts a marquee around the range cells it used (see **Figure 17**).

3. If the range in the formula is incorrect, type or select the correct range. Since the reference for the range of cells is selected in the formula, anything you type or select will automatically replace it.

4. When the formula is correct, press Return or Enter, click the Enter button on the formula bar, or click the AutoSum button on the Standard toolbar a second time.

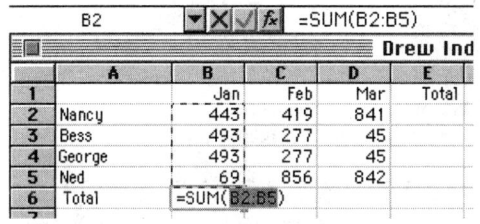

Figure 17. *Clicking the AutoSum button automatically writes a formula that adds up a column (or row) of numbers.*

Chapter 5

To use the AutoSum button on multiple cells

1. Select a range of cells adjacent to the columns or rows you want to add (see **Figure 18a**).
2. Click the AutoSum button once. ∑

   Excel writes the formulas in the cells you selected (see **Figure 18b**).

   or

1. Select the cells containing the columns you want to add (see **Figure 19a**).
2. Click the AutoSum button once. ∑

   Excel writes all the formulas in the row of cells immediately below the ones you selected (see **Figure 19b**).

   or

1. Select the cells containing the columns and rows you want to add, along with the empty row beneath them and the empty column to the right of them (see **Figure 20a**).
2. Click the AutoSum button once. ∑

   Excel writes all the formulas in the bottom and rightmost cells (see **Figure 20b**).

✔ Tip

- Be sure to check the formulas Excel writes when you use the AutoSum button. Excel is smart, but it's no mind-reader. The cells it includes may not be the ones you had in mind!

	A	B	C	D
1		Jan	Feb	Mar
2	Nancy	443	419	841
3	Bess	493	277	45
4	George	493	277	45
5	Ned	69	856	842
6	Total			

Figure 18a. *Select the cells adjacent to the columns (or rows) of cells you want to add…*

	A	B	C	D	E
1		Jan	Feb	Mar	To
2	Nancy	443	419	841	
3	Bess	493	277	45	
4	George	493	277	45	
5	Ned	69	856	842	
6	Total	1498	1829	1773	

Figure 18b. *…then click the AutoSum button to write all the formulas at once.*

	A	B	C	D
1		Jan	Feb	Mar
2	Nancy	443	419	841
3	Bess	493	277	45
4	George	493	277	45
5	Ned	69	856	842
6	Total			

Figure 19a. *Select the cells containing the columns you want to add…*

	A	B	C	D
1		Jan	Feb	Mar
2	Nancy	443	419	841
3	Bess	493	277	45
4	George	493	277	45
5	Ned	69	856	842
6	Total	1498	1829	1773

Figure 19b. *…then click the AutoSum button to write all the formulas in the cells beneath the selection.*

	A	B	C	D	E
1		Jan	Feb	Mar	Total
2	Nancy	443	419	841	
3	Bess	493	277	45	
4	George	493	277	45	
5	Ned	69	856	842	
6	Total				

Figure 20a. *Select the cells you want to add, as well as the cells in which you want the totals to appear…*

	A	B	C	D	E
1		Jan	Feb	Mar	Total
2	Nancy	443	419	841	1703
3	Bess	493	277	45	815
4	George	493	277	45	815
5	Ned	69	856	842	1767
6	Total	1498	1829	1773	5100

Figure 20b. *…then click the AutoSum button to add up the columns and rows all at once.*

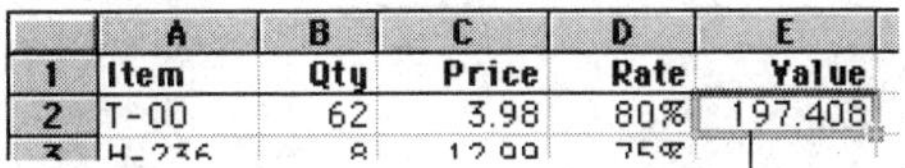

Using Functions in Formulas

Figure 21. *Two ways to use the PRODUCT function to multiply numbers.*

=PRODUCT(B2:D2) **or**
=PRODUCT(B2,C2,D2)

About the PRODUCT Function

The PRODUCT function (see **Figure 21**) multiplies its arguments much like the SUM function adds them. It uses the following syntax:

PRODUCT(number1,number2,...)

Although the PRODUCT function can accept up to 30 arguments separated by commas, only one is required.

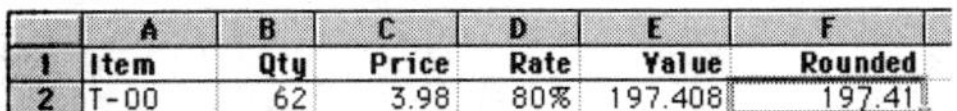

About the ROUND Function

Figure 22. *Use the ROUND function to round numbers to the number of decimal places you specify.*

=ROUND(E2,2)

The ROUND function (see **Figure 22**) rounds a number to the number of decimal places you specify. It uses the following syntax:

ROUND(number,num_digits)

Both arguments are required. The *num_digits* argument specifies how many decimal places the number should be rounded to. If 0, the number is rounded to a whole number. If less than 0, the number is rounded on the left side of the decimal point (see **Figure 23**).

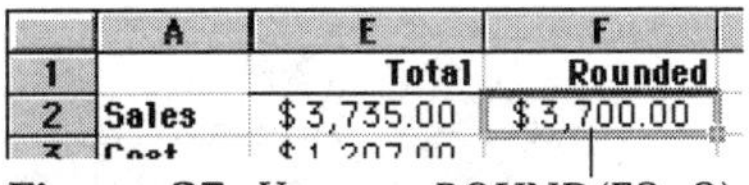

Figure 23. *You can also use the ROUND function to round a number to the left of the decimal point.*

=ROUND(E2,-2)

✔ Tips

- Rather than make a calculation in one cell and round it in another as shown in **Figures 22** and **23**, combine the two formulas in one cell (see **Figure 24**).

- The ROUNDUP function works like the ROUND function, but it always rounds up to the next higher number. The *num_digits* argument is not required; if omitted, the number is rounded to the next highest whole number.

- The ROUNDDOWN function works just like the ROUNDUP function, but it always rounds down.

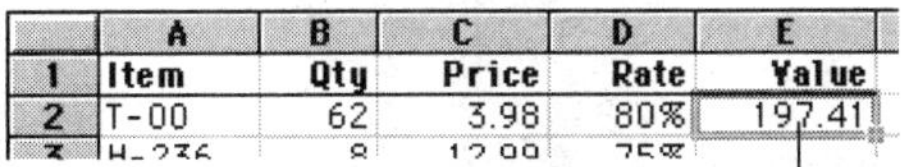

=ROUND(PRODUCT(B2:D2),2)

Figure 24. *You can also use the ROUND function to round the results of another formula or function.*

PRODUCT & ROUND

65

About the EVEN and ODD Functions

The EVEN function (see **Figure 25**) rounds a number up to the next even number. It uses the following syntax:

EVEN(number)

The *number* argument, which is required, is the number you want to round.

The ODD function works exactly the same way, but rounds a number up to the next odd number.

	A	B	
1	Number	Converted	
2	159.487	160	=EVEN(A2)
3	1647.1	1648	=EVEN(A3)
4	-14.48	-16	=EVEN(A4)

Figure 25. *Use the EVEN function to round a number up to the next even number.*

About the INT Function

The INT function (see **Figure 26**) rounds a number down to the nearest whole number or *integer*. It uses the following syntax:

INT(number)

The *number* argument, which is required, is the number you want to convert to an integer.

	A	B	
1	Number	Converted	
2	159.487	159	=INT(A2)
3	1647.1	1647	=INT(A3)
4	-14.48	-15	=INT(A4)

Figure 26. *Use the INT function to round a number down to the next whole number.*

About the ABS Function

The ABS function (see **Figure 27**) returns the absolute value of a number—it leaves positive numbers alone but turns negative numbers into positive numbers. (Is that high school math coming back to you yet?) It uses the following syntax:

ABS(number)

The *number* argument, which is required, is the number you want to convert to an absolute value.

	A	B	
1	Number	Converted	
2	159.487	159.487	=ABS(A2)
3	1647.1	1647.1	=ABS(A3)
4	-14.48	14.48	=ABS(A4)

Figure 27. *Use the ABS function to get the absolute value of a number.*

Using Functions in Formulas

	A	B
1	Number	Square Root
2	36	6 — =SQRT(A2)
3	22	4.69041576 — =SQRT(A3)
4	-10	#NUM! — =SQRT(A4)

Figure 28. *Use the SQRT function to find the square root of a number.*

	A	B
1	Number	Square Root
2	36	6 — =SQRT(ABS(A2))
3	22	4.69041576 — =SQRT(ABS(A3))
4	-10	3.16227766 — =SQRT(ABS(A4))

Figure 29. *Use the SQRT function to find the square root of a number.*

3.14159265358979 — =PI()

Figure 30. *The PI function calculates π up to 15 digits.*

Low	High	Random
0	1	0.29387186 — =RAND()
0	547	515.535806 — =RAND()*547
36	42	38.5474378 — =RAND()*(42-36)+36
164	4835	415.225341

=RAND()*(4835-164)+164

Figure 31. *The RAND function can be used alone or as part of a formula to generate random numbers within a certain range.*

About the SQRT Function

The SQRT function (see **Figure 28**) calculates the square root of a number. It uses the following syntax:

SQRT(number)

The *number* argument, which is required, is the number you want to find the square root of.

✔ Tip

■ You'll get a *#NUM!* error message if you try to use the SQRT function to calculate the square root of a negative number (see **Figure 28**). Prevent the error by using the ABS function in the formula (see **Figure 29**).

About the PI Function

The PI function (see **Figure 30**) returns the value of π, accurate up to 15 digits. It uses the following syntax:

PI()

About the RAND Function

The RAND (see **Figure 31**) function generates a random number greater than or equal to 0 and less than 1 each time the worksheet is calculated. It uses the following syntax:

RAND()

✔ Tips

■ Although there is no argument in either the PI or RAND function, if you fail to include the parentheses characters, you'll get a *#NAME?* error.

■ To generate a random number between two numbers (*low* and *high*), write a formula like this:

=RAND()(high-low)+low*

See **Figure 31** for some examples.

67

About the RADIANS and DEGREES Functions

The RADIANS function (see **Figure 32**) converts degrees to radians. The DEGREES function converts radians to degrees. They use the following syntax:

> *RADIANS(angle)*
> *DEGREES(angle)*

The angle argument, which is required, is the angle you want converted. Use degrees in the RADIANS function and radians in the DEGREES function.

About the SIN Function

The SIN function (see **Figure 32**) calculates the sine of an angle. It uses the following syntax:

> *SIN(number)*

The *number* argument, which is required, is the angle, in radians, for which you want the sine calculated.

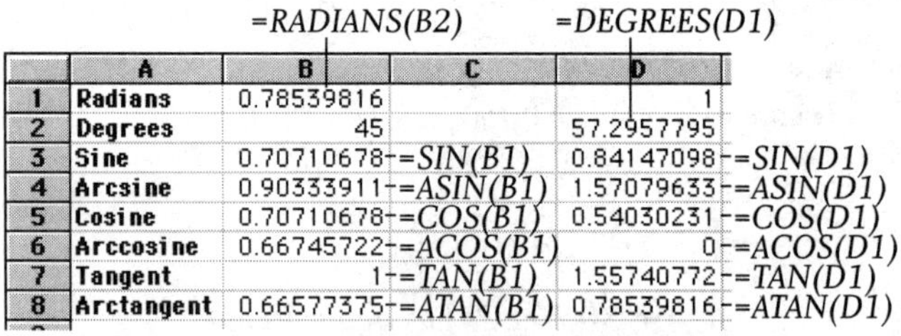

About the COS Function

The COS function (see **Figure 32**) calculates the cosine of an angle. It uses the following syntax:

> *COS(number)*

The *number* argument, which is required, is the angle, in radians, for which you want the cosine calculated.

About the TAN Function

The TAN function (see **Figure 32**) calculates the tangent of an angle. It uses the following syntax:

> *TAN(number)*

The *number* argument, which is required, is the angle, in radians, for which you want the tangent calculated.

	A	B	C	D
1	Radians	0.78539816		1
2	Degrees	45		57.2957795
3	Sine	0.70710678	=SIN(B1)	0.84147098	=SIN(D1)
4	Arcsine	0.90333911	=ASIN(B1)	1.57079633	=ASIN(D1)
5	Cosine	0.70710678	=COS(B1)	0.54030231	=COS(D1)
6	Arccosine	0.66745722	=ACOS(B1)	0	=ACOS(D1)
7	Tangent	1	=TAN(B1)	1.55740772	=TAN(D1)
8	Arctangent	0.66577375	=ATAN(B1)	0.78539816	=ATAN(D1)

=RADIANS(B2)   =DEGREES(D1)

Figure 32. *This example shows several trigonometry functions in action.*

✔ Tips

- To calculate the arcsine, arccosine, or arctangent of an angle, use the ASIN, ACOS, or ATAN function (see **Figure 32**). Each works in the same way as its counterpart.

- Excel has far more trigonometry functions than those mentioned here. At the end of this chapter, I tell you how to get more information on other Excel functions you may need to use.

About Statistical Functions

Excel has 71 statistical functions. On the next few pages, I tell you about a handful of the ones I think you'll use most.

About the AVERAGE Function

The AVERAGE function (see **Figure 33**) calculates the average or mean of its arguments. It uses the following syntax:

AVERAGE(number1,number2,...)

About the MEDIAN Function

The MEDIAN function (see **Figure 33**) calculates the median of its arguments. The median is the "halfway point" of the numbers—half the numbers have higher values and half have lower values. The MEDIAN function uses the following syntax:

MEDIAN(number1,number2,...)

About the MODE Function

The MODE function (see **Figure 33**) returns the mode of its arguments. The mode is the most common value. The MODE function uses the following syntax:

MODE(number1,number2,...)

If there are no repeated values, Excel returns a *#NUM!* error.

About the MIN and MAX Functions

The MIN function (see **Figure 33**) returns the minimum value of its arguments while the MAX function returns the maximum value of its arguments. They use the following syntax:

MIN(number1,number2,...)
MAX(number1,number2,...)

Figure 33. *This example shows a few of Excel's statistical functions at work.*

✔ Tips

- Excel's AVERAGE function does not include empty cells when calculating the average for a range of cells.
- Although the AVERAGE, MEDIAN, MODE, MIN and MAX functions can each accept up to 30 arguments separated by commas, only one argument is required.

Chapter 5

About the COUNT and COUNTA Functions

The COUNT function counts how many *numbers* are referenced by its arguments. The COUNTA function counts how many *values* are referenced by its arguments. Although this may sound like the same thing, it isn't. See **Figure 34** for an example of both that clarifies the difference.

The COUNT and COUNTA functions use the following syntax:

> *COUNT(number1,number2,...)*
>
> *COUNTA(number1,number2,...)*

Although either function can accept up to 30 arguments separated by commas, only one is required.

	A	B
1	987	
2	154.69	
3	chocolate	
4		
5	-745.145	
6	4/5/95	
7	ice cream	
8	$75	
9		
10	Numbers:	5 — =COUNT(A1:A8)
11	Values:	7 — =COUNTA(A1:A8)

Figure 34. *This example of the COUNT and COUNTA functions illustrates that while the COUNT function counts only cells containing numbers (including dates and times), the COUNTA function counts all non-blank cells.*

About the STDEV and STDEVP Functions

Standard deviation is a statistical measurement of how much values vary from the average or mean for the group. The STDEV function calculates the standard deviation based on a random sample of the entire population. The STDEVP function calculates the standard deviation based on the entire population. **Figure 35** shows an example of both.

The STDEV and STDEVP functions use the following syntax:

> *STDEV(number1,number2,...)*
>
> *STDEVP(number1,number2,...)*

Although either function can accept up to 30 arguments separated by commas, only one is required.

	A	B	C
1	Item	Qty	Price
2	T-00	62	3.98
3	H-236	8	12.99
4	F-734	54	15.99
5	D-154	108	9.99
6	S-48	34	14.99
7	D-183	69	19.99
8	P-139	75	24.99
9	W-87	87	12.99
10			
11	Average		14.489
12	STDEV:		6.3043 — =STDEV(C2:C9)
13	STDEVP:		5.8971 — =STDEVP(C2:C9)

Figure 35. *In this example, the STDEV function assumes that the range is a random sample from a larger population of information. The STDEVP function assumes that the same data is the entire population. That's why the results differ.*

✔ Tip

- To get accurate results from the STDEVP function, the arguments must include data for the entire population.

About Financial Functions

Excel has 53 financial functions that you can use to calculate depreciation, evaluate investment opportunities, or calculate the monthly payments on a loan. On the next few pages, I tell you about a few of the functions I think you'll find useful.

About the SLN Function

The SLN function (**see Figure 36**) calculates straight line depreciation for an asset. It uses the following syntax:

SLN(cost,salvage,life)

Cost is the acquisition cost of the asset, *salvage* is the salvage or scrap value, and *life* is the useful life expressed in years or months. All three arguments are required.

	A	B
1	Depreciation Comparison	
2		
3	Cost	1500
4	Salvage Value	150
5	Life (in Years)	3
6		
7	Year	1
8	Straight Line	$450.00
9	Declining Balance	$804.00
10	Double Declining Balance	$1,000.00
11	Sum of the Year's Digits	$675.00

=SLN(B3,B4,B5)
=DB(B3,B4,B5,B7)
=DDB(B3,B4,B5,B7)
=SYD(B3,B4,B5,B7)

Figure 36. *A simple worksheet lets you compare different methods of depreciation using the SLN, DB, DDB, and SYD functions.*

About the DB Function

The DB function (see **Figure 36**) calculates declining balance depreciation for an asset. It uses the following syntax:

DB(cost,salvage,life,period,month)

The *cost*, *salvage*, and *life* arguments are the same as for the SLN function. *Period*, which must be expressed in the same units as life, is the period for which you want to calculate depreciation. These first four arguments are required. *Month* is the number of months in the first year of the asset's life. If omitted, 12 is assumed.

About the DDB Function

The DDB function calculates the double-declining balance depreciation for an asset. It uses the following syntax:

DDB(cost,salvage,life,period,factor)

The *cost*, *salvage*, *life*, and *period* arguments are the same as for the DB function and are required. *Factor* is the rate at which the balance declines. If omitted, 2 is assumed.

About the SYD Function

The SYD function calculates the sum-of-years' digits depreciation for an asset. It uses the following syntax:

DDB(cost,salvage,life,period)

The *cost*, *salvage*, *life*, and *period* arguments are the same as for the DB and DDB functions. All arguments are required.

Chapter 5

About the PMT Function

The PMT function calculates the periodic payment for an annuity based on constant payments and interest rate. This function is commonly used for two purposes: to calculate the monthly payments on a loan and to calculate the monthly contribution necessary to reach a specific savings goal.

The PMT function uses the following syntax:

PMT(rate,nper,pv,fv,type)

Rate is the interest rate per period, *nper* is the total number of periods, and *pv* is the present value or current worth of the total payments. These three arguments are required. The *fv* argument is the future value or balance desired at the end of the payments. If omitted, 0 is assumed. *Type* indicates when payments are due: use 0 for payments at the end of the period and 1 for payments at the beginning of the period. If omitted, 0 is assumed.

To calculate loan payments

1. Enter the text and number values shown in **Figure 37a** in a worksheet. If desired, use your own amounts.

2. Enter the following formula in cell *B5*:

    =PMT(B2/12,B3,B1)

    This formula uses only the first three arguments of the PMT function. The rate argument is divided by 12 to arrive at a monthly interest rate since the number of periods is expressed in months and payments will be made monthly (all time units must match).

3. Press Return or Enter or click the Enter button on the formula bar.

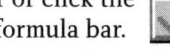

The result of the formula is expressed as a negative number (see **Figure 37b**) because it is an outgoing cash flow. (A minus sign or parentheses indicates a negative number.)

	A	B
1	Loan Amount	10000
2	Annual Interest Rate	9.50%
3	Loan Term (in Months)	48
4		
5	Monthly Payment	

Figure 37a. *A basic structure for a worksheet that calculates loan payments.*

	A	B
1	Loan Amount	10000
2	Annual Interest Rate	9.50%
3	Loan Term (in Months)	48
4		
5	Monthly Payment	($251.23)

=PMT(B2/12,B3,B1)

Figure 37b. *The PMT function calculates loan payments based on only three pieces of information.*

	A	B
1	Loan Amount	10000
2	Annual Interest Rate	9.50%
3	Loan Term (in Months)	36
4		
5	Monthly Payment	($320.33)

Figure 37c. *Playing "what-if." Change one of the constants and the result of the formula changes.*

✔ Tips

- If you prefer, you can use the Function Wizard to write the formula in step 2. Be sure to include the formula *B2/12* in the *rate* edit box. Leave the *fv* and *type* edit boxes blank.

- You can calculate loan payments without creating a whole worksheet—simply enter values rather than cell references as arguments for the PMT function. But using cell references makes it easy to play "what-if"—see how payments change when the loan amount, rate, and number of periods changes. **Figure 37c** shows an example.

Using Functions in Formulas

Figure 38a. *Start with this simple worksheet to create an amortization table...*

Figure 38b. *...add formulas to calculate interest, principal, and beginning balance...*

Figure 38c. *...then copy the formulas down each column for all months of the loan term.*

Figure 38d. *If desired, add column totals to sum the interest and principal paid.*

To create an amortization table

1. Create a loan payment worksheet following the steps on the previous page.
2. Enter text and number values for headings as shown in **Figure 38a**. Make sure there is a row with a payment number for each month of the loan term in cell *B3*.
3. In cell *B8*, enter *=B1*.
4. In cell *C8*, enter the following formula:

    *=ROUND(B8*$B$2/12,2)*

    This formula calculates the interest for the period and rounds it to two decimal places.
5. In cell *D8*, enter the following formula:

    =-$B$5-C8

    This formula calculates the amount of principal paid for the current month.
6. In cell *B9*, enter the following formula:

    =B8-D8

    This formula calculates the current month's beginning balance.

    At this point, your worksheet should look like the one in **Figure 38b**.
7. Use the fill handle to copy the formula in cell *B9* down the column for each month.
8. Use the Fill handle to copy the formulas in cells *C8* and *D8* down the columns for each month.

Your amortization table is complete. It should look like the one in **Figure 38c**.

✓ Tip

- If desired, you can add column totals at the bottom of columns *C* and *D* (see **Figure 38d**) to total interest (you may be shocked) and principal (which should match cell *B1*).

Creating an Amortization Table

73

Chapter 5

To calculate contributions to reach a savings goal

1. Enter the text and number values shown in **Figure 39a** in a worksheet. If desired, use your own amounts.

2. Enter the following formula in cell *B5*:

    =PMT(B2/12,B3,,B1)

    This formula uses the first *four* arguments of the PMT function, although the *pv* argument is left blank—that's why there are two commas after *B3*. The rate argument is divided by 12 to arrive at a monthly interest rate.

3. Press Return or Enter or click the Enter button on the formula bar.

    The result of the formula is expressed as a negative number (see **Figure 39b**) because it is an outgoing cash flow. (A minus sign or parentheses indicates a negative number.)

✔ Tips

- If you prefer, you can use the Function Wizard to write the formula in step 2. Be sure to include the formula *B2/12* in the *rate* edit box. Leave the *pv* and *type* edit boxes blank.

- You can calculate the amount of a monthly contribution to reach a savings goal without creating a whole worksheet—simply enter values rather than cell references as arguments for the PMT function. But using cell references makes it easy to play "what-if"—see how contributions change when the desired amount, rate, and number of periods changes. **Figure 39c** shows an example.

- To force an outgoing cash flow to be expressed as a positive number, simply include a minus sign (-) right after the equals sign (=) at the beginning of the formula.

	A	B
1	Desired Amount	100000
2	Annual Interest Rate	7.50%
3	Months	240
4		
5	Monthly Contribution	

Figure 39a. *A basic structure for a worksheet to calculate contributions to reach a savings goal.*

	A	B
1	Desired Amount	100000
2	Annual Interest Rate	7.50%
3	Months	240
4		
5	Monthly Contribution	($180.59)

=PMT(B2/12,B3,,B1)

Figure 39b. *The PMT function calculates the monthly contribution.*

	A	B
1	Desired Amount	250000
2	Annual Interest Rate	7.50%
3	Months	240
4		
5	Monthly Contribution	($451.48)

Figure 39c. *Change one constant and the result of the formula changes.*

Using Functions in Formulas

	A	B
1	Monthly Payment	150
2	Annual Interest Rate	8.50%
3	Number of Months	12
4		
5	Future Value	$1,871.81

=FV(B2/12,B3,-B1)

Figure 40. *Use the FV function to calculate the future value of constant cash flows, like those of periodic payroll savings deductions.*

	A	B
1	Initial Investment	-25000
2		
3	Monthly Cash In	200
4	Annual Interest Rate	9%
5	Number of Months	360
6		
7	Present Value	($24,856.37)

=PV(B4/12,B5,B3)

Figure 41. *This example uses the PV function to determine whether an investment is a good one. (It isn't good because the present value is less than the initial investment.)*

	A	B
1	Year 1	-500
2	Year 2	150
3	Year 3	100
4	Year 4	125
5	Year 5	135
6	Year 6	200
7		
8	Internal Rate of Return:	12%

=IRR(B1:B6)

Figure 42. *This worksheet calculates the internal rate of return of an initial $500 investment that pays out cash over the next few years.*

About the FV Function

The FV function (see **Figure 40**) calculates the future value of an investment with constant cash flows and a constant interest rate. It uses the following syntax:

FV(rate,nper,pmt,pv,type)

Rate is the interest rate per period, *nper* is the total number of periods, and *pmt* is the amount of the periodic payments. These three arguments are required. The *pv* argument is the present value of the payments. *Type* indicates when payments are due: use 0 for payments at the end of the period and 1 for payments at the beginning of the period. If either optional argument is omitted, 0 is assumed.

About the PV Function

The PV function (see **Figure 41**) calculates the total amount that a series of payments in the future is worth now. It uses the following syntax:

PV(rate,nper,pmt,fv,type)

The *rate, nper, pmt,* and *type* arguments are the same in the FV function. Only the first three are required. The *fv* argument is the amount left after the payments have been made. If omitted, 0 is assumed.

About the IRR Function

The IRR Function (see **Figure 42**) calculates the internal rate of return for a series of periodic cash flows. It uses the following syntax:

IRR(values,guess)

The *values* argument, which is required, is a range of cells containing the cash flows. The *guess* argument, which is optional, is for your guess of what the result could be. Although seldom necessary, *guess* could help Excel come up with an answer when performing complex calculations.

FV, PV, & IRR

75

Chapter 5

About Logical Functions

Excel has 6 logical functions you can use to evaluate conditions and act accordingly. I tell you about the most useful one: IF.

About the IF Function

The IF function (see **Figure 43b**) evaluates a condition and returns one of two different values depending on whether the condition is met (true) or not met (false). It uses the following syntax:

IF(logical_test,value_if_true,value_if_false)

The *logical_test* argument is the condition you want to meet. This argument is required. The *value_if_true* and *value_if_false* arguments are the values to return if the condition is met or not met. If omitted, the values *TRUE* and *FALSE* are returned.

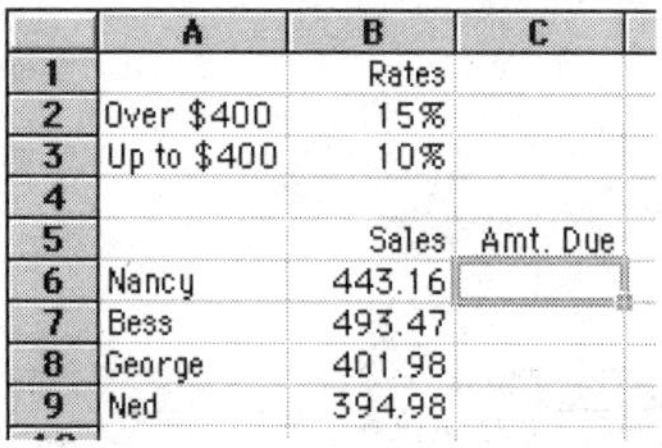

To use the IF function

This example uses the IF function to calculate commissions based on two different commission rates.

1. Create a worksheet with text and number values as shown in **Figure 43a**.

2. In cell C6, enter the following formula:

   =IF(B6>400,$B$2*B6,$B$3*B6)

   This formula begins by evaluating the sales amount to see if it's over $400. If it is, it moves to the *value_if_true* argument and multiplies the higher commission rate by the sales amount. If it isn't, it moves on to the *value_if_false* argument and multiplies the lower commission rate by the sales amount.

3. Press Return or Enter or click the Enter button on the formula bar (see **Figure 43b**).

4. Use the fill handle to copy the formula down the column for the rest of the salespeople (see **Figure 43c**).

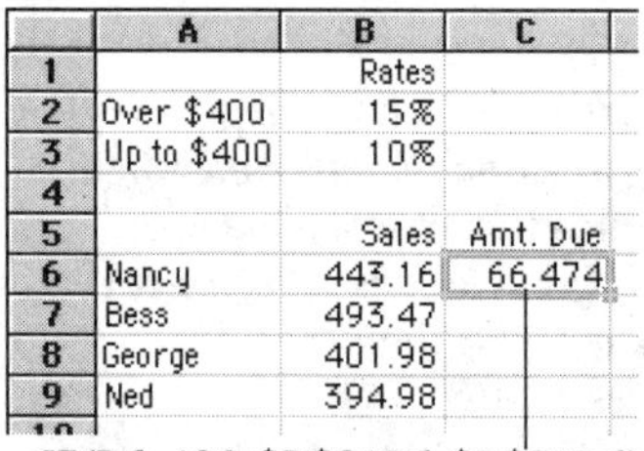

	A	B	C
1		Rates	
2	Over $400	15%	
3	Up to $400	10%	
4			
5		Sales	Amt. Due
6	Nancy	443.16	
7	Bess	493.47	
8	George	401.98	
9	Ned	394.98	

Figure 43a. *To try the IF function for yourself, start with a basic worksheet...*

	A	B	C
1		Rates	
2	Over $400	15%	
3	Up to $400	10%	
4			
5		Sales	Amt. Due
6	Nancy	443.16	66.474
7	Bess	493.47	
8	George	401.98	
9	Ned	394.98	

=IF(B6>400,$B$2*B6,$B$3*B6)

Figure 43b. *...enter the IF function formula shown here...*

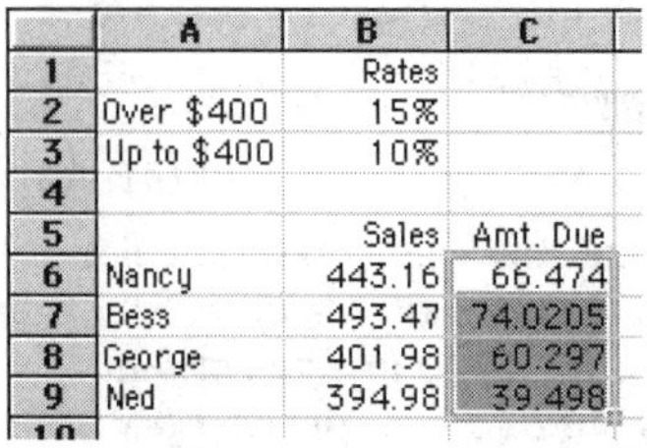

	A	B	C
1		Rates	
2	Over $400	15%	
3	Up to $400	10%	
4			
5		Sales	Amt. Due
6	Nancy	443.16	66.474
7	Bess	493.47	74.0205
8	George	401.98	60.297
9	Ned	394.98	39.498

Figure 43c. *...then use the fill handle to copy the formula to other cells.*

About Lookup and Reference Functions

Excel has 15 lookup and reference functions. These functions return values based on information stored elsewhere in the workbook or in a linked worksheet.

=VLOOKUP(B1,A5:D12,4,FALSE)

	A	B	C	D
1	Item Number:	S-48		
2	Price:	14.99		
3				
4	**Item Number**	**Item Name**	**Qty**	**Price**
5	D-154	Deuce Anaheim	108	14.99
6	D-183	David Silvermeadow	69	19.99
7	F-734	Franklin in Paris	54	15.99
8	H-236	Home with Fred	8	12.99
9	P-139	Pulp Fractions	75	24.99
10	S-48	Star Wreck	34	14.99
11	T-00	Blank Tapes	62	3.98
12	W-87	Woodland Gulch	87	12.99

Figure 44a. *This example illustrates the VLOOKUP function. When you enter an item number in cell B1, the formula in B2 attempts to match it to a value in the first column of the lookup table below it (A5:D12). If it finds a match, it returns the value in the fourth column of the same row as the match.*

	A	B	C	D
1	Item Number:	K-123		
2	Price:	#N/A		
3				
4	**Item Number**	**Item Name**	**Qty**	**Price**
5	D-154	Deuce Anaheim	108	14.99
6	D-183	David Silvermeadow	69	19.99
7	F-734	Franklin in Paris	54	15.99
8	H-236	Home with Fred	8	12.99
9	P-139	Pulp Fractions	75	24.99
10	S-48	Star Wreck	34	14.99
11	T-00	Blank Tapes	62	3.98
12	W-87	Woodland Gulch	87	12.99

Figure 44b. *If the formula in B2 doesn't find a match, it returns the* #N/A *error value, since the optional* range_lookup *argument is set to* FALSE.

About the VLOOKUP and HLOOKUP Functions

The VLOOKUP (see **Figures 44a** and **44b**) and HLOOKUP functions return information based on data stored in a *lookup table.* The function attempts to match a value in one of its arguments to values in the first column (VLOOKUP) or first row (HLOOKUP) of the lookup table. If it finds a match, it returns the associated value.

The VLOOKUP and HLOOKUP functions use the following syntax:

VLOOKUP(lookup_value,table_array, col_index_num, *range_lookup* ***)***

HLOOKUP(lookup_value,table_array, row_index_num, *range_lookup* ***)***

Lookup_value is the value you want to match in the table. *Table_array* is the cell reference for the lookup table. *Col_index_num* or *row_ref_number* is the number of the column or row, relative to the table, that contains the values you want returned. These three arguments are required. *Range_lookup,* which is not required, tells Excel what it should do if it can't match the *lookup_value.* TRUE tells Excel to return the value associated with the next lowest value; FALSE tells Excel to return the #N/A error value. If omitted, TRUE is assumed.

✔ Tip

- The first column or row of the lookup table must be sorted in ascending order for the VLOOKUP or HLOOKUP function to work properly.

Chapter 5

To use the VLOOKUP function

This example is similar to the one for the IF function in that it calculates commissions based on a sales-driven commission rate. But in this example, there are six rates, all included in a lookup table.

1. Enter text and number values to create a worksheet like the one in **Figure 45a**.

2. In cell *C2*, enter the following formula:

   =VLOOKUP(B2,$A$9:$B$14,2)*B2

   This formula tells Excel to match the sales amount to an amount in the first column of the commission rates table in *A9:B14*. If it finds a match, multiply the corresponding commission rate by the sales amount. It it doesn't find a match, use the rate corresponding to the next lowest value in the first column of the commission rates table.

3. Press Return or Enter or click the Enter button on the formula bar (see **Figure 45b**).

4. Use the fill handle to copy the formula in cell *C2* down the column for the other salespeople (see **Figure 45c**).

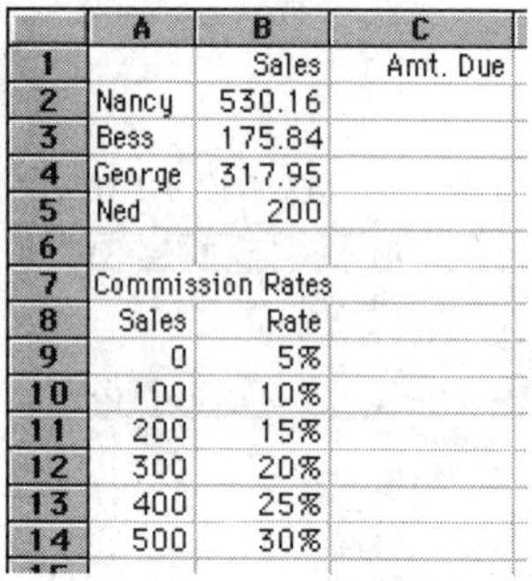

Figure 45a. *To try the VLOOKUP function, begin with a simple worksheet like this…*

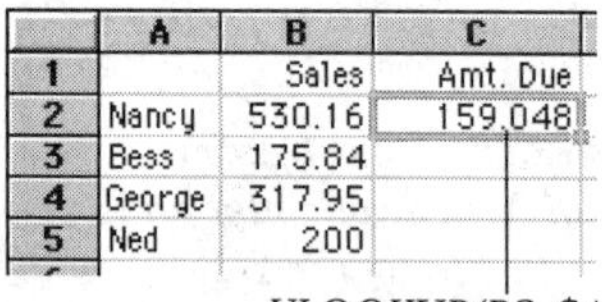

Figure 45b. *…enter the LOOKUP function formula…*

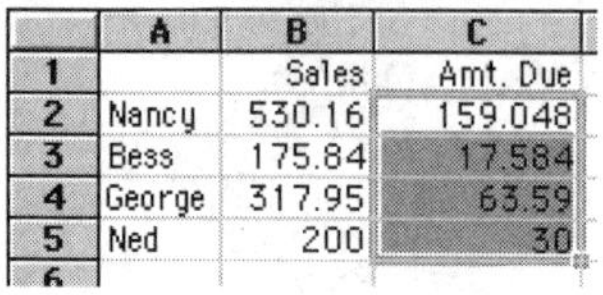

=VLOOKUP(B2,$A$9:$B$14,2)*B2

Figure 45c. *…then use the fill handle to copy the formula to other cells.*

✔ Tips

- The lookup table can be on any sheet of the workbook or on a linked worksheet. I tell you about 3D references in Chapter 12.

- Any changes you make to the lookup table are instantly reflected in the results of any formula that reference the table.

- When copying a formula containing a VLOOKUP or HLOOKUP function, be sure to use absolute references if necessary (see **Figure 45b**) in the formula you copy. Otherwise, the references to the table might change.

About Information Functions

Excel has 18 information functions. These functions return information about other cells.

About the IS Functions

	A	B	C	D	E
1	Test Values	673.24	anchovy		#N/A
2	Blank Cell	FALSE	FALSE	TRUE	FALSE
3	Error other than #N/A	FALSE	FALSE	FALSE	FALSE
4	Any error	FALSE	FALSE	FALSE	TRUE
5	Logical Value	FALSE	FALSE	FALSE	FALSE
6	#N/A Error	FALSE	FALSE	FALSE	TRUE
7	Not text	TRUE	FALSE	TRUE	TRUE
8	Number	TRUE	FALSE	FALSE	FALSE
9	Cell Reference	TRUE	TRUE	TRUE	TRUE
10	Text	FALSE	TRUE	FALSE	FALSE

Figure 46. *In this example, the nine built-in IS functions were used to evaluate the contents of the cells in row 1 of the worksheet. The results of each function appear below the value.*

Excel has nine built-in IS functions (see **Figure 46**), each with the following syntax:

ISBLANK(value)
ISERR(value)
ISERROR(value)
ISLOGICAL(value)
ISNA(value)
ISNONTEXT(value)
ISNUMBER(value)
ISREF(value)
ISTEXT(value)

In each case, Excel tests for a different thing. The value argument is the value or cell reference to be tested.

✔ Tip

■ Use an IS function in conjunction with the IF function to return a value based on the condition of a cell (see **Figures 47a&b**).

	A	B
1	Name:	
2		
3	Message:	You did not enter your name.
4		

=IF(ISTEXT(B1),"Hello "&B1,"You did not enter your name.")

	A	B
1	Name:	Maria
2		
3	Message:	Hello Maria

Figure 47a&b. *In this silly little example, a formula in cell B3, which utilizes the IF and ISTEXT functions, scolds the user for not entering a name, then greets her by name when she does enter it.*

About the COUNTBLANK Function

The COUNTBLANK function (see **Figure 48**) counts the blank cells in a range. It uses the following syntax:

COUNTBLANK(range)

The *range* argument, which is required, is the range for which you want Excel to count the blank cells.

	A	B	C
1	34		384.48
2	98		0
3		adios	384.48
4		65 goodbye	
5		hello	total
6			
7	Blank Cells:		5

=COUNTBLANK(A1:C5)

Figure 48. *The COUNTBLANK function counts blank cells in a range.*

✔ Tip

■ If a cell contains a space character, it will not be counted as blank.

Chapter 5

About Date and Time Functions

Excel has 19 functions you can use for working with dates and times. I tell you about the most useful ones here.

✔ Tips

- Excel treats dates and times as *serial numbers*. This means that although you may enter information as a date or time—like 10/15/95 or 2:45 PM—Excel converts what you type into a number for its own internal use (see **Table 1**). A date is the number of days since January 1, 1904. A time is the portion of a day since midnight. Excel's formatting makes the number look like a date or time. I tell you about cell formatting in Chapter 6.

- You can change Excel's date system from the Macintosh 1904 system to the Windows 1900 system. Choose Options from the Tools menu, click the Calculation tab, and turn off the 1904 Date System check box (see **Figure 49**). This will change the serial numbers for dates for all worksheets in the current workbook.

You Enter	Excel "Sees"
10/15/95	33525
6/30/61	21000
2:45 PM	0.61458333
10:02:56 AM	0.4187037
1/1/04	0
12:00 AM	0

Table 1. *How Excel interprets dates and times.*

☒ 1904 Date System

Figure 49. *The Options dialog box lets you switch between the standard 1904 date system and the Windows 1900 date system.*

About the DATE Function

The DATE function (see **Figure 50**) returns the serial number for a date. It uses the following syntax:

=DATE(year,month,day)

The *year* argument is the year number, the *month* argument is the month number, and the *day* argument is the day number. All arguments are required.

10/15/95 —=DATE(95,10,15)

Figure 50. *The DATE function returns the serial number for a date, which Excel formats as a date.*

	A	B
1	First Date	8-May-95
2	Second Date	15-Oct-95
3	Days Between	160

=B2-B1

Figure 51. *Calculating the number of days between two dates is as simple as subtracting the contents of two cells.*

To calculate the number of days between two dates

Enter the two dates into separate cells of a worksheet, then write a formula using the subtraction operator (-) to subtract the earlier date from the later date (see **Figure 51**).

or

In a worksheet cell, write a formula using the date function, like this:

=DATE(95,10,15)-DATE(95,5,8)

5/9/95 10:34	=NOW()
5/9/95	=TODAY()

Figure 52. *The NOW function returns the current date and time while the TODAY function returns just the current date.*

About the NOW and TODAY Functions

The NOW and TODAY functions (see **Figure 52**) return the serial number for the current date and time (NOW) or current date (TODAY). Results are automatically formatted and will change each time the worksheet is recalculated or opened. They use the following syntax:

NOW()

TODAY()

Although there are no arguments, the parentheses characters must be included.

	A	B	
1		15-Apr-96	
2	Day	15	=DAY(B1)
3	Weekday	2	=WEEKDAY(B1)
4	Month	4	=MONTH(B1)
5	Year	1996	=YEAR(B1)

Figure 53. *The DAY, WEEKDAY, MONTH, and YEAR functions extract portions of a date.*

About the DAY, WEEKDAY, MONTH, and YEAR Functions

The DAY, WEEKDAY, MONTH, and YEAR functions (see **Figure 53**) return the day of the month, the day of the week, the month number, or the year number for a serial number. They use the following syntax:

DAY(serial_number)
WEEKDAY(serial_number)
MONTH(serial_number)
YEAR(serial_number)

The serial_number argument can be a cell reference, number, or date written as text, like "10/15/95" or "15-April-96."

Chapter 5

About Text Functions

Excel includes 23 text functions you can use to extract, convert, concatenate, and get information about text. I tell you about a few of the more commonly used ones here.

About the LOWER, UPPER, and PROPER Functions

The LOWER, UPPER, and PROPER functions (see **Figure 54**) convert text to lowercase, uppercase, and title case. They use the following syntax:

> *LOWER(text)*
> *UPPER(text)*
> *PROPER(text)*

	A	B	
1	Original	This IS an eXample	
2	Lowercase	this is an example	—=LOWER(B1)
3	Uppercase	THIS IS AN EXAMPLE	—=UPPER(B1)
4	Title Case	This Is An Example	—=PROPER(B1)

Figure 54. *Use the LOWER, UPPER, and PROPER functions to change the case of text.*

The *text* argument, which is required, is the text you want converted.

About the LEFT, RIGHT, and MID Functions

The LEFT, RIGHT, and MID functions (see **Figure 55**) return the leftmost, rightmost, or middle characters of a text string. They use the following syntax:

> *LEFT(text,num_chars)*
> *RIGHT(text,num_chars)*
> *MID(text,start_num,num_chars)*

	A	B	
1	Original Text	sassafras	
2	First 4 Characters	sass	—=LEFT(B1,4)
3	Last 4 Characters	fras	—=RIGHT(B1,4)
4	4 Chars Starting with 3rd	ssaf	—=MID(B1,3,4)

Figure 55. *Use the LEFT, RIGHT, and MID functions to extract characters from text.*

The *text* argument, which is required, is the text characters extracted from. The *num_chars* argument is the number of characters you want extracted. If omitted from the LEFT or RIGHT function, 1 is assumed. The MID function has an additional argument, *start_num*, which is the number of the first character from which you want to extract text. The MID function requires all arguments.

About the CONCATENATE Function and Operator

The CONCATENATE function (see **Figure 56**) joins or concatenates two or more strings of text. It uses the following syntax:

CONCATENATE(text1,text2,...)

Each text argument can include single cell references, text, or numbers you want to join. The CONCATENATE function can accept up to 30 arguments, but only two are required.

	A	B	C
1	Last Name	First Name	Full Name
2	Twain	Mark	Mark Twain

=CONCATENATE(B2," ",A2) **or** *=B2&" "&A2)*

Figure 56. *Use the CONCATENATE function or operator to join strings of text.*

✔ Tips

- Excel recognizes the ampersand character (&) as a concatenation operator in formulas. You can concatenate text by including an ampersand between cells or text strings in a formula, like this:

  =B2&" "&A2

- If you want spaces between the strings, be sure to include the space character, between double quote characters, as an argument (see **Figure 56**).
- Creative use of the CONCATENATE function or operator makes it possible to give documents a personal touch. **Figure 57** shows an example.

	A	B	C	D
1	$124.90			
2	10/15/95			
3				
4	The total amount due is $124.90. Please pay by 11/14/95.			

="The total amount due is "&DOLLAR(A1)&". Please pay by "&TEXT(A2+30,"mm/dd/yy")&"."

Figure 57. *This formula writes a sentence using the contents of two cells, the contatenate operator, and two text functions.*

To get more information about a function

1. Double-click the Help button on the Standard toolbar.
2. In the keyword list dialog box that appears, type the name of the function in the edit box (see **Figure 58a**).
3. Make sure the function name is selected in the top scrolling window and click the Show Topics button.
4. Make sure the function name is selected in the bottom scrolling window and click the Go To button.

Excel displays a help window for the function (see **Figure 58b**). It completely describes the function and its arguments, provides examples, and lets you quickly move to other help windows for related functions. I tell you more about Microsoft Excel Help in Chapter 1.

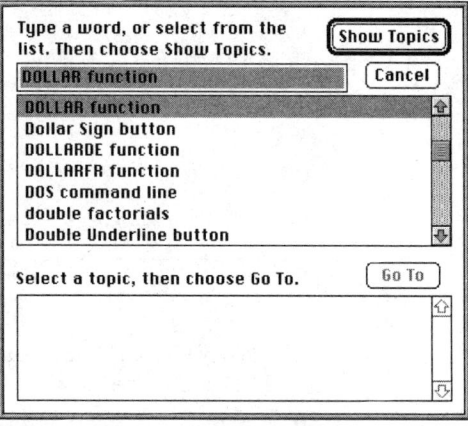

Figure 58a. *Use the Search feature in Excel Help to enter the name of a function for which you want more information.*

✔ Tips

- You can write formulas that reference cells in other worksheets or other workbook files. I tell you how in Chapter 12.
- Naming cells or ranges of cells makes cell references easier to remember and use. I tell you how to use names in Chapter 12.

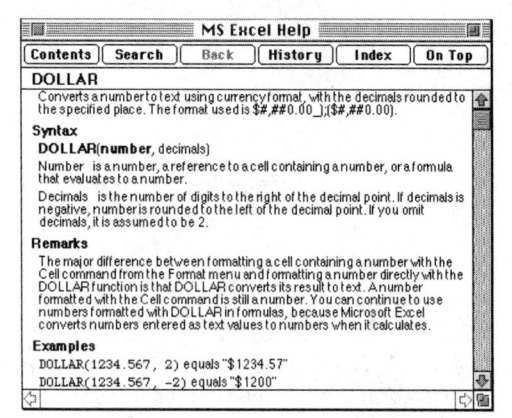

Figure 58b. *The MS Excel Help window displays complete information about functions.*

FORMATTING WORKSHEET CELLS 6

Drew Industries				
First Quarter Sales Results				
	Jan	Feb	Mar	Total
Nancy	443	419	841	1703
Bess	493	277	45	815
George	493	277	45	815
Ned	69	856	842	1767
Total	1498	1829	1773	5100

Figure 1a. *While content should be more important than appearance, you can bet that this worksheet won't get as much attention…*

Drew Industries				
First Quarter Sales Results				
	Jan	Feb	Mar	**Total**
Nancy	443	419	841	1703
Bess	493	277	45	815
George	493	277	45	815
Ned	69	856	842	1767
Total	1498	1829	1773	5100

Figure 1b. *…as this one!*

About Formatting

To paraphrase an old Excel mentor of mine, formatting a worksheet is like putting on its makeup. The worksheet's contents may be perfectly correct, but by applying formatting, you can increase its impact to make an impression on the people who see it (see **Figures 1a** and **1b**).

Excel offers a wide range of formatting options you can use to beautify your worksheets:

- *Number formatting* lets you change the appearance of numbers, dates, and times.
- *Alignment* lets you change the way cell contents are aligned within the cell.
- *Font formatting* lets you change the appearance of text and number characters.
- *Borders* let you add lines around cells.
- *Patterns* let you add color, shading, and patterns to cells.
- *Column and row formatting* let you change column width and row height.

You can apply formatting to cells using a variety of techniques: with toolbar buttons, shortcut keys, menu commands, or the AutoFormat feature.

✔ Tips

- Excel may automatically apply formatting to cells, depending on what you enter. For example, if you use a date function, Excel formats the results of the function as a date. You can change Excel's formatting at any time to best meet your needs.

Chapter 6

About Number Formatting

By default, Excel applies the General format to all cells on a worksheet. This format displays numbers just as they're entered. If the integer part of the number is longer than the width of the cell or 11 digits, it displays them in scientific notation. **Figure 2** shows some examples.

Change number formatting with toolbar buttons or the Format Cells dialog box.

Figure 2. *General formatting displays the numbers just as they're typed in and uses scientific notation when they're very big.*

✔ Tips

- Number formatting changes only the *appearance* of a number. Although formatting may remove decimal places from displayed numbers, it does not round numbers. **Figure 3** illustrates this. Use the ROUND function, which I discuss in Chapter 5, to round numbers in formulas.

- If you include characters like dollar signs or percent symbols with a number you enter, Excel automatically assigns an appropriate built-in format to the cell.

Figure 3. *The two columns contain identical values, but the column on the right has been formatted with the Currency Style. Because Excel performs calculations with the numbers underlying any formatting, the total on the right appears incorrect!*

To format numbers with toolbar buttons

1. Select the cell(s) containing the number(s) you want to format.
2. Click the Formatting toolbar button for the number format you want to apply (see **Figure 4**):

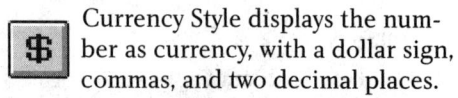

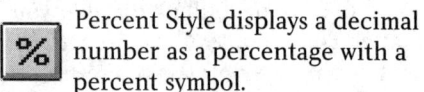

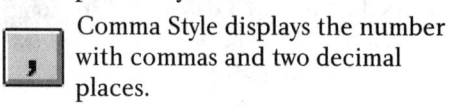

   Currency Style displays the number as currency, with a dollar sign, commas, and two decimal places.

   Percent Style displays a decimal number as a percentage with a percent symbol.

   Comma Style displays the number with commas and two decimal places.

Figure 4. *This example shows three different numbers with each of the Formatting toolbar's number formatting options applied.*

Increase Decimal displays an additional digit after the decimal point.

Decrease Decimal displays one less digit after the decimal point.

Applying Number Formatting

86

Formatting Worksheet Cells

Figure 5a. *Choose Cells from the Format menu...*

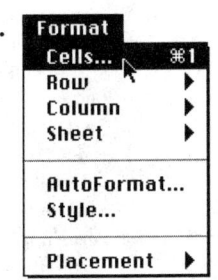

To format numbers with the Format Cells dialog box

1. Select the cell(s) containing the number(s) you want to format.
2. Choose Cells from the Format menu (see **Figure 5a**).

   or

   Press ⌘1.

3. The Format Cells Dialog box appears. If necessary, click the Number tab to display the number formatting options (see **Figure 5b**).
4. Choose a category from the Category scrolling list.
5. Choose a code from the Format Codes scrolling list. A sample of the number in the active cell appears near the bottom of the dialog box with the format applied. (see **Figure 5c**).
6. Click OK or press Return or Enter to accept the formatting.

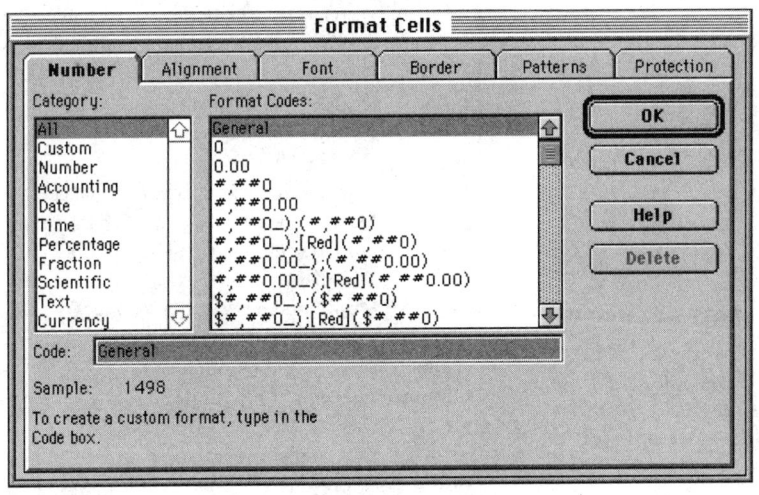

Figure 5b. *...to display the Format Cells dialog box.*

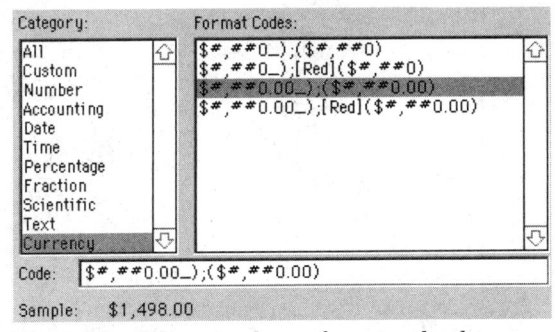

Figure 5c. *When you choose format code, the number in the active cell appears in the Sample area with the format applied.*

✔ Tip

- Take advantage of the sample area at the bottom of the dialog box to preview the effect of several format codes. This way, you can choose the perfect code on the first try.

Applying Number Formatting

87

Chapter 6

About Number Format Codes

Number format codes provide Excel with formatting instructions. They use symbols to tell Excel how to treat a number's digits and where to place other characters like spaces, commas, and dollar signs. **Table 1** lists most of the symbols that can be included in a number format code.

The symbols in number format codes are organized in up to four sections separated by semicolons (;):

1. Format for positive numbers.
2. Format for negative numbers.
3. Format for zeros.
4. Format for text.

✔ Tips

- To learn more about how the number format codes and their symbols work, pay close attention to the formatting applied when you choose options in the Number tab of the Format Cells dialog box.

- To create custom number formats, enter the appropriate symbols in the Code edit box of the Number tab (see **Figures 5b** and **5c**). When you click OK or press Return or Enter, the code you create is applied. The next time you open the Number tab of the Format Cells dialog box, you'll see the code you created. It is saved with the workbook file and can be applied to other cells.

- Don't be afraid to experiment with custom number format codes. This is one of Excel's most powerful features!

Symbol	Purpose
#	Optional digit placeholder
0	Required digit placeholder
?	Required digit placeholder for aligning decimal places and fraction bars
.	Decimal point
,	Thousands separator
%	Percentage; Excel multiplies by 100 and appends the % character
$	Displays the character
-	Displays the character
+	Displays the character
/	Displays the character
(&)	Displays the character
:	Displays the character
space	Displays the character
*	Repeats the next character to fill cell
_	Skips the width of the next character
"text"	Displays the text inside the quotes
@	Text placeholder for text in cell
m	Month number without leading 0
mm	Month number with leading 0
mmm	Abbreviated month name
mmmm	Spelled out month name
d	Day number without leading 0
dd	Day number with leading 0
ddd	Abbreviated day name
dddd	Spelled out day name
yy	Two-digit year number
yyyy	Four-digit year number
h	Hour without leading 0
hh	Hour with leading 0
m	Minute without leading 0; must follow h or hh symbol
mm	Minute with leading 0; must follow h or hh symbol
s	Second without leading 0
ss	Second with leading 0
AM/PM	Displays AM or PM after time; uses 12-hour clock
[color]	Displays characters in *color*. Options are BLACK, BLUE, CYAN, GREEN, MAGENTA, RED, WHITE, YELLOW

Table 1. *Symbols used in Excel's number format codes.*

Formatting Worksheet Cells

About Alignment

By default, within each cell, Excel left aligns text and right aligns numbers. This is called General alignment. You can change alignment to position cell contents exactly the way you want. **Figure 6** shows some examples.

You change alignment with toolbar buttons or the Format Cells dialog box.

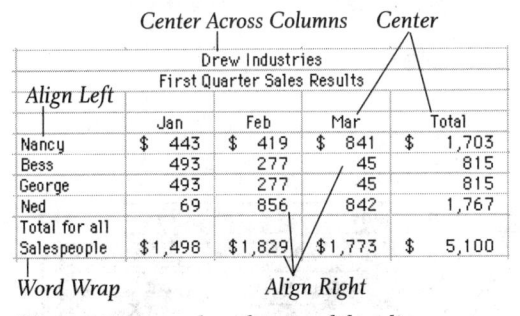

Figure 6. *Examples of some of the alignment options Excel offers.*

✔ Tips

- Although it's common to center headings over columns containing numbers, the worksheet may actually look better with headings right aligned. **Figures 7a&b** show an example.

- Alignment is applied to cells, not cell contents. If you use the Clear Contents command or ⌘B shortcut to clear a cell, the formatting remains and will be applied to whatever data is next entered into it.

Figures 7a&b. *Which looks better: centered or right aligned headings?*

To align cell contents with toolbar buttons

1. Select the cell(s) whose contents you want to align (see **Figure 8a**).
2. Click the Formatting toolbar button for the alignment you want to apply (see **Figure 8b**):

    The Align Left button aligns cell contents against the left side of the cell.

    The Center button centers cell contents between the left and right sides of the cell.

    The Align Right button aligns cell contents against the right side of the cell.

    The cell contents shift accordingly (see **Figure 8c**).

Figure 8a. *Begin by selecting the cells whose alignment you want to change…*

Figure 8b. *…then click the appropriate alignment toolbar button.*

Figure 8c. *The alignment you chose is applied.*

Aligning Cell Contents

89

Chapter 6

Aligning Cell Contents

To align cell contents with the Format Cells dialog box

1. Select the cell(s) whose contents you want to align (see **Figure 8a**).
2. Choose Cells from the Format menu (see **Figure 5a**).

   or

   Press ⌘1.
3. The Format Cells dialog box appears. If necessary, click the Alignment tab to display the alignment options (see **Figure 9**).
4. Choose a radio button for the kind of alignment you want.
5. Click OK or press Return or Enter.

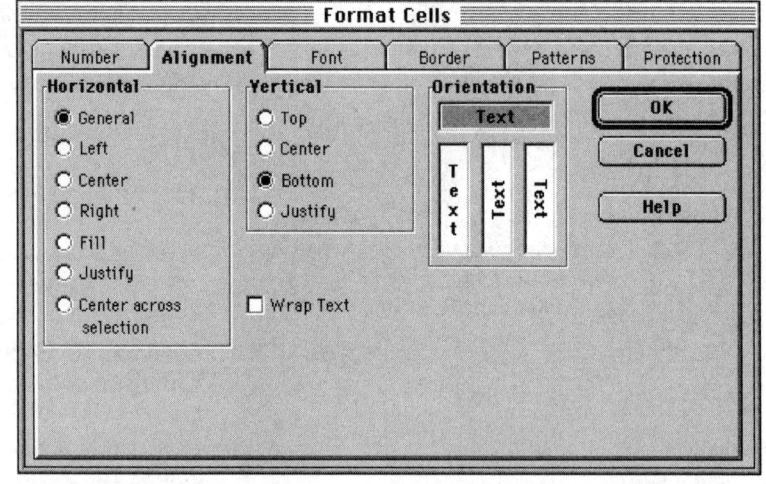

Figure 9. *The Alignment tab of the Format Cells dialog box offers many alignment options.*

To center cells across columns

1. Select the cell(s) whose contents you want to center, along with the cells of the columns to the right that you want to center across (see **Figure 10a**).
2. Click the Center Across Columns button on the Formatting toolbar (see **Figure 10b**).

   or

   Follow steps 2 and 3 above to display the Alignment tab of the Format Cells dialog box, select the Center Across Selection radio button (see **Figure 10c**), and click OK.

The cell contents shift so they're centered between the left and right sides of the selected area (see **Figure 10d**).

Figure 10a. *Select the cells whose contents you want to center, as well as the cells you want to center across…*

Figure 10b. *…then click the Center Across Columns button.*

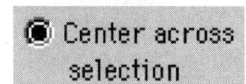

Figure 10c. *…or select the Center Across Selection radio button.*

Figure 10d. *The cells on the far left of the selection are centered across the entire selection.*

90

Formatting Worksheet Cells

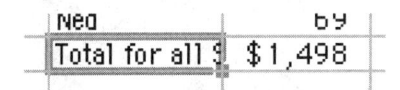

Figure 11a. *Select the cell whose contents you want to word wrap…*

Figure 11b. *…then turn on the Wrap Text check box.*

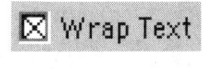

Figure 11c. *The text wraps within the cell.*

Figure 12a. *Select the cell whose orientation you want to change…*

Figure 12b. *…then choose the orientation option you want.*

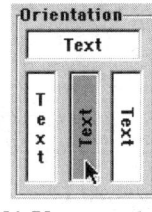

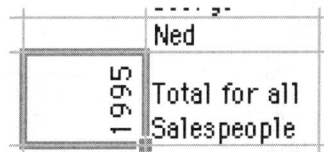

Figure 12c. *The cell's orientation shifts.*

To word wrap cell contents

1. Select the cell(s) whose contents you want to word wrap (see **Figure 11a**).
2. Choose Cells from the Format menu or press ⌘1.
3. The Format Cells dialog box appears. If necessary, click the Alignment tab (see **Figure 9**).
4. Turn on the check box beside Wrap Text (see **Figure 11b**).
5. Click OK or press Return or Enter.

   The cell's contents word wrap within the cell (see **Figure 11c**). The entire row's height changes to accommodate the additional lines of text within it.

✔ Tip

- In order for word wrap to occur, the text within the cell must be too wide to fit into the cell. I tell you how to change column widths and row heights later in this chapter.

To change the orientation of cell contents

1. Select the cell(s) whose orientation you want to change (see **Figure 12a**).
2. Choose Cells from the Format menu or press ⌘1.
3. The Format Cells dialog box appears. If necessary, click the Alignment tab (see **Figure 9**).
4. Choose an orientation option by clicking it (see **Figure 12b**).
5. Click OK or press Return or Enter.

   The cell's contents change orientation (see **Figure 12c**). If necessary, the entire row's height changes to accommodate the shifted characters.

Wrapping Text & Changing Orientation

91

Chapter 6

About Font Formatting

Excel uses 10 point Geneva as the default font or typeface for worksheets. You can change the font applied to text, number, or symbol characters, as well as its size and its style using toolbar buttons, shortcut keys, and the Format Cells dialog box.

✔ Tip

- You can change the formatting of individual characters within a cell (see **Figure 12b**) by double-clicking the cell to make it active, selecting the characters you want to change (see **Figure 12a**), and then using the appropriate font formatting technique to change the characters.

To change a font with the Formatting toolbar

1. Select the cell(s) or character(s) whose font you want to change.

2. Click on the arrow beside the Font box on the Formatting toolbar to display a menu of all fonts installed in your system (see **Figure 13**) and choose the font you want to apply.

    or

    Click on the Font box to select its contents (see **Figure 14a**), type in the name of the font you want to apply (see **Figure 14b**), and press Return or Enter.

    The font you chose is applied to the selected cell(s).

✔ Tip

- Your font menu won't look exactly like the one illustrated here. The fonts that appear on the font menu are those installed in your Macintosh system.

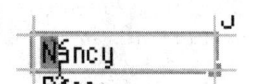

Figure 12a. *Double-click the cell and select the character(s) you want to format.*

Figure 12b. *When you make the change, only the selected character(s) are affected.*

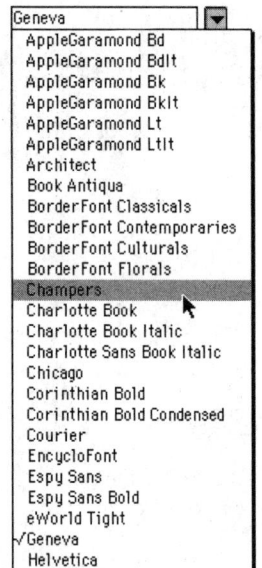

Figure 13. *The Font menu on the Formatting toolbar lets you choose from all the fonts installed in your system.*

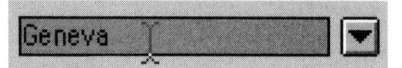

Figure 14a. *Click in the font box to select its contents…*

Figure 14b. *…then type in the name of a font installed in your system and press Return.*

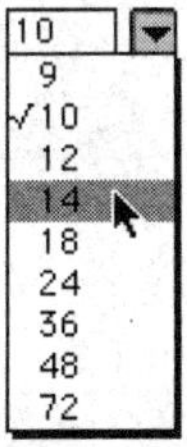

Figure 15. *The Font Size menu on the Formatting toolbar lets you change the size of characters in selected cells.*

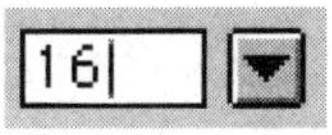

Figure 16. *You can type almost any size you like into the Font box.*

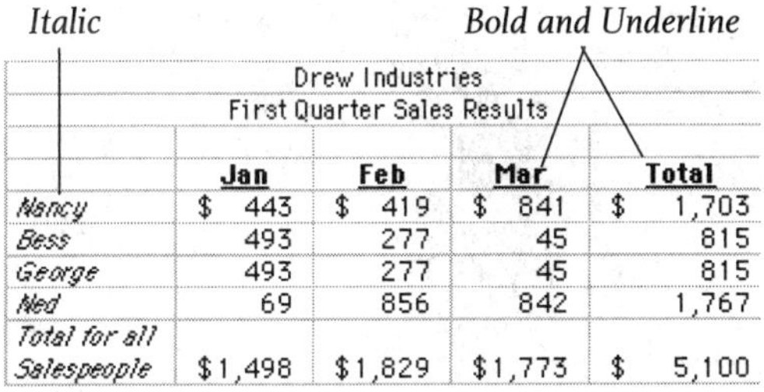

	Drew Industries			
	First Quarter Sales Results			
	Jan	Feb	Mar	Total
Nancy	$ 443	$ 419	$ 841	$ 1,703
Bess	493	277	45	815
George	493	277	45	815
Ned	69	856	842	1,767
Total for all Salespeople	$1,498	$1,829	$1,773	$ 5,100

Figure 17. *Examples of style options that can be applied with Formatting toolbar buttons.*

✔ Tip

■ Use border formatting or accounting underlines rather than the Underline button to put lines at the bottom of columns being totalled. I tell you about border formatting and accounting underlines later in this chapter.

To change font size with the Formatting toolbar

1. Select the cell(s) or character(s) whose font size you want to change.
2. Click on the arrow beside the Font Size box on the Formatting toolbar to display a menu of sizes (see **Figure 15**) and choose the size you want to apply.

   or

   Click on the Font Size box to select its contents, type in a size to apply (see **Figure 16**), and press Return or Enter.

   The font size you chose is applied to the selected cell(s).

✔ Tips

■ The sizes offered in the Font Size menu will vary depending on the font.

■ Font size must be between 1 and 409 points in half-point increments. (In case you're wondering, 72 points equals 1 inch.)

To change font style with the Formatting toolbar or shortcut keys

1. Select the cell(s) whose font style you want to change.
2. Click the Formatting toolbar button for the style you want to apply (see **Figure 17**):

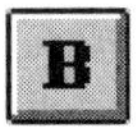

The Bold button or ⌘Shift-B makes characters in the selected cell(s) appear in a bold style.

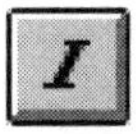

The Italic button or ⌘Shift-I makes characters in the selected cell(s) appear in an italic style.

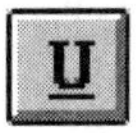

The Underline button or ⌘Shift-U puts a single underline under characters in the selected cell(s).

Chapter 6

To change font formatting with the Format Cells dialog box

1. Select the cell(s) or character(s) whose font you want to change.

2. Choose Cells from the Format menu or press ⌘1.

3. The Format Cells dialog box appears. If necessary, click the Font tab to display the font formatting options (see **Figure 18a**).

4. Select a font from the Font scrolling list or type a font name into the edit box above the list.

5. Select a font style from the Font Style scrolling list or type a style name into the edit box above the list.

6. Select a font size from the Size scrolling list or type a size into the edit box above the list.

7. Choose an underline style from the Underline pop-up menu (see **Figure 18b**). Accounting underlines stretch almost the entire width of the cell.

8. Choose a color from the Color pop-up menu (see **Figure 18c**). Automatic color is determined by formatting options on the Number tab. I tell you about them earlier in this chapter.

9. Use the Effects check boxes to turn different character effects on or off.

10. When the sample text in the Preview area looks just the way you want, click OK or press Return or Enter.

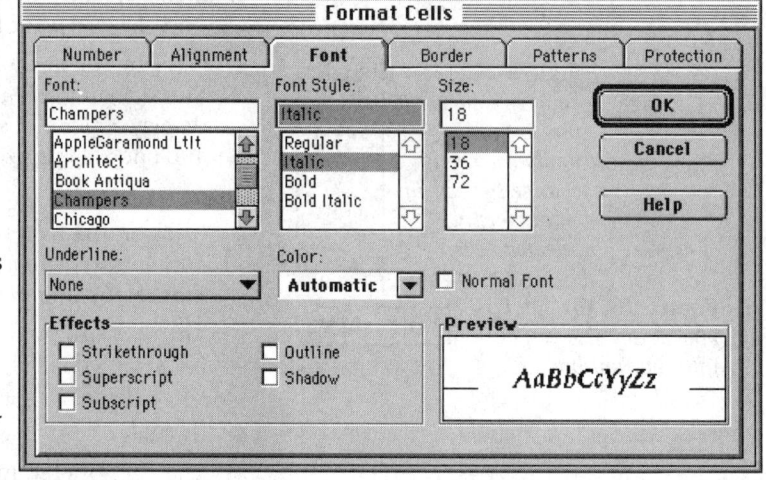

Figure 18a. *The Font tab of the Format Cells dialog box offers all kinds of font formatting options.*

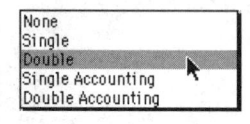

Figure 18b. *The Underline pop-up menu offers five options.*

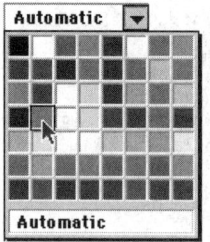

Figure 18c. *Use the color pop-up menu to choose a color for the characters of selected cells.*

✔ Tips

- The Font Color button/menu on the Formatting toolbar works the same way as the Color menu in the Format cells dialog box (see **Figure 17c**).

- To return a selection to the default font, turn on the Normal Font check box.

Formatting Worksheet Cells

Drew Industries
First Quarter Sales Results

	Jan	Feb	Mar	Total
Nancy	$ 443	$ 419	$ 841	$ 1,703
Bess	493	277	45	815
George	493	277	45	815
Ned	69	856	842	1,767
Total for all Salespeople	$1,498	$1,829	$1,773	$ 5,100

Figure 19. *Use borders to place "accounting underlines" above and below column totals.*

Figure 20a. *Click the Borders button to apply the currently displayed border style...*

Figure 20b. *...or click the triangle to display a menu of border styles and choose one.*

About Borders

Excel offers a number of different border styles that you can apply to separate cells or a selection of cells (see **Figure 19**). Use the Formatting toolbar or the Format Cells dialog box to add borders.

To add borders with the Borders button

1. Select the cell(s) to which you want to add borders.

2. Click on the picture part of the Borders button (see **Figure 20a**) to apply the border style illustrated on the button.

   or

   Click on the triangle on the right side of the Borders button to pull down a menu of border styles (see **Figure 20b**) and choose the style you want.

✔ Tips

- All of the border styles on the Borders menu except the last two apply borders to each cell in the selection. The last two choices apply borders around the outside of the entire selection.

- The last border selection you made from the Borders menu is the one that is illustrated on the button. This makes it quick and easy to apply the same border formatting again.

- To remove borders from a selection, choose the first (top left) border style. If the border does not disappear, it may be applied to a cell adjoining the one you selected.

- The accounting underlines available from the Underline pop-up menu in the Format Cells dialog box are *not* the same as borders. They do not stretch the entire width of the cell and they only appear when the cell is not blank.

Adding Borders

Chapter 6

To add borders with the Format Cells dialog box

1. Select the cell(s) to which you want to add borders.

2. Choose Cells from the Format menu or press ⌘1.

3. The Format Cells dialog box appears. If necessary, click the Border tab to display the border options (see **Figure 21**).

4. Select a line style from the Style section.

5. If desired, select a color from the Color pop-up menu. This menu looks and works exactly like the one on the Font tab (see **Figure 18c**).

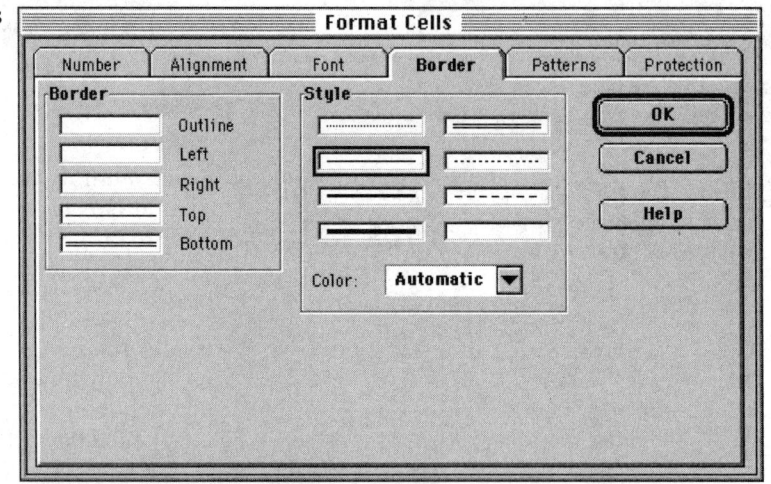

Figure 21. *You can add borders to selected cells with options from the Borders tab of the Format Cells dialog box.*

6. Click on a border position option in the Border section. This places the line style you chose in that position for each of the selected cells. If you choose Outline, the line is placed around the selection.

7. Repeat steps 4, 5, and 6 until all the line styles, colors, and positions for the selected cells are set.

8. Click OK or press Return or Enter.

✔ Tip

- To get the borders in your worksheet to look just the way you want, be prepared to make several selections and trips to either the Borders button on the Formatting toolbar or the Borders tab of the Format Cells dialog box.

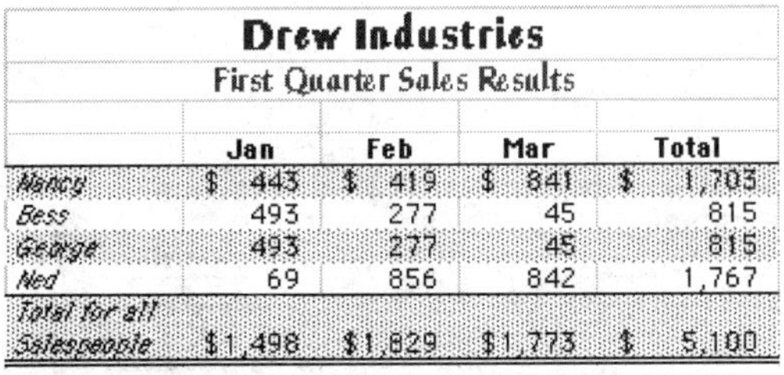

Formatting Worksheet Cells

About Colors, Patterns, and Shading

Excel's pattern feature lets you add color to cells (see **Figure 22**), either with or without patterns. Although the Color button/menu on the Formatting toolbar lets you add color to cells, the Format Cells dialog box offers far more flexibility.

✔ Tip

- By combining two colors with a pattern, you can create various colors and levels of shading.

To add color with the Color button

1. Select the cell(s) to which you want to add color.
2. Click on the picture part of the Color button (see **Figure 23a**) to apply the color illustrated on the button.

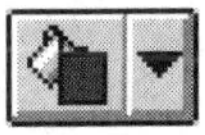

   or

   Click on the triangle on the right side of the Color button to pull down a menu of colors (see **Figure 23b**) and choose the color you want.

✔ Tips

- The last color selection you made from the Color menu is the one that is illustrated on the button. This makes it easy to apply the same color again and again.
- To remove colors from a selection, choose None from the Color menu.

Figure 22. *Use Excel's pattern feature to add color, patterns, and shading to cells.*

Figure 23a. *Click the Color button to apply the currently displayed color…*

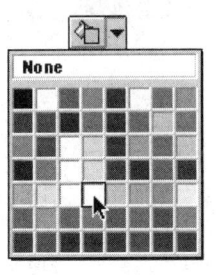

Figure 23b. *…or click the triangle to display a menu of colors and choose one.*

Adding Color

Chapter 6

To add color, pattern, and shading with the Format Cells dialog box

1. Select the cell(s) to which you want to add colors, patterns, or shading.
2. Choose Cells from the Format menu or press ⌘1.
3. The Format Cells dialog box appears. If necessary, click the Patterns tab to display the color and pattern options (see **Figure 24a**).
4. Select a color from the Color palette in the Cell Shading area of the dialog box. This is the foreground color.
5. If desired, choose a background color and pattern from the Pattern pop-up menu (see **Figure 24b**).
6. When the Sample area of the dialog box looks just the way you want your selection to look, click OK or press Return or Enter.

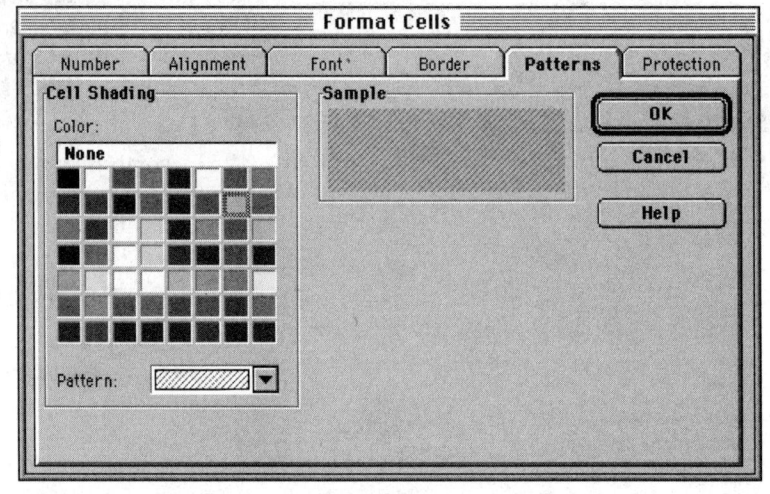

Figure 24a. Use the Patterns tab of the Format Cells dialog box to add color, patterns, and shading to selected cells.

Figure 24b. Choose a pattern from the top of the Pattern pop-up menu and a background color from the bottom.

✔ Tips

- Be careful when adding colors to cells! If the color is too dark, cell contents may not be legible.
- To improve the legibility of cell contents in colored cells, try making the characters bold.
- For a different look, use a dark color for the cell and make its characters white.

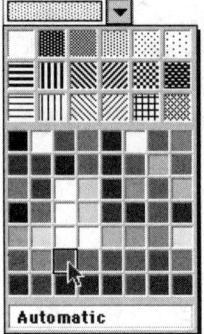

Formatting Worksheet Cells

About the Format Painter

The Format Painter button lets you copy cell formatting and apply it to other cells. This can help you format worksheets quickly and consistently.

Figure 25a. *Click the Format Painter button on the Standard toolbar.*

To copy formatting with the Format Painter

1. Select a cell with the formatting you want to copy.
2. Click the Format Painter button on the Standard toolbar (see **Figure 25a**). The mouse pointer turns into a little plus sign with a paintbrush beside it and a marquee appears around the original selection (see **Figure 25b**).
3. Use the Format Painter pointer to select the cells you want to apply the formatting to (see **Figure 25c**). When you release the mouse button, the formatting is applied (see **Figure 25d**).

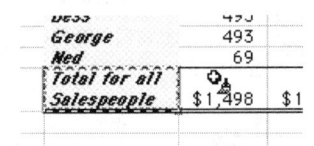

Figure 25b. *The mouse pointer changes and a marquee appears.*

✔ Tips

- Double-click the Format Painter button in step 1 above to keep applying a copied format throughout the worksheet. Press Esc or click the Format Painter button again to stop applying the format and return the mouse pointer to normal.
- If you copy a format that doesn't include number formatting to cells containing numbers, you'll have to apply (or reapply) appropriate number formatting. You can see an example of this in **Figures 25c** and **25d**.
- You can also use the Paste Special dialog box (which is discussed on the next page) to paste copied formats.

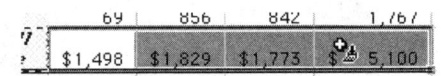

Figure 25c. *Drag the mouse over the cells you want to apply formatting to.*

Figure 25d. *When you release the mouse button, the formatting of the cells changes to match the originally selected cell.*

Copying Formatting

99

Chapter 6

To copy formatting with the Copy and Paste Special commands

1. Select a cell with the formatting you want to copy.
2. Choose Copy from the Edit menu, press ⌘C, or click the Copy button on the Standard toolbar.
3. Switch to the other worksheet and select the cell(s) to which you want to paste formatting.
4. Choose Paste Special from the Edit menu (see **Figure 26a**).
5. In the Paste Special dialog box that appears (see **Figure 26b**), select the Formats radio button.
6. Click OK or press Return or Enter.

To remove only formatting from cells

1. Select the cell(s) from which you want to remove just the formatting.
2. Choose Formats from the Clear submenu under the Edit menu (see **Figure 27**).

✔ Tip

- When you remove formats from a cell, you return font formatting to the normal font and number formatting to the General format. You also remove borders or colors added to the cell.

About Styles

Once you get the hang of using Excel's formatting options, check out its Style feature. This feature, which you access by choosing Styles from the Format menu, lets you combine formats into named styles that you can apply to any cell in the workbook. This can save time and ensure consistency.

Figure 26a. *To paste only formats from a copied cell, choose Paste Special from the Edit menu...*

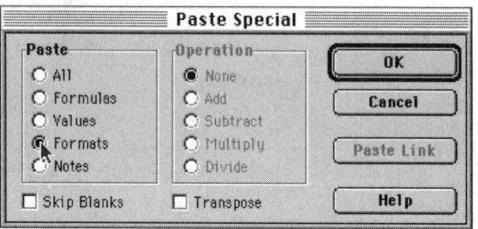

Figure 26b. *...then select the Formats radio button in the Paste Special dialog box and click OK.*

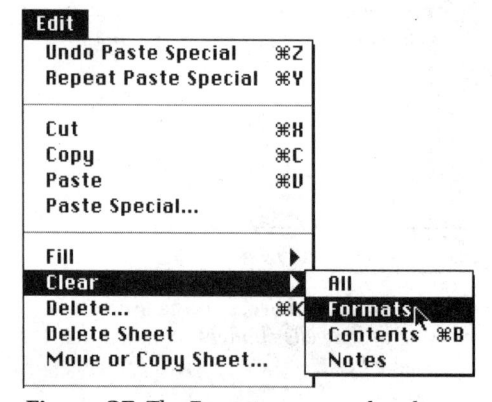

Figure 27. *The Formats command under the Clear submenu will clear all formatting from selected cells.*

100

Formatting Worksheet Cells

About Column Width and Row Height

If the data you enter into a cell doesn't fit, you can make the column wider to accommodate all the characters. You can also make columns narrower to use worksheet space more efficiently. And although Excel automatically adjusts row height when you increase the font size of cells within the row, you can increase or decrease row height as desired.

Excel offers two ways to change column width and row height: with the mouse and with Format menu commands.

✔ Tips

- If text typed into a cell does not fit, it appears to overlap into the cell to its right (see **Figure 28a**). Even though the text may appear to be in more than one cell, all of the text is really in the cell in which you typed it. (You can see for yourself by clicking in the cell to the right and looking at the formula bar—it will not contain any part of the text!) If the cell to the right of the text is not blank, the text appears truncated (see **Figure 28b**). Don't let appearances fool you. The text is still all there. The missing part is just hidden by the contents of the cell beside it.

- If a number doesn't fit in a cell, the cell fills up with pound signs (#) (see **Figure 29a**). To display the number, make the column wider (see **Figure 29b**) or change the number formatting to omit symbols and decimal places (see **Figure 29c**). I tell you how to change number formatting earlier in this chapter.

- Setting column width or row height to 0 (zero) hides the column or row.

Figure 28a. *When text doesn't fit in a cell, it appears to overlap into the cell beside it…*

Figure 28b. *…unless the cell beside it isn't blank.*

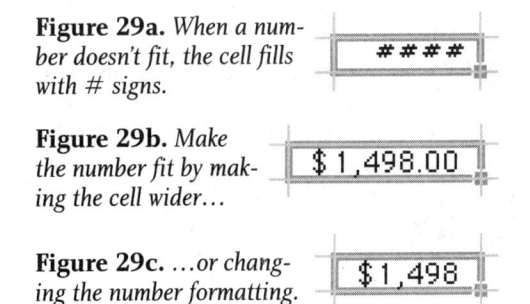

Figure 29a. *When a number doesn't fit, the cell fills with # signs.*

Figure 29b. *Make the number fit by making the cell wider…*

Figure 29c. *…or changing the number formatting.*

Column Width & Row Height

101

Chapter 6

To change column width or row height with the mouse

1. Position the mouse pointer on the line right after the column heading (see **Figure 30a**) or right below the row number (see **Figure 30b**) of the column or row you want to change. The mouse pointer turns into a line with two arrows coming out of it.
2. Press the mouse button down and drag.
   - ☞ To make a column narrower, drag to the left.
   - ☞ To make a column wider, drag to the right.
   - ☞ To make a row taller, drag down.
   - ☞ To make a row shorter, drag up.

   As you drag, a dotted line moves along with the mouse pointer (see **Figure 30c**). The width of the row or height of the column appears in the left end of the formula bar (see **Figure 30d**).
3. Release the mouse button. The column width or row height changes.

Figure 30a&b. Position the mouse pointer between column or row headings...

Figure 30c. ...and drag.

Figure 30d. As you drag, the column width or row height appears in the formula bar.

✔ Tips

- When you change column width or row height, you change the width or height for the entire column or row, not just selected cells.
- To change column width or row height for more than one column or row at a time, select multiple columns or rows and drag the border of one of them. I tell you how to select multiple columns or rows in Chapter 2.
- If you drag a column or row border all the way to the left or all the way up, you set the column width or row height to 0. The column or row disappears from view. I tell you more about hiding columns and rows on the next page.
- To quickly set the width or height of a column or row to fit its contents, double-click the column or row border. I tell you more about the AutoFit feature later in this chapter.

Formatting Worksheet Cells

Figure 31a. *Options under the Column submenu let you change column formatting.*

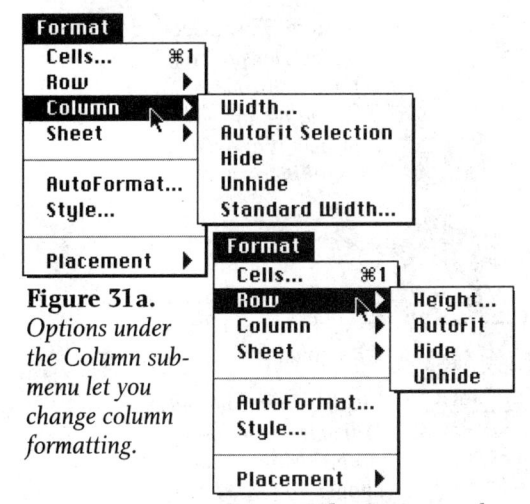

Figure 31b. *Options under the Row submenu let you change row formatting.*

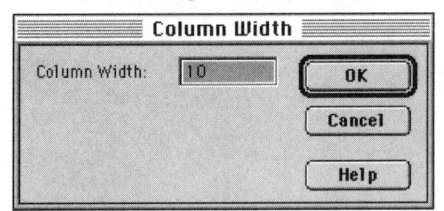

Figure 31c&d. *You're not seeing double. These two dialog boxes let you change column width and row height.*

Figure 32. *When you hide columns or rows, the data is still in the worksheet.*

To change column width or row height with menu commands

1. Select the column(s) or row(s) whose width or height you want to change.
2. Choose Width from the Column submenu under the Format menu (see **Figure 31a**) or choose Height from the Row submenu under the Format menu (see **Figure 31b**).
3. In the Column Width dialog box (see **Figure 31c**) or Row Height dialog box (see **Figure 31d**), enter a new value. Column width is expressed in standard font characters while row height is expressed in points.
4. Click OK or press Return or Enter.

To hide columns or rows

1. Select the column(s) or row(s) you want to hide.
2. Choose Hide from the Column submenu (see **Figure 31a**) or the Row submenu (see **Figure 31b**) under the Format menu.

   The selected columns or rows disappear (see **Figure 32**).

✔ Tip

- Hiding a column or row is not the same as deleting it. Data in a hidden column or row still exists in the worksheet and can be referenced by formulas.

To unhide columns or rows

1. Drag to select the columns or rows on both sides of the hidden column(s) or row(s).
2. Choose Unhide from the Column submenu (see **Figure 31a**) or the Row submenu (see **Figure 31b**) under the Format menu.

Changing Column Width or Row Height

103

Chapter 6

About AutoFit

Excel's AutoFit feature automatically adjusts a column's width or a row's height so it's only as wide or as high as it needs to be to display the information within it (see **Figure 33c**). This is a great way to adjust columns and rows to use worksheet space more efficiently.

To use AutoFit

1. Select the column(s) or row(s) for which you want to change the width or height (see **Figure 33a**).
2. Choose AutoFit Selection from the Column submenu or AutoFit from the Row menu under the Format menu (see **Figures 31a** and **31b**).

   or

   Double-click on the border to the right of the column heading or below the row heading (see **Figure 33b**).

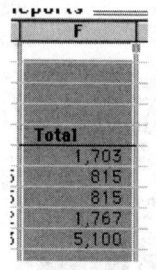

Figure 33a. Select the columns or rows for which you want to change the width or height and use the AutoFit command...

Figure 33b. ...or double-click the border between column or row headings.

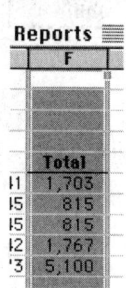

Figure 33c. The width or height is changed so it's just wide or tall enough to fit cell contents.

✔ Tips

- To adjust a column without taking every cell into consideration—for example, to exclude a cell containing a lot of text—select only the cells for which you want to adjust the column (see **Figure 34a**). When you choose AutoFit Selection from the Column submenu under the Format menu, only the cells you selected are measured for the AutoFit adjustment (see **Figure 34b**).
- By using the Wrap Text feature in conjunction with AutoFit, you can keep your columns narrow. I tell you about Wrap Text earlier in this chapter.

Figure 34a. To use AutoFit without taking every cell in the column into consideration, select only the cells for which you want the column adjusted.

Figure 34b. Using AutoFit Selection makes it possible to keep columns narrow when some column cells contain a lot of text.

Formatting Worksheet Cells

Figure 35a. *Select the portion of the worksheet you want to format…*

Figure 35b. *…choose AutoFormat from the Format menu…*

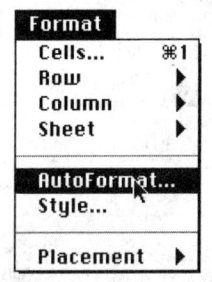

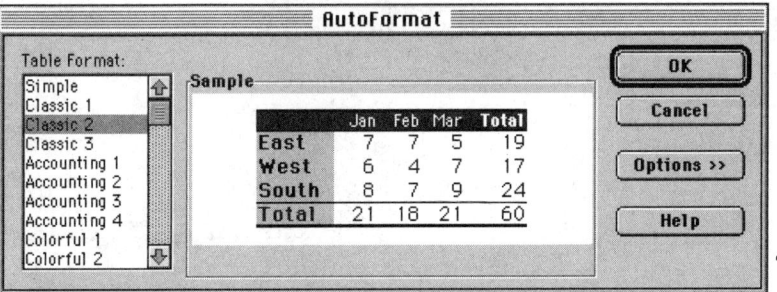

Figure 35c. *…then choose the predefined format you like best.*

Figure 35d. *Excel applies all kinds of formatting all at once.*

Figure 36. *Clicking the Options button expands the AutoFormat dialog box to display check boxes for the different kinds of formatting that can be applied.*

About AutoFormat

Excel's AutoFormat feature offers a quick way to dress up tabular data in worksheets by applying predefined formats. If you're like me and like to leave design for designers, you'll welcome this feature.

To use AutoFormat

1. Select the portion of the worksheet you want to format (see **Figure 35a**).
2. Choose AutoFormat from the Format menu (see **Figure 35b**).
3. In the AutoFormat dialog box that appears (see **Figure 35c**), choose a format from the Table Format scrolling list. A preview of the format appears in the Sample area so you can decide whether you like it before you apply it.
4. When you're satisfied with your selection, click OK or press Return or Enter. Your Worksheet is formatted instantly (see **Figure 35d**).

✔ Tip

- To pick and choose among the different kinds of formatting automatically applied, click the Options button in the AutoFormat dialog box. The box expands to display check boxes for each type of formatting (see **Figure 36**). To exclude a type of change from the AutoFormat process, turn off its check box.

Using AutoFormat

105

Chapter 6

About Cell Notes

Excel lets you add notes to any cell. You can use notes to annotate your worksheets, providing background information for complex or important calculations.

To add a Cell Note

1. Select the cell to which you want to add a note.
2. Choose Note from the Insert menu (see **Figure 37a**).

    or

    Press Shift-F2 (on an extended keyboard only).
3. In the Note dialog box that appears (see **Figure 37b**), enter the text for the note in the Text Note edit box.
4. Click the Add button.
5. Click OK or press Return or Enter.

    A tiny red mark appears in the upper right corner of the cell (see **Figure 37c**) to indicate that the cell has a note. This mark does not print.

Figure 37a. *Choose Note from the Insert menu…*

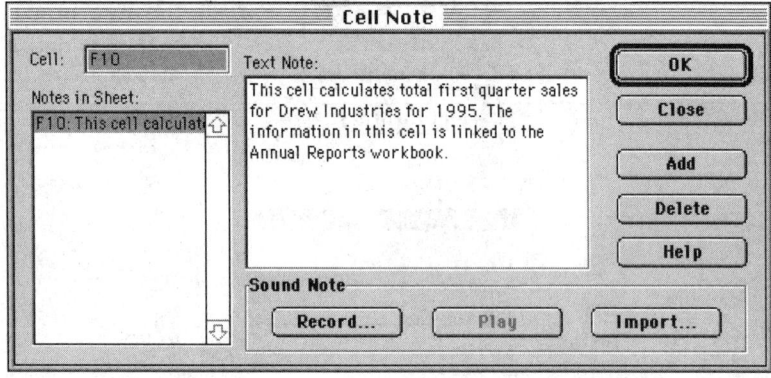

Figure 37b. *…then type your note into the Text Note edit box.*

Figure 37c. *A mark appears in the corner of a cell with a note.*

To view cell notes

1. Choose Note from the Insert menu (see **Figure 37a**).
2. In the Note dialog box that appears (see **Figure 37b**), select the cell containing the note you want to view from the Notes in Sheet scrolling list. The note appears in the Text Note edit box.

✔ Tips

- To add multiple notes, after you click Add for the first note, enter a new cell address in the Cell edit box and repeat steps 3 and 4 until all notes have been added.
- You can use the Record or Import buttons in the Sound Note area (see **Figure 37b**) to record or import sound notes.

Adding Cell Notes

106

DRAWING AND FORMATTING OBJECTS 7

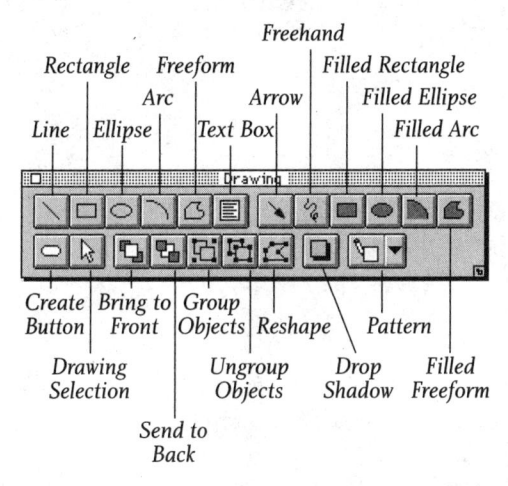

Freehand
Rectangle *Freeform* *Filled Rectangle*
Arc *Arrow* *Filled Ellipse*
Line *Ellipse* *Text Box* *Filled Arc*

Create Button | *Bring to Front* | *Group Objects* | *Reshape* | *Pattern*
Drawing Selection | *Ungroup Objects* | *Drop Shadow* | *Filled Freeform*
Send to Back

Figure 1. *The Drawing toolbar.*

Figure 2. *Click the Drawing button on the Standard toolbar.*

About Drawing Objects

Excel's Drawing toolbar (see **Figure 1**) includes a wide range of tools you can use to add lines, arrows, shapes, and text boxes to your worksheets and charts. Through creative use of these tools, you can add impact and improve appearance in all of your Excel documents.

To display the Drawing toolbar

Click the Drawing button on the Standard toolbar (see **Figure 2**). The button turns dark gray and the Drawing toolbar appears (see **Figure 1**).

✔ Tip

- If your Drawing toolbar doesn't look exactly like this one, don't panic. Although the Drawing toolbar is a floating toolbar by default, it may have been reshaped or anchored the last time it was used—Excel remembers the shape and position of all toolbars. I tell you more about toolbars in Chapter 14.

To hide the Drawing toolbar

Click the Drawing button on the Standard toolbar a second time.

or

If the Drawing toolbar's title bar is displayed, click its close box (see **Figure 3**).

Figure 3. *If the Drawing toolbar is floating, you can hide it by clicking its close box.*

Displaying & Hiding the Drawing Toolbar

107

Chapter 7

About Objects

Many of the tools on the Drawing toolbar let you draw *objects* in worksheet or chart windows. An object can be any line or shape. Excel lets you draw lines, rectangles, squares, ellipses, circles, arcs, freeform shapes, and text boxes. Objects you draw can be selected, resized, moved, or copied at any time.

To draw a line or arrow

1. Click the appropriate Drawing toolbar button once to select it:

    Use the Line tool to draw straight lines.

    Use the Arrow tool to draw straight lines with arrowheads on either or both ends.

    Use the Arc tool to draw arcs. An arc is a quarter of a circle or an ellipse.

    Use the Freehand tool to draw lines in any shape. You can even use it to sign your name!

    When you click the tool's button the mouse pointer turns into a cross hair pointer (see **Figure 4**).

2. Position the cross hair where you want to begin drawing the line.

3. Press the mouse button down and drag. As you move the mouse, a line is drawn (see **Figure 5**).

4. Release the mouse button to complete the line. The line appears with selection handles on either end (see **Figures 6a** and **6b**) or around it (see **Figures 6c** and **6d**). I tell you more about selection handles later in this chapter.

Figure 4. *When you click a drawing tool, the mouse pointer changes into a cross hair.*

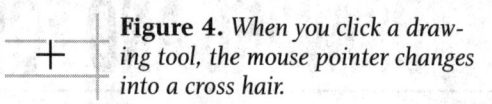

Figure 5. *Drag the cross hair pointer to draw a line.*

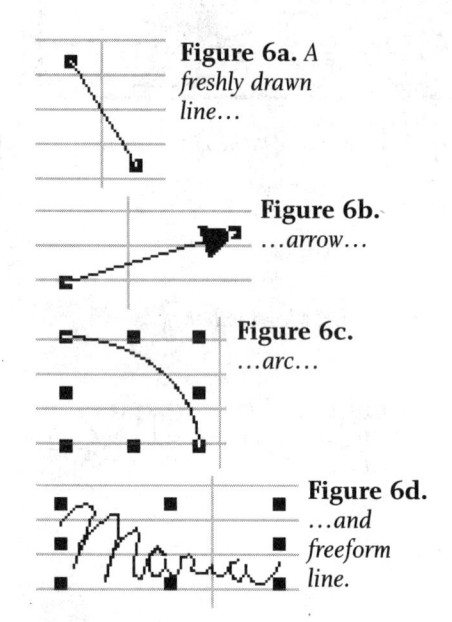

Figure 6a. *A freshly drawn line…*

Figure 6b. *…arrow…*

Figure 6c. *…arc…*

Figure 6d. *…and freeform line.*

✔ Tips

- The Freehand tool's cross hair pointer turns into a pencil as you draw.

- To draw a line or arrow that's perfectly vertical, horizontal, or at a 45° angle, hold down the Shift key as you press down the mouse button and draw.

- To draw multiple lines with the same tool, double-click its button to select it. The tool remains active until you either click the button again, click another button, or press Esc.

Drawing and Formatting Objects

To draw a rectangle, square, ellipse, or circle

1. Click the appropriate Drawing toolbar button once to select it:

   Use the Rectangle tool to draw rectangles or squares.

   Use the Ellipse tool to draw ovals and circles.

   When you click the tool's button the mouse pointer turns into a cross hair pointer (see **Figure 4**).

2. Position the cross hair where you want to begin drawing the shape.

3. Press the mouse button down and drag. As you move the mouse, the shape begins to take form (see **Figure 7**).

4. Release the mouse button to complete the shape. The shape appears with selection handles around it (see **Figures 8a** and **8b**). I tell you more about selection handles later in this chapter.

Figure 7. *Drag the cross hair pointer to draw a shape.*

Figure 8a. *A freshly drawn rectangle…*

Figure 8b. *…and ellipse.*

✔ Tips

- When you draw with the rectangle or ellipse tool, you draw from corner to corner.

- To draw a square or a circle, click the Rectangle or Ellipse button, then hold down the Shift key as you press down the mouse button and draw. The drawing movements are restricted so only perfectly square or perfectly round shapes can be drawn.

- To draw multiple shapes with the same tool, double-click its button to select it. The tool remains active until you either click the button again, click another button, or press Esc.

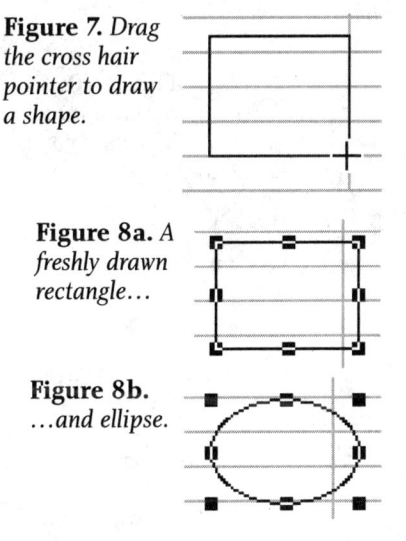

109

Chapter 7

To draw a freeform shape

1. Click the Freeform button on the Drawing toolbar once to select it. The mouse pointer turns into a cross hair pointer (see **Figure 4**).
2. Position the cross hair where you want to begin drawing the shape.
3. Press the mouse button down and drag to draw freehand lines (see **Figure 9a**).

   and/or

   Click where you want the corners of the shape to have Excel draw straight lines between them (see **Figure 9b**).
4. Click at the starting point of the shape to complete a closed shape (see **Figure 10a**).

   or

   Double-click at the ending point of the shape to complete an open shape (see **Figure 10b**).

   The finished shape appears with selection handles around it (see **Figures 10a** and **10b**). I tell you more about selection handles later in this chapter.

✔ Tips

- A freeform shape can combine the dragging and clicking techniques in step 3 above to make shapes that have straight and curved edges (see **Figure 11**).
- To draw multiple freeform shapes, double-click the Freeform button to select it. The Freeform tool remains active until you either click the button again, click another button, or press Esc.
- The best way to learn how to use the Freeform tool is by practicing!

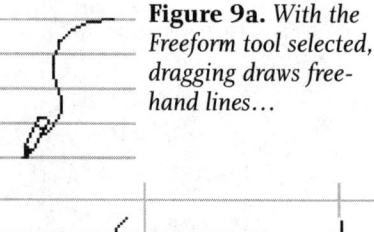

Figure 9a. With the Freeform tool selected, dragging draws free-hand lines…

Figure 9b. …while clicking specifies corners that Excel joins with straight lines.

Figure 10a. A freshly drawn closed freeform shape…

Figure 10b. …and an open freeform shape.

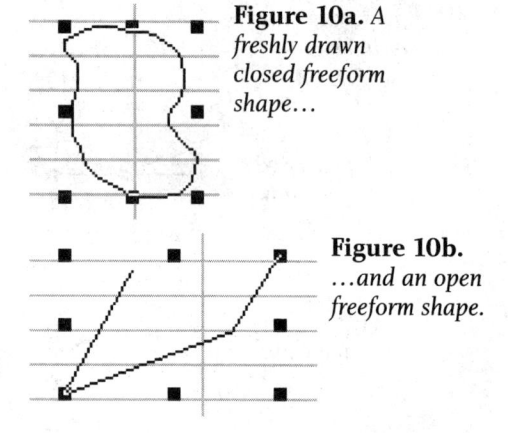

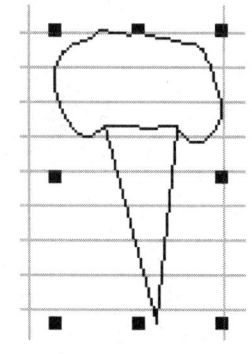

Figure 11. An example of a freeform shape that combines straight lines with curves. Any resemblance to an ice cream cone is purely coincidental.

Drawing and Formatting Objects

About Filled Shapes

Four of Excel's Drawing toolbar buttons activate tools for drawing filled shapes:

Use the Filled Rectangle tool to draw rectangles or squares.

Use the Filled Ellipse tool to draw ovals and circles.

Use the Filled Arc tool to draw arcs.

Use the Filled Freeform tool to draw freeform shapes.

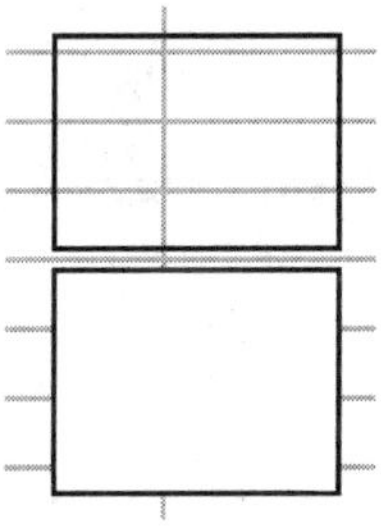

Figure 12.
Two shapes: one unfilled, the other filled with the default color, white. See the difference?

While an unfilled shape is simply a line with a specific form, a filled shape consist of an outline that defines the shape plus a fill color, pattern, and background color. **Figure 12** shows side-by-side examples of both an unfilled and filled shape.

You draw filled shapes the same way you draw unfilled shapes—I explain how to do that on the previous few pages.

✔ Tips

- The default fill color is white. I tell you how to change fill color later in this chapter.

- You can convert an unfilled shape to a filled shape by applying a fill color or pattern. You can also convert a filled shape to an unfilled shape by removing its fill color or pattern. I tell you how to do both of these things later in this chapter.

111

Chapter 7

About Modifying Objects

Any object you draw in Excel can also be edited in Excel. You can resize and reshape objects, move and copy objects, and group objects together. You can also change the color and thickness of lines and the color and pattern of fill. If you decide you don't like the object, you can delete it.

In order to make any changes to an object, however, you must begin by selecting it.

To select an object

1. Position the mouse pointer on a line, on the border of an unfilled object, or anywhere on a filled object. The mouse pointer turns into a selection pointer (see **Figure 13a**) rather than the standard worksheet pointer (see **Figure 13b**).
2. Click. Selection handles appear around the object (see **Figure 14**).

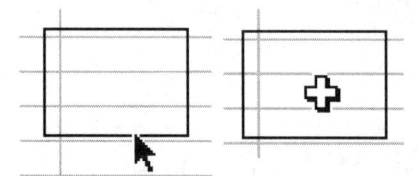

Figure 13a. *This mouse pointer will select this object.*

Figure 13b. *This mouse pointer will only select the cell beneath the object.*

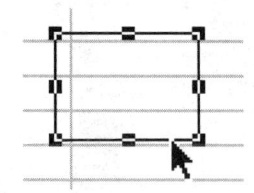

Figure 14. *Black boxes called selection handles appear around selected objects.*

✔ Tip

- To convert the mouse pointer into a selection pointer so the standard worksheet pointer doesn't appear while you're working with drawing objects, click the Drawing Selection button on the Drawing toolbar. The button turns dark gray and the mouse pointer changes to an arrow. To get the regular pointer back, click the Drawing Selection button again, double-click any worksheet cell, or press Esc once or twice.

To deselect an object

Click on any other object or anywhere else in the window. The selection handles disappear.

Selecting Objects

Drawing and Formatting Objects

Figure 15a.
Hold down the Shift key and click on each object…

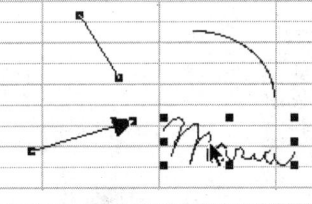

Figure 15b.
…or use the selection pointer to drag a rectangle around all objects.

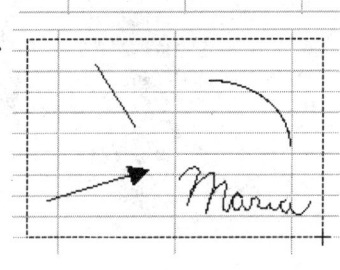

Figure 15c.
Selection handles appear around each object.

To select multiple objects

Follow steps 1 and 2 on the previous page to select the first object, then hold down the Shift key and continue to select objects (see **Figure 15a**) until all have been selected (see **Figure 15c**).

or

Click the Drawing Selection button on the Drawing toolbar to activate the selection pointer, then use the pointer to drag a rectangle that completely surrounds all the objects you want to select (see **Figure 15b**). When you release the mouse button, selection handles appear around each object (see **Figure 15c**).

✔ Tips

- To select all the objects on a worksheet, click the Drawing Selection button on the Drawing toolbar and press ⌘A.
- To deselect objects from a multiple selection, hold down the Shift key while clicking on the objects you want to deselect.

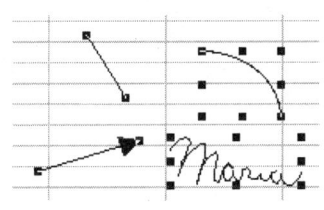

Figure 16.
Grouped objects share one set of selection handles.

To group objects

1. Select all the objects you want to include in the group.
2. Click the Group Objects button on the Drawing toolbar.

The objects are grouped together, with only one set of selection handles (see **Figure 16**).

✔ Tips

- Grouping objects makes it easier to move, copy, or resize them when you want them to stay together.
- In addition to grouping separate objects, you can also group groups of objects.

To ungroup objects

1. Select the grouped object you want to ungroup.
2. Click the Ungroup Objects button on the Drawing toolbar.

Separate selection handles appear for each object.

Selecting & Grouping Multiple Objects

113

Chapter 7

To move an object

1. Position the mouse pointer on the object so that the selection pointer appears.
2. Press the mouse button down and drag. An outline of the object moves along with the mouse pointer (see **Figure 17**).
3. When the object's outline is in the desired position, release the mouse button. The object moves.

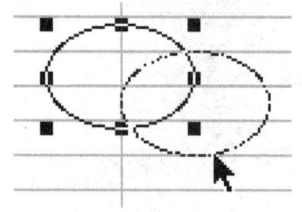

Figure 17. To move an object, simply drag it.

✔ Tips

- To restrict an object's movement so that it moves only horizontally or vertically, hold down the Shift key while dragging.
- To restrict an object's movement so that it snaps to the worksheet gridlines, hold down the Command (⌘) key while dragging.

To copy an object with the Copy and Paste commands

1. Select the object you want to copy.
2. Choose Copy from the Edit menu, press ⌘C, or click the Copy button on the Standard toolbar.
3. If you want to paste the object into a different worksheet or chart sheet, switch to that sheet.
4. Choose Paste from the Edit menu, press ⌘V, or click the Paste button on the Standard toolbar.

✔ Tip

- To remove the original object from the sheet, choose Cut from the Edit menu, press ⌘X, or click the Cut button on the Standard toolbar in step 2 above.

To copy an object by dragging

1. Position the mouse pointer on the object so it turns into a selection pointer.
2. Hold down the Option key, press the mouse button down, and drag. A tiny plus sign appears beside the mouse pointer. As you drag, an outline of the object moves along with the mouse pointer (see **Figure 18**).
3. When you release the mouse button, a copy of the object appears at the outline's position.

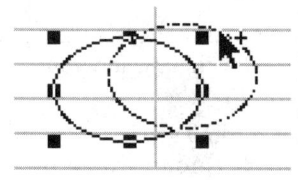

Figure 18. *If you hold down the Option key while dragging, a copy of the object is made.*

114

Drawing and Formatting Objects

To delete an object

1. Select the object(s) or group of objects you want to delete.
2. Press the Delete key.

   or

   Press the Del key (on an extended keyboard only).

   or

   Choose All from the Clear submenu under the Edit menu (see **Figure 19**).

   or

   Press ⌘B.

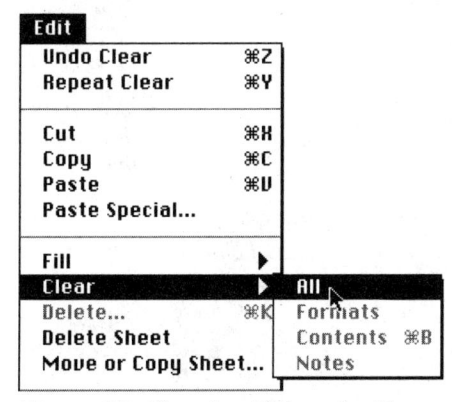

Figure 19. *Choosing All from the Clear submenu is only one way to delete a selected object.*

Figures 20a, 20b, & 20c. *Positioning the mouse pointer over a selection handle turns it into a resize pointer.*

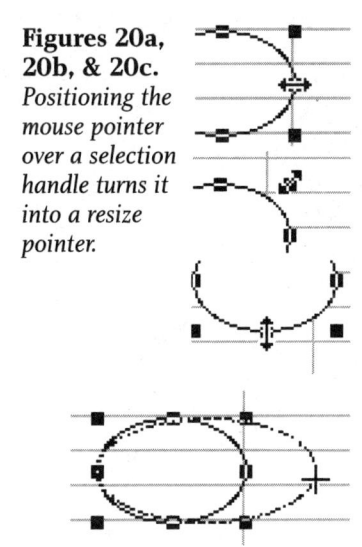

Figure 21. *To resize an object, drag one of its selection handles.*

To resize an object

1. Select the object you want to resize.
2. Position the mouse pointer on a selection handle. The mouse pointer turns into a double-headed arrow (see **Figures 20a**, **20b**, and **20c**).
3. Press the mouse button down and drag to stretch or shrink the object. The mouse pointer turns into a cross hair and an outline of the edge of the object moves with your mouse pointer as you drag (see **Figure 21**).
4. When the outline of the object reflects the size you want, release the mouse button. The object is resized.

✔ Tips

- To resize an object or group proportionally, hold down the Shift key while dragging a corner selection handle.
- To resize the object so that the handle you drag snaps to the worksheet gridlines, hold down the Command (⌘) key while dragging.
- To resize multiple objects at the same time, select the objects, then resize one of them. All selected objects will stretch or shrink.

Deleting & Resizing Objects

115

Chapter 7

To reshape an object

1. Select the object you want to reshape. The object must be a *polygon* (a multi-sided object).
2. Click the Reshape button on the Drawing toolbar. Handles for *vertices* appear at the ends of straight lines and along freehand curves (see **Figures 22a** and **22b**).
3. Position the mouse pointer on a vertex handle. The mouse pointer turns into a cross hair.
4. Press the mouse button down and drag (see **Figure 23a**). As you drag, an outline of the edge of the object moves with your mouse pointer.
5. When the vertex is in the proper position, release the mouse button. The object reshapes (see **Figure 23b**).
6. Repeat steps 3, 4, and 5 for any other vertices you need to move.

Figure 22a. Vertices appear at the ends of straight lines...

Figure 22b. ...and along freehand curves.

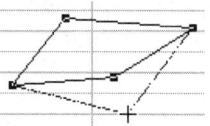

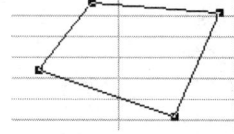

Figure 23a. Drag a vertex to reshape an object.

Figure 23b. When you release the mouse button, the object reshapes.

✔ Tips

- The vertices will remain on the selected object (or will appear on any other polygon you select) until you click the Reshape button again.
- To add a vertex, hold down the Option key and drag the edge of the polygon (see **Figure 24**). This inserts and positions the new vertex.
- To delete a vertex, hold down the Option key and click on the vertex handle (see **Figure 25a**). The vertex is removed and the polygon reshapes accordingly (see **Figure 25b**).

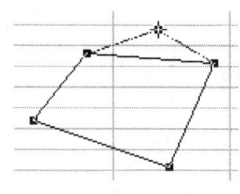

Figure 24. Hold down the Option key and drag a polygon side to insert a vertex.

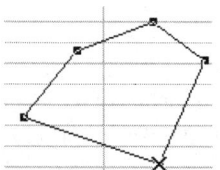

Figure 25a. Hold down the Option key and click on a vertex handle.

Figure 25b. The vertex disappears and the shape of the polygon changes accordingly.

Drawing and Formatting Objects

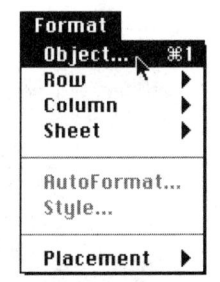

Figure 26a. *Select the line you want to change and choose Object from the Format menu.*

To change the style, color, and weight of lines

1. Click on the line you want to change to select it and choose Object from the Format menu (see **Figure 26a**) or press ⌘1.

   or

   Double-click on the line you want to change.

2. The Format Object dialog box appears. Click the Patterns tab if necessary to display its options (see **Figure 26b**).

3. To change the line style, choose a style from the Line Style pop-up menu (see **Figure 26c**).

4. To change the line color, choose a color from the Line Color pop-up menu (see **Figure 26d**).

5. To change the line weight or thickness, choose a weight from the Line Weight pop-up menu (see **Figure 26e**).

6. When the line in the Sample area looks like the line you want, click OK or press Return or Enter to apply the formatting.

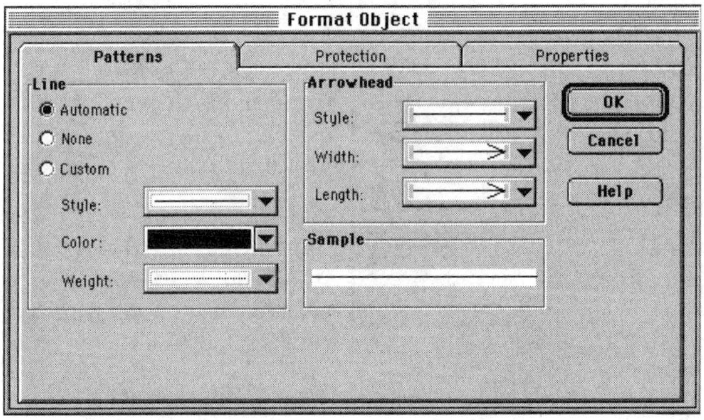

Figure 26b. *When a line or arrow is selected, the Patterns tab of the Format Objects dialog box offers these options.*

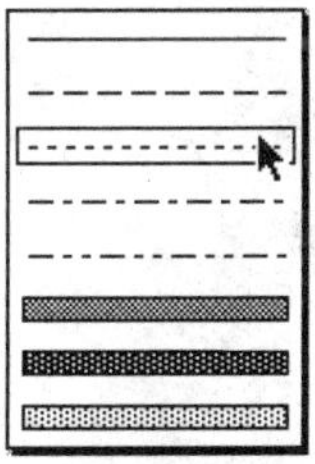

Figure 26c. *Use the Line Style pop-up menu to choose a line style.*

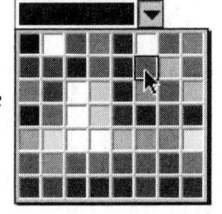

Figure 26d. *Use the Line Color pop-up menu to choose a line color.*

Figure 26e. *Use the Line Weight pop-up menu to choose a line thickness.*

✔ Tip

- To return to default line formatting, select the Automatic radio button in the Format Object dialog box.

Changing Line Style, Color, & Weight

117

Chapter 7

Modifying Arrowheads

To change or add arrowheads

1. Click on the line or arrowhead you want to change to select it and choose Object from the Format menu (see **Figure 26a**) or press ⌘1.

   or

   Double-click on the line you want to change.

2. The Format Object dialog box appears. Click the Patterns tab if necessary to display its options (see **Figure 26b**).

3. To change the arrowhead style or add an arrowhead to a plain line, choose a style from the Style pop-up menu (see **Figure 26f**).

4. To change the arrowhead width, choose a width from the Width pop-up menu (see **Figure 26g**).

5. To change the arrowhead length, choose a length from the Length pop-up menu (see **Figure 26h**).

6. If desired, make changes in the Style, Color, and Weight pop-up menus on the left side of the dialog box. I tell you how on the previous page.

7. When the arrow in the Sample area looks like the arrow you want, click OK or press Return or Enter to apply the formatting.

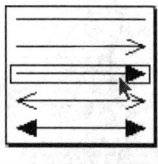

Figure 26f. *Use the Arrowhead Style pop-up menu to choose an arrowhead style.*

Figure 26g. *Use the Arrowhead Width pop-up menu to choose an arrowhead width.*

Figure 26h. *Use the Arrowhead Length pop-up menu to choose an arrowhead length.*

✔ Tips

- To remove an arrowhead from a line, choose the first line style from the Arrowhead Style pop-up menu (see **Figure 26f**).

- When you draw an arrow, you always draw from the tail to the head. To switch arrowhead sides, drag the selection handle for the head around so that the arrow points in the opposite direction. Then drag the selection for the tail to adjust the line length.

Drawing and Formatting Objects

To change the style, color, and weight of shape borders

1. Click on the shape you want to change to select it and choose Object from the Format menu (see **Figure 26a**) or press ⌘1.

   or

   Double-click on the shape you want to change.

2. The Format Object dialog box appears. Click the Patterns tab if necessary to display its options (see **Figure 27**).

3. To change the border style, choose a style from the Style pop-up menu (see **Figure 26c**).

4. To change the border color, choose a color from the Color pop-up menu (see **Figure 26d**).

5. To change the border weight or thickness, choose a weight from the Weight pop-up menu (see **Figure 26e**).

6. To add a drop shadow border to the object, turn on the Shadow check box.

7. To round the corners of rectangles or squares, turn on the Round Corners check box. (This option is not available for ellipses and circles.)

8. When the border around the shape in the Sample area looks like the border you want, click OK or press Return or Enter to apply the formatting.

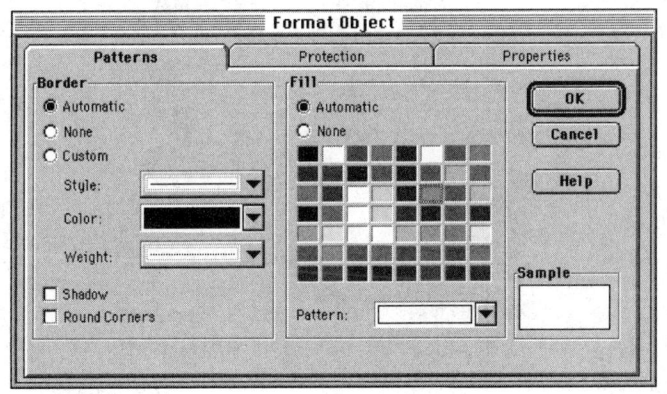

Figure 27. *When a shape is selected, the Patterns tab of the Format Object dialog box offers these options.*

✔ Tips

- To add just a drop shadow border around a selected object, click the Drop Shadow button on the Drawing toolbar.

- To return to default border formatting, select the Automatic radio button on the left side of the Format Object dialog box.

- To remove the border from the object, select the None radio button on the left side of the Format Object dialog box.

To change or add fill colors and patterns to shapes

1. Click on the shape you want to change to select it and choose Object from the Format menu (see **Figure 26a**) or press ⌘1.

   or

   Double-click on the shape you want to change.

2. The Format Object dialog box appears. Click the Patterns tab if necessary to display its options (see **Figure 27**).

3. To change or add the fill color, click the color you want on the Fill color palette. This is the foreground color.

4. To change the fill pattern and background color, choose a pattern and color from the Pattern pop-up menu (see **Figure 28**).

5. If desired, make additional changes in the Border area of the dialog box. I tell you how on the previous page.

6. When the shape in the Sample area looks just the way you want it to, click OK or press Return or Enter to apply the formatting.

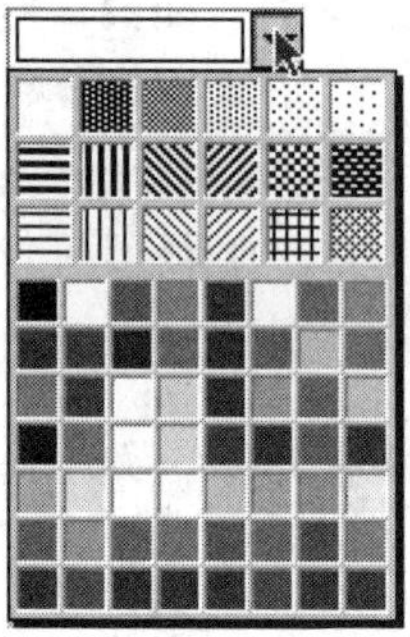

Figure 28. *Use the Fill Pattern pop-up menu to choose a pattern and background color for object fill.*

✔ Tips

- To add or change just the fill pattern or background color for a selected object, use the Pattern menu/button on the Drawing toolbar. Click the button to apply the pattern and background color illustrated on it. Click the arrow on the right side of the button to display a menu identical to the Pattern pop-up menu in the Format Object dialog box (see **Figure 28**).

- To remove colors or patterns from the object fill, select the Automatic radio button in the Fill area of the Format Object dialog box. This sets the fill to the default color—white.

- To remove the fill color and pattern from the object, select the None radio button in the Fill area of the Format Object dialog box.

Drawing and Formatting Objects

Figure 29. *Each object you draw gets its own drawing layer.*

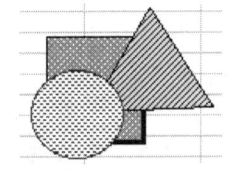

Figure 30a. *Select the object you want to move to another layer…*

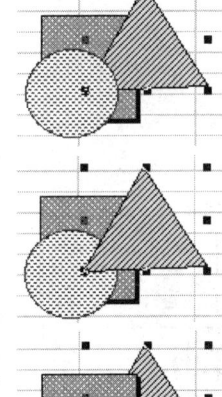

Figure 30b. *…then click the Bring to Front button…*

Figure 30c. *…or click the Send to Back button.*

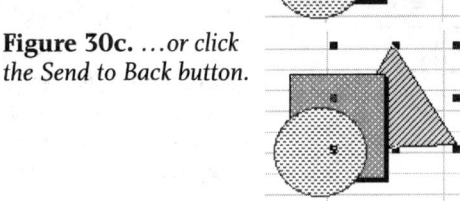

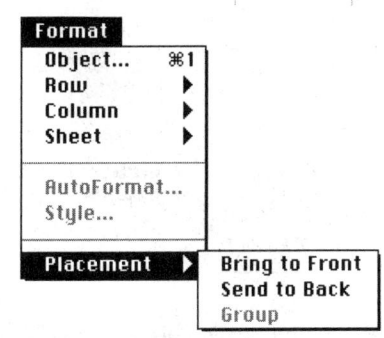

Figure 31. *If you prefer, you can use the Bring to Front and Send to Back commands rather than toolbar buttons.*

About Stacking Order

Each time you draw a shape, Excel puts it on a new drawing layer. So when you draw a shape that overlaps another shape, the first shape may be partially obscured by the one "on top" of it (see **Figure 29**).

To change stacking order

1. Select the object(s) you want to move to another layer (see **Figure 30a**).
2. To bring the object(s) to the top layer (see **Figure 30b**), click the Bring to Front button on the Drawing toolbar or choose Bring to Front from the Placement submenu under the Format menu (see **Figure 31**).

   or

   To send the object(s) to the bottom layer (see **Figure 30c**), click the Send to Back button on the Drawing toolbar or choose Send to Back from the Placement submenu under the Format menu (see **Figure 31**).

✔ Tips

- Since there are no commands to move an object one layer at a time, you may need to move more than one object to achieve certain stacking orders.
- Once you've gotten objects in the order you want, consider grouping them so they stay just the way you want them to. I tell you how to group objects earlier in this chapter.
- You cannot move graphic objects behind the worksheet layer.

Chapter 7

About Text Boxes

A text box is like a little word processing document on an Excel sheet. Once created, you can enter and format text within it. Text boxes offer far more flexibility than worksheet cells when entering long passages of text.

To add a text box

1. Click the Text box button on the Drawing or Standard toolbar. The mouse pointer turns into a cross hair pointer.
2. Position the cross hair where you want to begin drawing the text box.
3. Press the mouse button down and drag. As you move the mouse, the text box begins to take form (see **Figure 32a**).
4. Release the mouse button to complete the text box. An insertion point appears within it (see **Figure 32b**).
5. Enter the text you want in the text box (see **Figure 32c**).

✔ Tips

- You can move, copy, and resize a text box just like any other object.
- To edit text in a text box, click on the box to select it, then click inside the text box to position an insertion point or drag over text in the text box to select it. Standard editing techniques apply.
- To format text in a text box (see **Figure 32d**), select the text you want to change, then use keyboard shortcuts, toolbar buttons, or options in the Format Object dialog box to make the changes. All of these techniques and options are discussed in Chapter 6.

Figure 32a. *Drag with the text box tool to create a text box.*

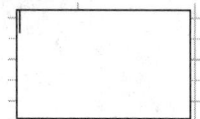

Figure 32b. *When you release the mouse button, an insertion point appears.*

Figure 32c. *Enter the text you want in the box.*

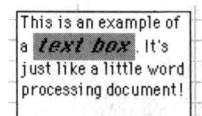

Figure 32d. *Select and format text as discussed in Chapter 6.*

- To change the border or fill of a text box, click on its border to select it and choose Object from the Format menu or press ⌘1. I tell you how to use the Patterns tab options in the Format Object dialog box earlier in this chapter.

Adding Text Boxes

About External Graphics

You can add graphics created with other programs to your Excel sheets. You might find this handy if you need to include a company logo or other graphic in a file.

To paste in graphic objects

1. Use the Copy command in Excel or another application to copy the object to the Clipboard (see **Figure 33a**).

2. If necessary, switch to the sheet in which you want to place the object.

3. Choose Paste from the Edit menu, press ⌘V, or click the Paste button on the Standard toolbar. The object appears and you can drag it into position on the sheet. (see **Figure 33b**).

✔ Tip

- Once you put a graphic object in an Excel sheet, it can be moved, copied, or resized just like any other graphic object.

- Use the Apple Scrapbook desk accessory (available under the Apple menu) to store graphics you use often. You'll find that Excel documents aren't the only ones into which you can paste graphics!

Figure 33a. *Here's a company logo created in Photoshop being copied to the Clipboard.*

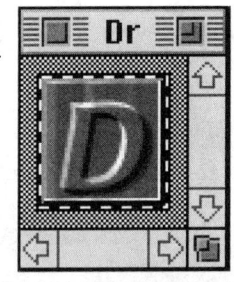

Figure 33b. *The logo can then be pasted into a worksheet to impress the stockholders.*

Chapter 7

Inserting ClipArt

To insert Microsoft ClipArt

1. Choose Object from the Insert menu (see **Figure 34a**).
2. In the Create New dialog box that appears (see **Figure 34b**), choose Microsoft ClipArt Gallery and click OK.
3. In the Microsoft ClipArt Gallery dialog box that appears (see **Figure 34c**), choose a category and then an image to insert in your sheet.
4. Click OK. After a moment, the image appears in your worksheet.

✔ Tips

- The Microsoft ClipArt Gallery must be installed in order to use this feature. If the ClipArt Gallery option does not appear in step 2 above, use your Microsoft Excel or Microsoft Office installation disks to install the ClipArt Gallery.

- In order to use the ClipArt Gallery, your Macintosh must have enough random access memory (RAM) to run Excel and the ClipArt Gallery application at the same time.

- If this is the first time you've used the ClipArt Gallery, you may be prompted to update or add images to the gallery. If a message like this appears, click OK.

- You can move, copy, or resize ClipArt images like any other graphic image.

- ClipArt images are *embedded* into your sheets. This means there's a live link between the sheet and the image file. I tell you more about links in Chapter 12.

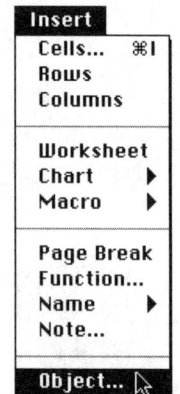

Figure 34a. *Choose Object from the Insert menu.*

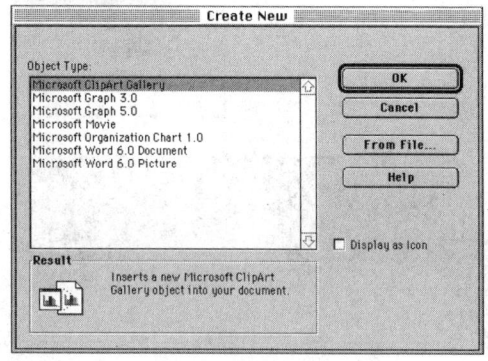

Figure 34b. Choose Microsoft ClipArt Gallery in the Create New dialog box and click OK.

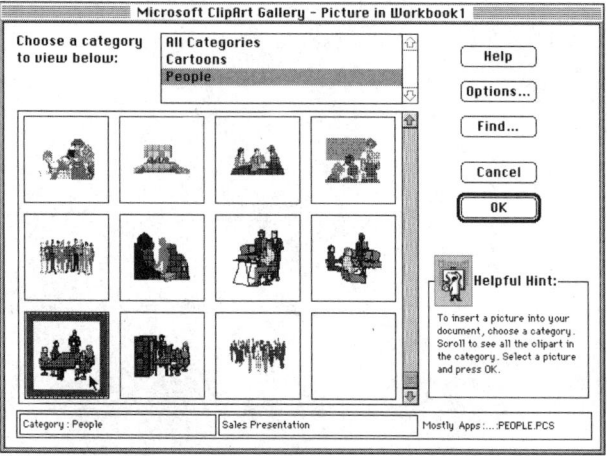

Figure 34c. Finally, choose the category and image you want and click OK.

124

CREATING CHARTS 8

About Charts

A chart is a graphic representation of data. A chart can be embedded in a worksheet (see **Figure 1**) or can be a chart sheet of its own (see **Figure 2**).

With Excel, you can create 14 different types of charts. The 3-D pie chart and 3-D column chart shown here (see **Figures 1** and **2**) are only two examples. Since each type of chart has at least one variation and you can customize any chart you create, there's no limit to the number of ways you can present data graphically with Excel.

Figure 1. *Here's a 3-D pie chart embedded in a worksheet file.*

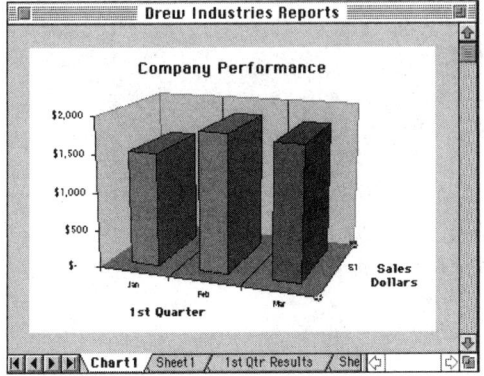

Figure 2. *Here's a 3-D column chart on a chart sheet of its own.*

✔ Tips

- Include charts with worksheets whenever you want to emphasize worksheet results. Charts can often communicate information like trends and comparitive results better than numbers alone.

- A skilled chartmaker can, through choice of data, chart format, and scale, get a chart to say almost anything about the data it represents!

About the ChartWizard

Excel's ChartWizard walks you step-by-step through the creation of a chart. It uses illustrated dialog boxes to prompt you for information. In the final steps of the ChartWizard, you get to see what your chart looks like. At any point, you can go back and make changes to selections. When you're finished, your chart appears. You can then use a variety of chart formatting commands and buttons to change the look of your chart.

To embed a chart on a worksheet

1. Select the data you want to include in the chart (see **Figure 3a**). Your selection can include text to use as headings as well as the numbers the chart will represent.

2. Click the ChartWizard button on the Standard toolbar.

   or

   Choose On This Sheet from the Chart submenu under the Insert menu (see **Figure 3b**).

   The mouse pointer turns into a cross hair with a tiny chart icon beside it and the cells you selected become surrounded with a marquee (see **Figure 3c**).

3. Use the mouse pointer to drag a box the size and shape of the chart you want (see **Figure 3d**).

4. Release the mouse pointer. The first dialog box of the ChartWizard appears. Continue following the instructions on the next page to use the ChartWizard.

To insert a chart as a separate sheet

1. Select the data you want to include in the chart (see **Figure 3a**). Your selection can include text to use as headings as well as the numbers the chart will represent.

2. Choose As a New Sheet from the Chart submenu under the Insert menu (see **Figure 3b**).

   Excel inserts a chart sheet in front of the active sheet and displays the first dialog box of the ChartWizard. Continue following the instructions on the next page to use the ChartWizard.

Figure 3a. *Select the data you want to chart.*

Figure 3b. *Tell Excel where to put the chart by choosing from the Chart submenu.*

Figure 3c. *The mouse pointer changes and a marquee appears around selected cells.*

Figure 3d. *Drag a box the size and shape of the chart you want.*

Creating Charts

To use the ChartWizard

Follow the steps on the previous page to tell Excel where to put the chart and activate the ChartWizard. Then:

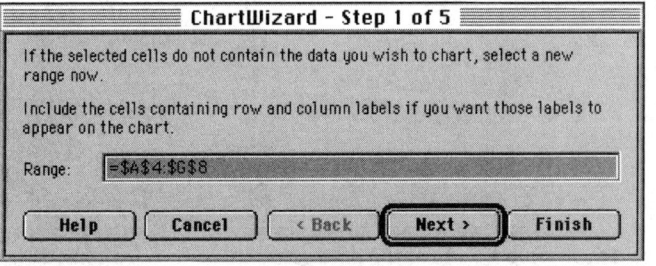

Figure 4a. *In Step 1, select the range(s) you want to chart.*

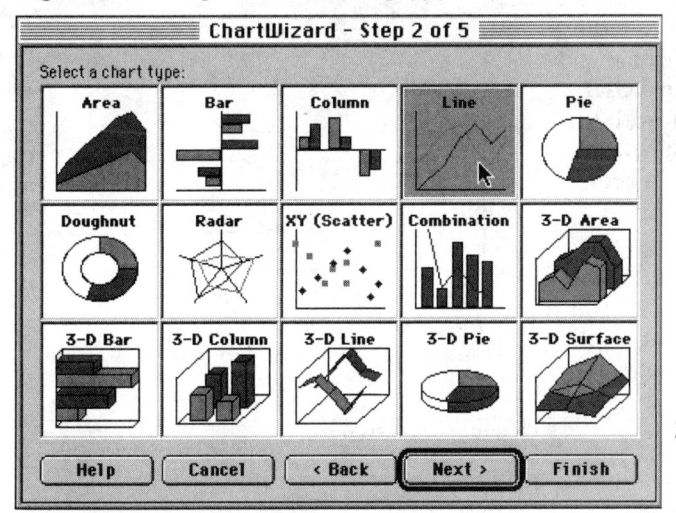

Figure 4b. *In Step 2, select a chart type.*

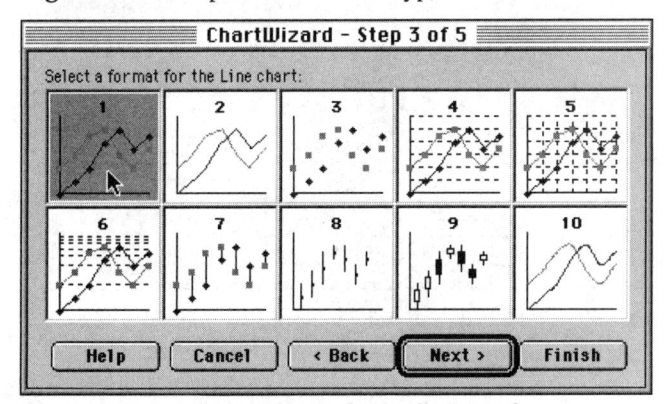

Figure 4c. *In Step 3, select a chart subtype or format.*

1. In the ChartWizard – Step 1 dialog box (see **Figure 4a**), check the contents of the Range edit box to assure that it indicates the data you want to chart. You can see which data range(s) will be charted by dragging the ChartWizard dialog box aside so you can see the sheet behind it. If incorrect, select the correct range(s). The ChartWizard window remains in the foreground as you make your changes, recording the new range(s) for you. When you're satisfied with your selection, click Next or press Return or Enter.

2. In the ChartWizard – Step 2 dialog box (see **Figure 4b**), select one of the 15 chart types by clicking it. Then click Next or press Return or Enter.

3. In the ChartWizard – Step 3 dialog box (see **Figure 4c**), select one of the formats for the chart by clicking it. The options offered vary depending on the selection you made in step 2. When you've made your selection, click Next or press Return or Enter.

Using the ChartWizard

127

Chapter 8

4. In the ChartWizard – Step 4 dialog box (see **Figure 4d**), you get your first look at your chart. The options offered vary depending on the selections you made in steps 2 and 3. In **Figure 4d**, for example, I can change the data series and row(s) or column(s) containing text for labels or the chart legend. If I select the Columns radio button under Data Series, I completely change the look of the sample chart (see **Figure 4e**). Experiment with the options that appear until the chart looks right, then click Next or press Return or Enter.

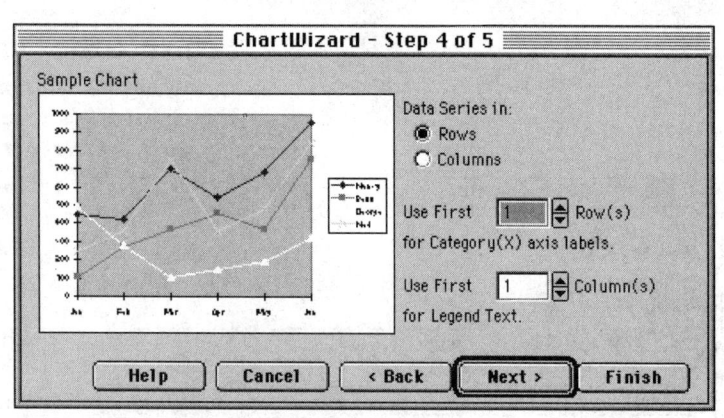

Figure 4d. *In Step 4, adjust the data series and text selections.*

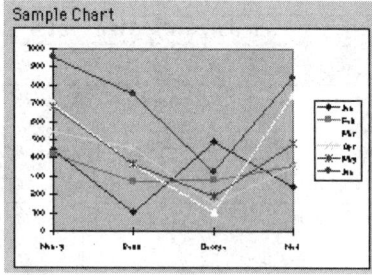

Figure 4e. *As this example illustrates, changing the data series in Step 4 can completely change the chart!*

5. In the ChartWizard – Step 5 dialog box (see **Figure 4f**), use radio buttons to add or remove a chart legend and use edit boxes to specify a chart title and axis labels. All of your changes are reflected in the Sample Chart area of the dialog box. When you're done, click Finish or press Return or Enter.

   Excel inserts the chart you created with the ChartWizard's help (see **Figure 5a**).

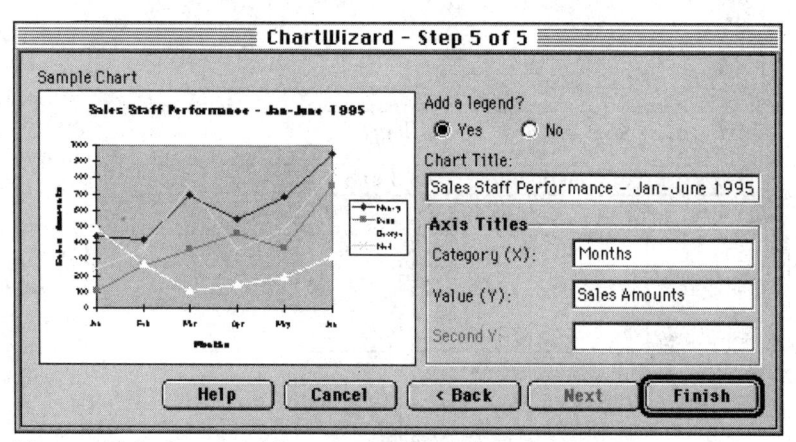

Figure 4f. *In Step 5, add or remove a legend, chart title, and axis labels.*

Creating Charts

Selection Handles

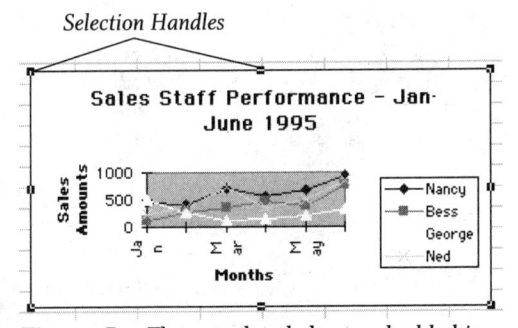

Figure 5a. *The completed chart embedded in a worksheet file. If the information is packed so tightly that you can't read it...*

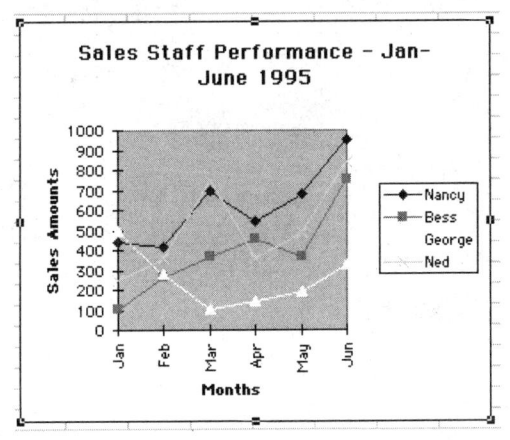

Figure 5b. *...stretch the box containing the chart so everything displays properly.*

✔ Tips

- At any time while using the ChartWizard, you can click the Back button to move to a previous step. Any changes you make in a previous step are carried forward when you continue.

- If your chart is too small to show everything it needs to display (see **Figure 5a**), you can resize it by dragging one of its selection handles. I tell you how to resize graphics in Chapter 7; resizing a chart works the same way. **Figure 5b** shows the same chart resized to display everything properly.

- A chart embedded in a worksheet or a chart sheet is a special kind of graphic. You can move, copy, resize, or delete it just like any other graphic object. I tell you how to work with graphics in Chapter 7.

- Although Excel will automatically include many formatting options in charts created with the ChartWizard, you can edit, move, format, or delete almost any chart element. I tell you how in Chapter 9.

- Don't be afraid to experiment with the ChartWizard. Try different options to see what effects you can achieve. You can always delete the chart and start fresh. Deleting the chart does not change the data.

ChartWizard Tips

129

Chapter 8

About Worksheet and Chart Links

When you create a chart based on worksheet data, the worksheet and chart are linked. Excel knows exactly which worksheet and cells it should look at to plot the chart. If the contents of one of those cells changes, the chart changes accordingly (see **Figures 6a** and **6b**).

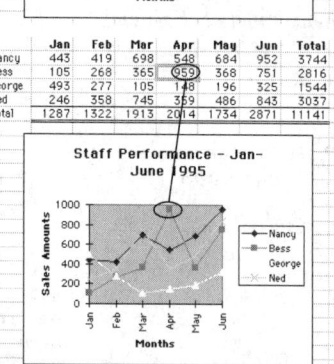

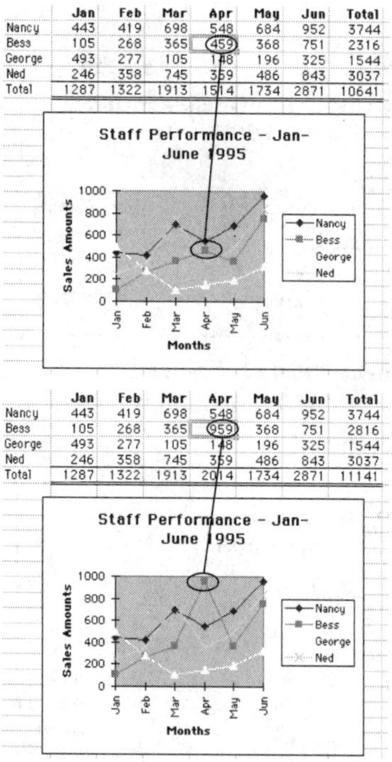

✔ Tips

- The link works both ways. With some chart types, you can drag a data point to change the data in the source worksheet (see **Figure 7**). This makes an good planning tool for businesses interested in maintaining trends.

- You can see (and edit) the links between a chart and a worksheet by activating the chart, selecting one of the data series, and looking at the formula bar. You should see a formula with a SERIES function that specifies the sheet name and absolute cell references for the range making up that series. **Figures 8a** and **8b** show an example.

- If you delete worksheet data or an entire worksheet that is linked to a chart, Excel warns you with a dialog box like the one in **Figure 9**. If you removed the data by mistake, immediately choose Undo Delete Cells from the Edit menu, click the Undo button on the Standard toolbar, or press ⌘Z to get the deleted data back.

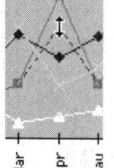

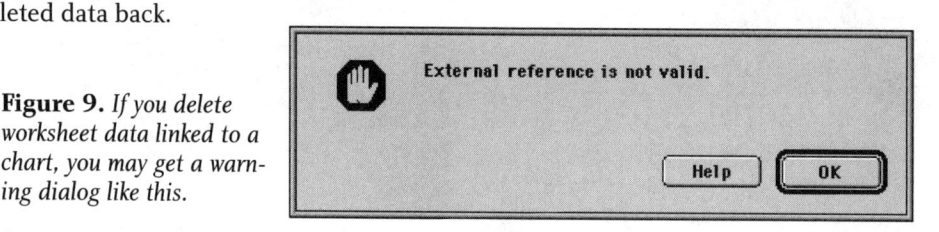

Figure 9. *If you delete worksheet data linked to a chart, you may get a warning dialog like this.*

Figures 6a&b. *A linked worksheet and chart before (top) and after (bottom) a change to a cell's contents. When you change one, the other changes automatically.*

Figure 7. *Dragging a point on a chart also changes the corresponding value in a linked worksheet.*

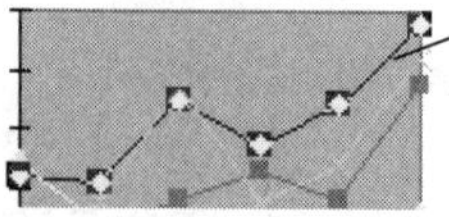

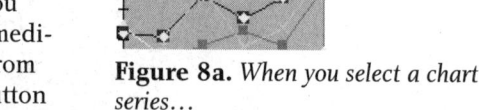

Figure 8a. *When you select a chart series…*

=SERIES(Sheet15!$A$5,Sheet15!$B$4:$G$4,Sheet15!$B$5:$G$5,1)

Figure 8b. *…you can see (and edit) its link in the formula bar.*

To add or remove chart data with the ChartWizard

1. Activate the chart by switching to its chart sheet or, if it's an embedded chart, double-clicking it.
2. Click the ChartWizard button on the Standard or Chart toolbar.
3. In the ChartWizard – Step 1 dialog box (see **Figure 10a**), select the range(s) of cells that include all the data you want to chart. Then click Next or press Return or Enter.
4. In the ChartWizard – Step 2 dialog box (see **Figure 10b**), make changes as necessary to properly display your data in the Sample Chart area. Then click OK or press Return or Enter.

   The revised chart appears, using the new data range(s) you selected.

Figure 10a. *Use Step 1 of the ChartWizard to choose the range(s) to chart.*

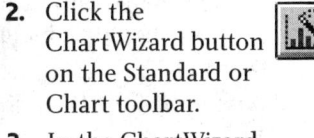

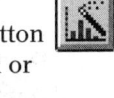

Figure 10b. *Then use Step 2 of the ChartWizard to fine-tune the revised chart if necessary.*

✔ Tip

- If all you're doing is adding or removing chart data, you shouldn't need to make any changes in the second step of the ChartWizard dialog box.

Chapter 8

To add chart data with the Copy and Paste commands

1. In the worksheet, select the data you want to add to the chart (see **Figure 11a**). Be sure to include column or row headings if they should be included as labels.

2. Choose Copy from the Edit menu.

   or

   Press ⌘C.

   or

   Click the Copy button on the Standard toolbar.

   A marquee appears around the selected cells.

3. Activate the chart to which you want to add the data.

4. Choose Paste from the Edit menu.

   or

   Press ⌘V.

   or

   Click the Paste button on the Standard toolbar.

   The chart changes to include the additional data (see **Figure 11b**).

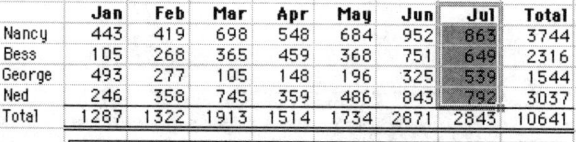

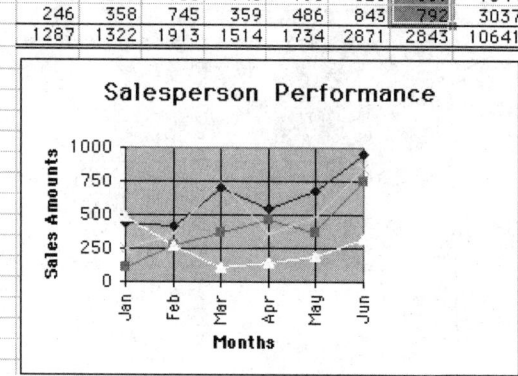

Figure 11a. *Select the range for the data you want to add to the chart and copy it to the Clipboard.*

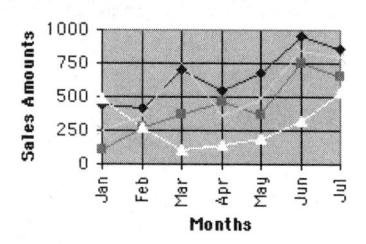

Figure 11b. *When you paste it into the chart, the chart changes to include it.*

✔ Tips

- In order for this to work properly, the data you add must be the same kind of data originally charted. For example, if you originally plotted totals to create a pie chart, you can't successfully add a series of numbers that aren't totals to the chart.

- For additional control over how data is pasted into a chart, choose Paste Special from the Edit menu in step 4 above. This dialog box will sometimes appear on its own when you paste a range.

Creating Charts

Figure 12a. *Position the mouse pointer on the border of the selection you want to drag.*

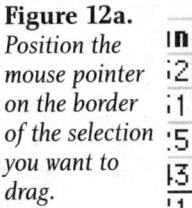

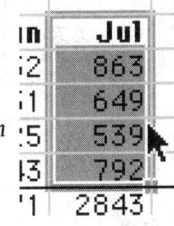

Figure 12b. *As you drag cells onto a chart, the mouse pointer changes and a striped border appears around the chart.*

To add chart data with drag and drop

1. In the worksheet, select the data you want to add to the chart (see **Figure 11a**). Be sure to include column or row headings if they should be included as labels.
2. Position the mouse pointer on the border of the selection. The mouse pointer turns into an arrow (see **Figure 12a**).
3. Press the mouse button down and drag the selection on top of the chart. The mouse pointer gets a little plus sign next to it and the chart border changes (see **Figure 12b**).
4. Release the mouse button.

   The chart changes to include the additional data (see **Figure 11b**).

✔ Tips

- This technique only works on charts that are embedded in the worksheet containing the original data since you can't drag and drop onto another worksheet. To add data from one worksheet to a chart on another, use the ChartWizard or Copy and Paste commands as discussed on the previous two pages.

- To add data contained in noncontiguous ranges, use the New Data command on the Edit menu, use copy and paste as discussed on the previous page, or use the ChartWizard to reselect the data range(s) from scratch.

- In order for this technique to work properly, the data you add must be the same kind of data originally charted. For example, if you originally plotted totals to create a pie chart, you can't successfully add a series of numbers that aren't totals to the chart.

Chapter 8

To remove a data series

1. Select the series you want to remove (see **Figure 13a**).
2. Choose Series from the Clear submenu under the Edit menu (see **Figure 13b**).

   or

   Press ⌘B.

   or

   Press the Del key on an extended keyboard.

   The series disappears (see **Figure 13c**). If the chart included a legend, it is revised to exclude the deleted data.

✔ Tips

- Removing a series from a chart does not remove it from the source worksheet. It simply tells Excel that you no longer want it included in the chart.
- You can also remove a data series by using the ChartWizard to redefine the ranges you want to chart. I tell you how earlier in this chapter.

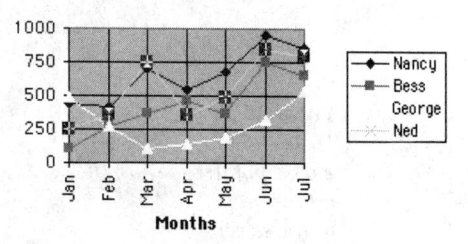

Figure 13a. *Select the series you want to remove…*

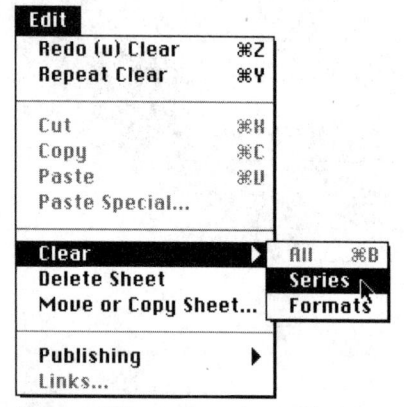

Figure 13b. *…then choose Series from the Clear menu under the Edit menu.*

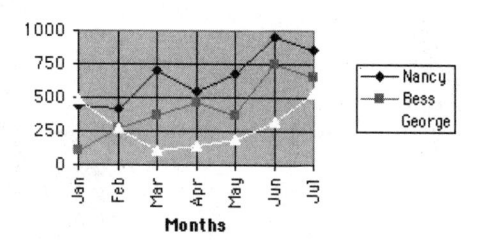

Figure 13c. *The series is removed and the legend (if any) is updated.*

EDITING AND FORMATTING CHARTS

9

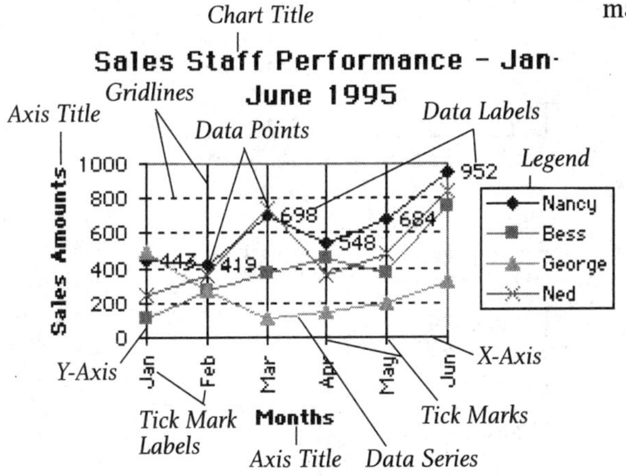
Chart Title
Sales Staff Performance - Jan-June 1995
Gridlines
Axis Title
Data Points
Data Labels
Legend
Sales Amounts
1000
800
600
400
200
0
952
698
684
548
443
419
Nancy
Bess
George
Ned
X-Axis
Y-Axis
Jan
Feb
Mar
Apr
May
Jun
Tick Mark Labels
Months
Tick Marks
Axis Title
Data Series

Figure 1. *The anatomy of a chart.*

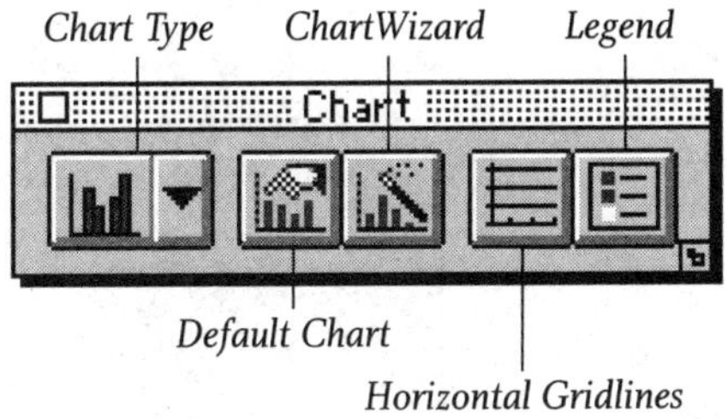
Chart Type
ChartWizard
Legend
Chart
Default Chart
Horizontal Gridlines

Figure 2. *The Chart toolbar.*

About Editing and Formatting Charts

Once you've created a chart, you can make a wide variety of changes to it.

- Add, remove, or change the text and formatting of titles and legends.
- Change the color, pattern, and background color of any chart item.
- Change the appearance, tick marks, and scale of axes.
- Move chart items almost anywhere within the chart area.
- Rotate 3-D charts to make charted data easier to view.

Figure 1 identifies most of the chart elements you'll work with.

About the Chart Toolbar

The Chart toolbar (see **Figure 2**) appears automatically whenever a chart is selected. It includes tools you can use to change the appearance of a chart. I tell you about Chart tools throughout this chapter.

✔ Tips

- The Chart toolbar only appears when a chart is selected. As soon as you click on a worksheet cell or switch to a sheet that does not contain a selected chart, the Chart toolbar disappears.
- You can move the Chart toolbar anywhere in the window by dragging its title bar. I tell you more about working with toolbars in Chapter 14.

About Activating Charts and Selecting Chart Items

To edit or format a chart, you *must* begin by activating it. Once a chart is activated, the chart commands and options are available (see **Figures 3a**, **3b**, **4a**, and **4b**). You can then select and modify various chart items or the entire chart.

To activate a chart

If the chart is embedded in a worksheet, double-click it. A thick, striped border appears around it (see **Figure 5**).

or

If the chart is on a chart sheet, activate it by clicking its sheet tab to display it.

To deactivate a chart

If the chart is embedded in a worksheet, click a worksheet cell. This deactivates the chart. Double-clicking a worksheet cell or pressing Esc several times also deselects the chart.

or

If the chart is on a chart sheet, click a different sheet tab.

To select a chart item

Once a chart has been activated, click on any chart item to select it. The name of the item appears in the far left side of the formula bar.

✔ Tip

- You can often select separate items within groups. For example, if you click a data series, you select the whole series. If you then click one point in the series, you select just that point.

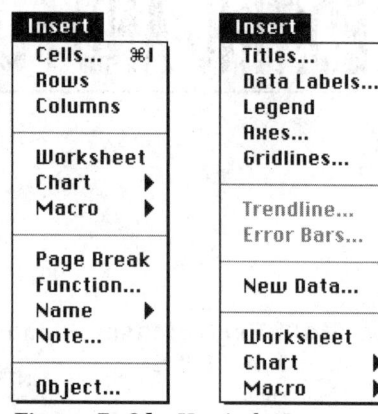

Figure 3a&b. *Here's the Insert menu with a worksheet active (left) and with a chart active (right).*

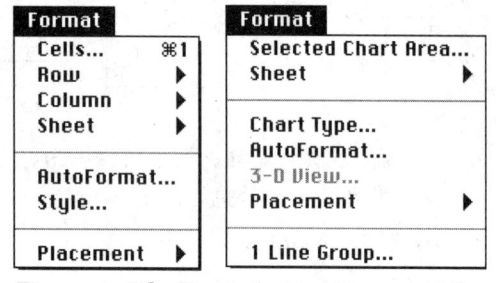

Figure 4a&b. *Here's the Format menu with a worksheet active (left) and with a chart active (right).*

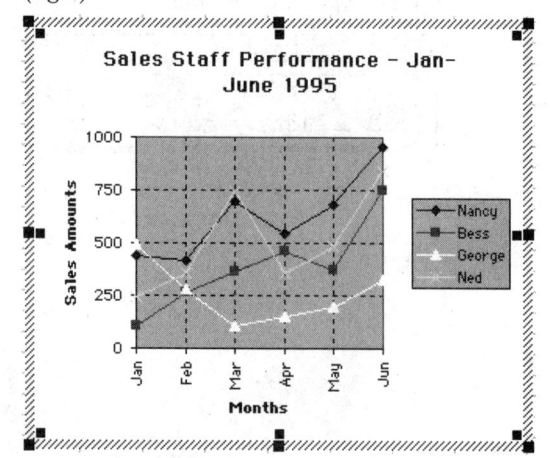

Figure 5. *An embedded chart gets a thick, striped border around it when activated.*

Editing & Formatting Charts

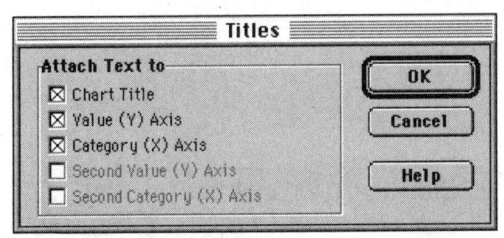

Figure 6. *Use the Titles dialog box to add a chart title or axis titles.*

Figure 7a. *Click the title to select it…*

Figure 7b. *…then use standard editing techniques to change the text and click anywhere to accept it.*

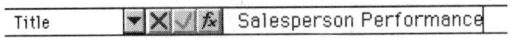

Figure 7c. *…or enter new text in the formula bar and press Return or Enter to accept it.*

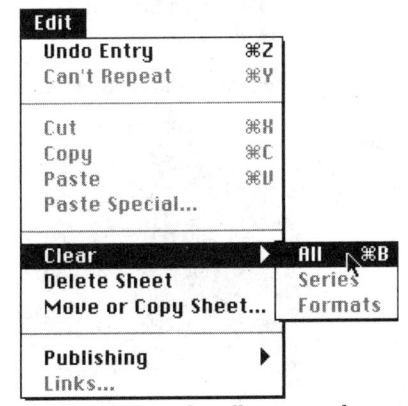

Figure 8. *Use the All command under the Clear submenu to delete selected chart items like titles.*

To add titles

1. Choose Titles from the Insert menu (see **Figure 3b**).
2. In the Titles dialog box (see **Figure 6**), turn on the check boxes for the kinds of titles you want. The available options vary depending on the type and format of the chart.
3. Click OK or press Return or Enter.

To edit titles

1. If necessary, click on the title you want to edit to select it. A box with selection handles appears around it (see **Figure 7a**).
2. Click inside the box to position an insertion point or drag over the contents of the box to select all or part of its contents. The box disappears. Make changes using standard editing techniques (see **Figure 7b**). When you're finished, click elsewhere on the chart to accept the changes.

    or

    Enter new text. It appears in the formula bar (see **Figure 7c**) and overwrites the existing title. Press Return or Enter or click the Enter button on the formula bar to accept the changes.

To remove titles

1. Choose Titles from the Insert menu (see **Figure 3b**).
2. In the Titles dialog box (see **Figure 6**), turn off the check boxes for the title(s) you want to remove.
3. Click OK or press Return or Enter.

    or

1. Select the title you want to remove.
2. Choose All from the Clear submenu under the Edit menu (see **Figure 8**) or press ⌘B.

Adding, Editing, & Removing Titles

137

Chapter 9

Adding Data Labels

About Data Labels

A data label is text or a number that labels a data series. The options are:

- Value displays the number represented in the chart.
- Percent displays the percentage represented in the chart.
- Label displays the name of the item represented in the chart.
- Label and Percent displays both the percentage and label for the item represented in the chart.

✔ Tip

- The available options depend on the type and format of the chart. Percent, for example, is not available with line or bar charts.

To add data labels

1. Choose Data Labels from the Insert menu (see **Figure 3b**).
2. In the Data Labels dialog box (see **Figure 9a**), select the radio button for the kind(s) of data labels you want.
3. Click OK or press Return or Enter.

   The data labels are applied (see **Figure 9b**).

✔ Tips

- To add data labels to only one data series (see **Figure 9c**), select that data series first. Otherwise, the labels will be applied to all data series in the chart (see **Figure 9b**).
- To display the legend color for the series beside its label, turn on the Show Legend Key next to Label check box in step 2 above.
- To turn off the data labels, select None in the Data Labels dialog box.

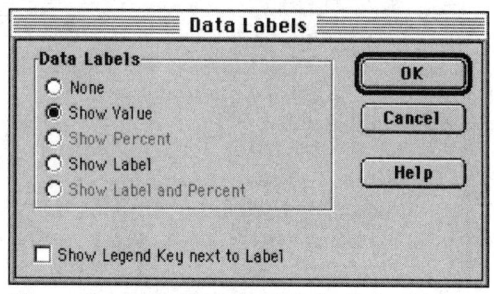

Figure 9a. *Use the Data Labels dialog box to choose a type of data label.*

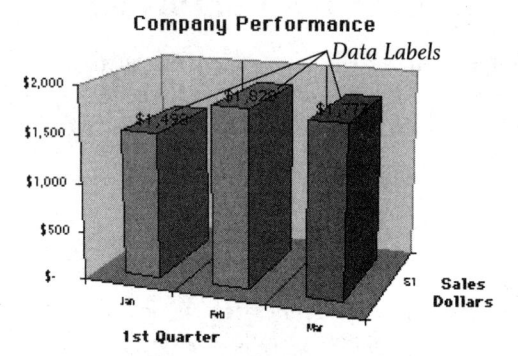

Figure 9b. *This chart has value data labels on all data series...*

Figure 9c. *...while this chart has value data labels on only one data series.*

138

Editing & Formatting Charts

Figure 10. Add or remove a legend with the Legend command or button.

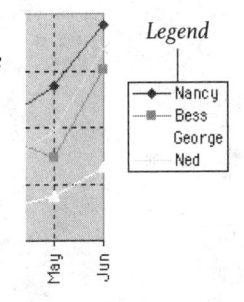

Figure 11a. A 3-D chart has 3 axes; in this illustration, all are displayed.

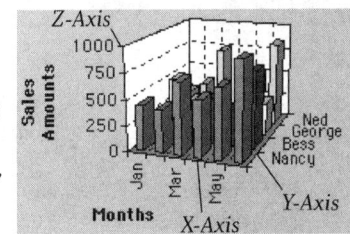

Figure 11b. A 2-D chart has 2 axes; in this illustration, only the Y-axis is displayed.

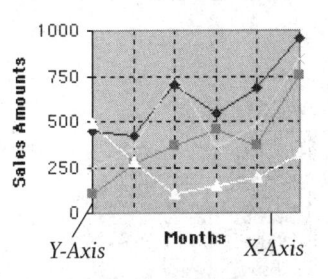

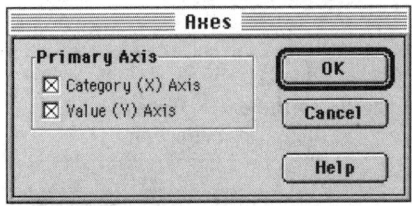

Figures 12a&b. The Axes dialog box displays different options for 2-D (above) and 3-D (below) charts.

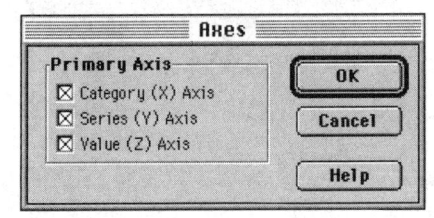

To add a legend

Choose Legend from the Insert menu (see **Figure 3b**).

or

Click the Legend button on the Chart toolbar.

The legend appears (see **Figure 10**).

To remove a legend

Click the Legend button on the Chart toolbar.

or

Click the legend once to select it and choose All from the Clear submenu under the Edit menu (see **Figure 8**) or press ⌘B.

✔ Tip

■ The Legend button on the chart toolbar looks dark gray when turned on.

About Axes

Most kinds of charts use two or three axes to plot the values. Excel lets you decide which axes should display on your chart. **Figures 11a** and **11b** show two examples.

✔ Tip

■ Axes options depend on the type and format of the chart. Pie charts, for example, do not have axes.

To add or remove axes

1. Choose Axes from the Insert menu (see **Figure 3b**).

2. In the Axes dialog box (see **Figures 12a** and **12b**), turn on the check box for the axis you want to display and turn off the check box for the axis you don't want to display.

3. Click OK or press Return or Enter.

Adding & Removing Legends & Axes

139

Chapter 9

About Gridlines

Gridlines are solid, dashed, or dotted lines on the plot area of a chart. They help chart viewers follow the lines for values and labels. **Figures 13a**, **13b**, and **13c** show examples of a chart with various gridline options turned on or off.

✔ Tip

- Gridlines options depend on the type and format of the chart. Pie charts, for example, do not have gridlines.

To add or remove gridlines

1. Choose Gridlines from the Insert menu (see **Figure 3b**).
2. In the Gridlines dialog box (see **Figures 14a** and **14b**), turn on the check boxes for the kinds of gridlines you want to display and turn off the check boxes for the kinds of gridlines you don't want to display.
3. Click OK or press Return or Enter.

or

To turn only major horizontal gridlines on or off, click the Horizontal Gridlines button on the Chart toolbar.

✔ Tips

- If you want to use both major and minor gridlines, format the lines differently. I tell you how to format gridlines later in this chapter.
- The Horizontal Gridlines button on the Chart toolbar looks dark gray when turned on.

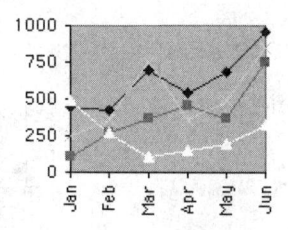

Figure 13a. *A chart with gridlines turned off.*

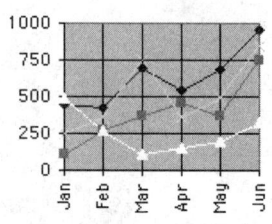

Figure 13b. *A chart with only major gridlines (on both axes) turned on.*

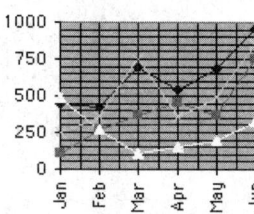

Figure 13c. *A chart with both major and minor gridlines (on both axes) turned on.*

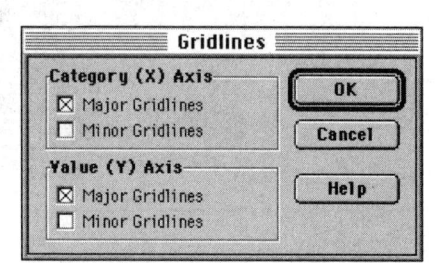

Figures 14a&b. *The Gridlines dialog box offers different options for 2-D (above) and 3-D (below) charts.*

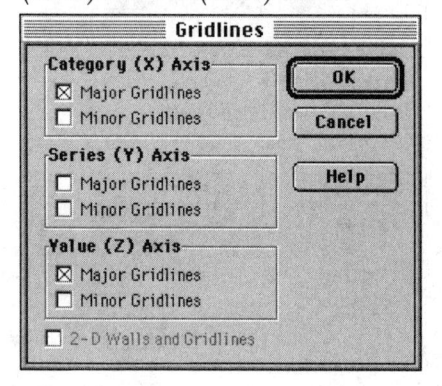

Adding & Removing Gridlines

140

Editing & Formatting Charts

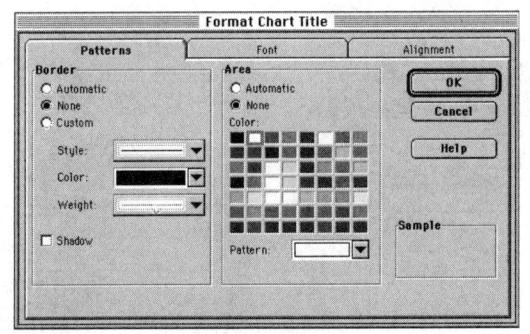

Figure 15. *The Format Chart Title and Format Axis Title dialog boxes let you format title text and the area around it.*

Figure 16a. *Select the title you want to format...*

Figures 16b&c. *...then choose Selected Chart Title or Selected Axis Title from the Format menu. (The command name changes depending on what's selected.)*

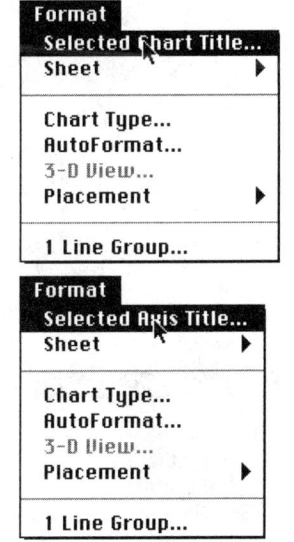

About Formatting Titles

The Format Chart Title dialog box (see **Figure 15**) lets you format chart titles in the following ways:

- Use the Patterns tab to add, remove, or format borders around titles and the area containing the title text.
- Use the Font tab to change the font, size, style, and color of title text.
- Use the Alignment tab to change the alignment and orientation of title text.

As you may have guessed, these tabs are almost identical to the ones I tell you about in Chapter 6, so if you need help using them, check the information I provide there.

To format titles

1. Select the title you want to format (see **Figure 16a**) and choose Selected Chart Title or Selected Axis Title from the Format menu (see **Figures 16b** and **16c**).

   or

   Double-click the border of the title you want to format.

2. In the Format Chart Title (see **Figure 15**) or Format Axis Title dialog box that appears, choose the tab corresponding to the type of formatting you want to do.

3. When you're finished making changes in the dialog box, click OK or press Return or Enter to accept them.

✔ Tip

- You can also use buttons on the Formatting toolbar to format selected titles. I tell you how to use them in Chapter 6, too.

Chapter 9

About Formatting Data Labels

The Format Data Labels dialog box (see **Figure 17**) lets you format data labels in the following ways:

- Use the Patterns tab to add, remove, or format borders around data labels and the area around data label text.
- Use the Font tab to change the font, size, style, and color of data label text.
- Use the Number tab to change the number formatting of data label values.
- Use the Alignment tab to change the alignment and orientation of data label text.

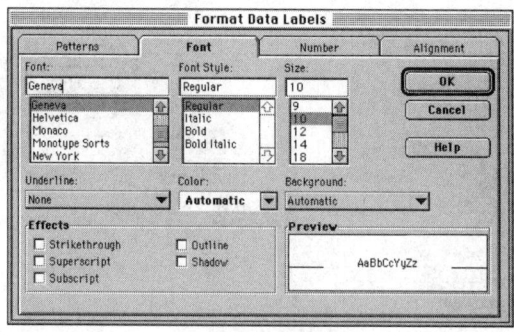

Figure 17. *The Format Data Labels dialog box lets you format data labels and the area around them.*

These tabs are almost identical to the ones I tell you about in Chapter 6, so if you need help using them, check the information I provide there.

To format data labels

1. Select the data label(s) you want to format (see **Figure 18a** and **18b**) and choose Selected Data Labels (see **Figure 18c**) from the Format menu.

   or

   Double-click one data label in the series you want to format.

2. In the Format Data Labels dialog box (see **Figure 17**), choose the tab corresponding to the type of formatting you want to do.

3. When you're finished making changes in the dialog box, click OK or press Return or Enter to accept them.

✔ Tip

- You can also use buttons on the Formatting toolbar to format selected data labels. I tell you how to use them in Chapter 6, too.

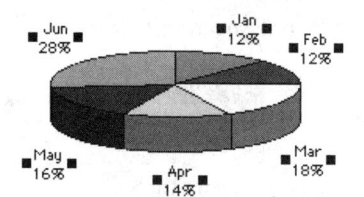

Figure 18a. *Select the data labels you want to format...*

Figure 18b. *...or one of the data labels in a data series...*

Figure 18c. *...and choose Selected Data Labels from the Format menu.*

142

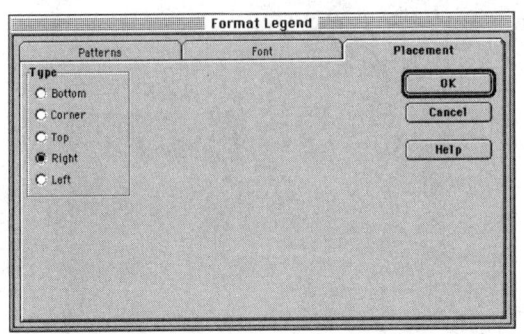

Editing & Formatting Charts

Figure 19. *The Format Legend dialog box lets you format the borders, fill, font, and placement of a legend.*

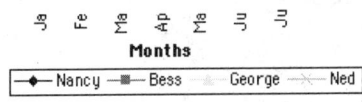

Figure 20. *The Bottom option on the Placement tab of the Format Legend dialog box changes the position and shape of the legend.*

Figure 21a. *Select the legend...*

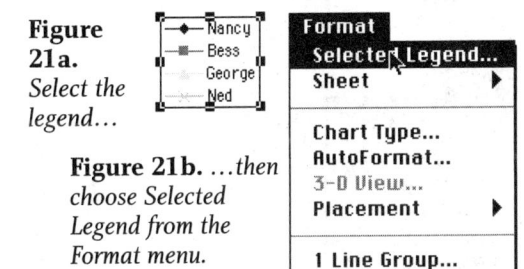

Figure 21b. *...then choose Selected Legend from the Format menu.*

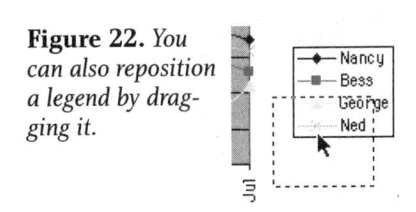

Figure 22. *You can also reposition a legend by dragging it.*

About Formatting Legends

The Format Legend dialog box (see **Figure 19**) lets you format legends in the following ways:

- Use the Patterns tab to add, remove, or format borders around a legend and the area around legend text.
- Use the Font tab to change the font, size, style, and color of legend text.
- Use the Placement tab to change the positioning of a legend.

The Patterns and Font tabs are almost identical to the ones I tell you about in Chapter 6, so if you need help using them, check the information I provide there.

The Placement tab (see **Figure 19**), offers five options for positioning the legend in relation to the chart area. Select the radio button for the option you want. **Figure 20** shows an example of a legend's position with the Bottom radio button selected.

To format a legend

1. Select the legend (see **Figure 21a**) and choose Selected Legend (see **Figure 21b**) from the Format menu.

   or

   Double-click the legend.

2. In the Format Legend dialog box (see **Figure 19**), choose the tab corresponding to the type of formatting you want to do.

3. When you're finished making changes in the dialog box, click OK or press Return or Enter to accept them.

✔ Tips

- You can also use buttons on the Formatting toolbar to format the borders, fill, and text of a legend. I tell you how to use them in Chapter 6.

- You can also change the placement of a legend by dragging it into a new position (see **Figure 22**). This is not the same as using options in the Placement tab.

143

Chapter 9

About Formatting Axes

The Format Axis dialog box (see **Figures 24**, **28a**, and **28b**) lets you format axes in the following ways:

- Use the Patterns tab to change the appearance of the axis and its tick marks and tick mark labels.
- Use the Scale tab to change the scale or units for the axis.
- Use the Font tab to change the font, size, style, and color of axis tick mark text.
- Use the Number tab to change the number formatting of axis tick mark value text.
- Use the Alignment tab to change the alignment of axis tick mark text.

The Font, Number, and Alignment tabs are almost identical to the ones I tell you about in Chapter 6, so if you need help using them, check the information I provide there. I tell you about the Patterns and Scale tabs on the next two pages.

Figure 23a. *Select the axis you want to format…*

To format an axis

1. Select the axis you want to format (see **Figure 23a**) and choose Selected Axis (see **Figure 23b**) from the Format menu.

   or

   Double-click the axis.

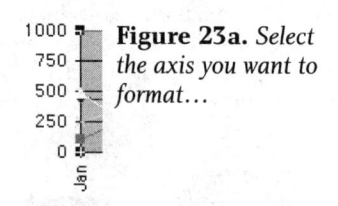

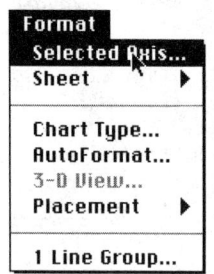

Figure 23b. *…then choose Selected Axis from the Format menu.*

2. In the Format Axis dialog box (see **Figures 24**, **28a**, and **28b**), choose the tab corresponding to the type of formatting you want to do.

3. When you're finished making changes in the dialog box, click OK or press Return or Enter to accept them.

✔ Tip

- You can also use buttons on the Formatting toolbar to format the text of axis tick marks. I tell you how to use them in Chapter 6.

144

Editing & Formatting Charts

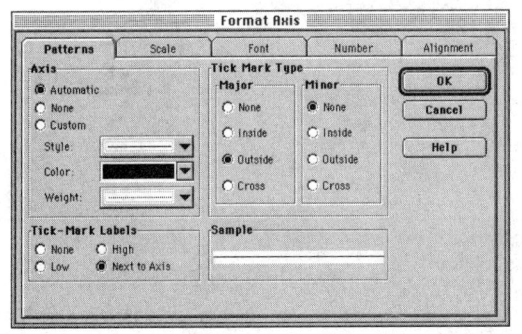

Figure 24. *The Patterns tab of the Format Axis dialog box is just one of five formatting tabs.*

Figure 25a&b. *This example takes the standard settings and removes the axis line.*

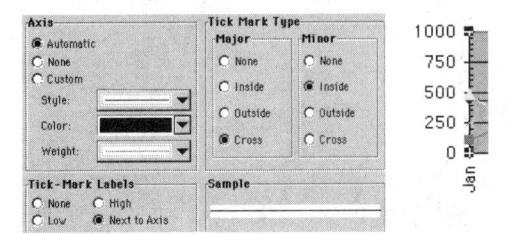

Figure 26a&b. *This example adds minor tick marks.*

Figure 27a&b. *This example, for minimalists, removes tick marks, tick mark labels, and the axis line.*

To change the appearance of an axis and its tick marks

1. Select the axis you want to format (see **Figure 23a**) and choose Selected Axis (see **Figure 23b**) from the Format menu.

   or

   Double-click the axis.

2. In the Format Axis dialog box, click the Patterns tab (see **Figure 24**).

3. To change the appearance of the axis line, choose options from the Style, Color, and Weight pop-up menus. These menus are identical to the ones in the Patterns tab of the Format Cells dialog box. I tell you about that in Chapter 6.

4. To change the positioning of the tick mark labels in relation to the tick marks, select one of the radio buttons in the Tick-Mark Labels area.

5. To change the positioning of the major and minor tick marks in relation to the axis, select radio buttons in the Major and Minor areas.

6. When you're finished making changes, click OK or press Return or Enter.

Figures 25a&b, **26a&b**, and **27a&b** show examples of some of the effects you can achieve with the Patterns tab of the Format Axis dialog box.

Changing Axis Lines & Tick Marks

145

Chapter 9

To change the axis scale

1. Select the axis whose scale you want to change (see **Figure 23a**) and choose Selected Axis (see **Figure 23b**) from the Format menu.

   or

   Double-click the axis.

2. In the Format Axis dialog box, click the Scale tab (see **Figures 28a** and **28b**).

3. Enter values in the edit boxes for the scale elements you want to change. These elements vary depending on whether the axis is a value axis (see **Figure 28a**) or a category axis (see **Figure 28b**). To have Excel automatically assign values for any of these elements, turn on the Auto check box before the element.

4. If desired, turn on check boxes for additional scale-related options at the bottom of the dialog box. These options will affect the tick marks and axis position.

5. When you're finished making changes, click OK or press Return or Enter.

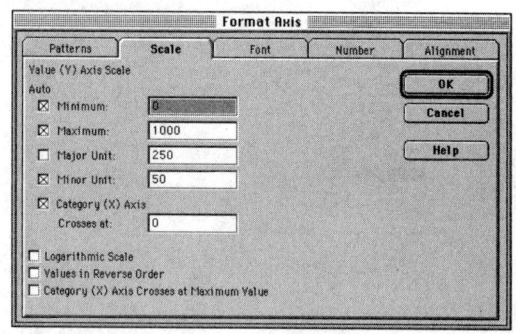

Figure 28a. *The Scale tab offers value-related options for value axes...*

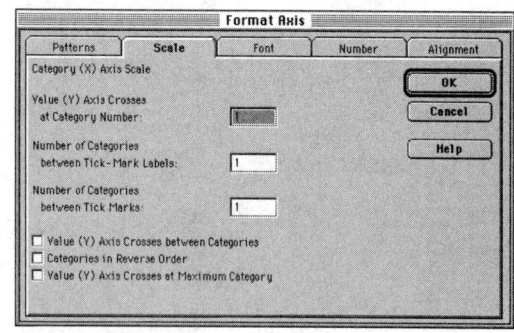

Figure 28b. *...and category-related options for category axes.*

✔ Tips

- To make results look more dramatic, set the minimum and maximum values the same as the minimum and maximum values of the data. **Figures 29a** and **29b** show an example.

- You can make results look even more dramatic by stretching the chart so it's long and narrow. **Figure 29c** shows an example.

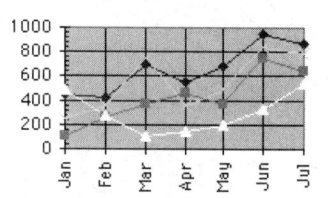

Figure 29a. *Here's a chart with automatic scale options set.*

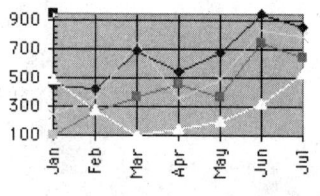

Figure 29b. *Changing the scale makes the lines a little steeper.*

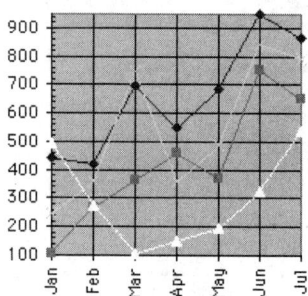

Figure 29c. *Stretching the chart makes the lines even steeper!*

Changing Axis Scale

Editing & Formatting Charts

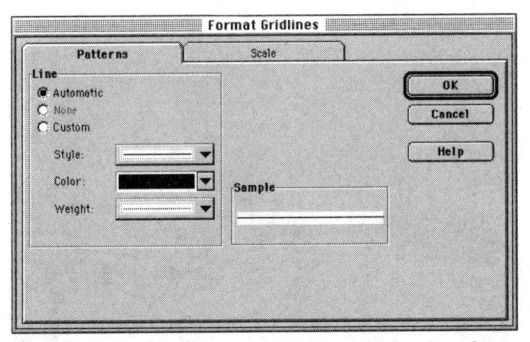

Figure 30. *The Format Gridlines dialog box lets you change the look and the scale of gridlines.*

Figure 31a. *Select a horizontal or vertical gridline...*

Figure 31b. *...then choose Selected Gridlines from the Format menu.*

About Formatting Gridlines

The Format Gridlines dialog box (see **Figure 30**) lets you format gridlines in the following ways:

- Use the Patterns tab to change the appearance of the gridlines.
- Use the Scale tab to change the scale or units for the gridlines.

The Patterns tab (see **Figure 30**) is an abbreviated version of the Patterns tab in the Format Axis dialog box. The Line options are the same as the Axis options. I tell you about them earlier in this chapter. The Scale tab is identical to the Scale tab for the Format Axis dialog box. I tell you about that on the previous page.

To format gridlines

1. Select one of the major or minor horizontal or vertical gridlines you want to format (see **Figure 31a**) and choose Selected Gridlines (see **Figure 31b**) from the Format menu.

   or

   Double-click the gridline.

2. In the Format Gridlines dialog box (see **Figure 30**), choose the tab corresponding to the type of formatting you want to do.

3. When you're finished making changes in the dialog box, click OK or press Return or Enter to accept them.

✔ Tip

- While gridlines can make it easier to read a chart, they can also obscure it. Formatting gridlines as dotted, dashed, or lightly colored lines can prevent them from cluttering the chart with lines and overpowering other chart elements.

147

Chapter 9

About Formatting the Chart Area

The *chart area* is the area around the chart. The Format Chart Area dialog box (see **Figure 32**) lets you format the chart area in the following ways:

- Use the Patterns tab to change the appearance of the border and fill for the chart area.
- Use the Font tab to change the font, size, and style for chart text.

These two tabs are almost identical to the ones I tell you about in Chapter 6, so if you need additional help using them, check the information I provide there.

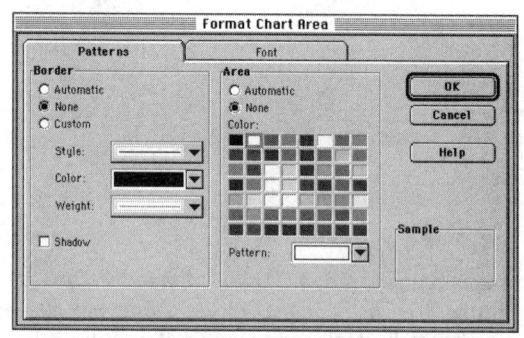

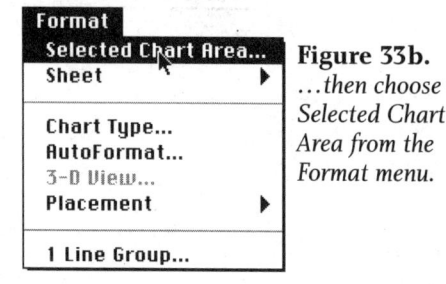

Figure 32. *Use the Format Chart Area dialog box to change the border, fill, and font formatting of the area around a chart.*

To format the chart area

1. Select the chart area (see **Figure 33a**) and choose Selected Chart Area (see **Figure 33b**) from the Format menu.

   or

   Double-click the chart area.

2. In the Format Chart Area dialog box (see **Figure 32**), choose the tab corresponding to the type of formatting you want to do.

3. When you're finished making changes in the dialog box, click OK or press Return or Enter to accept them.

✔ Tips

- If you decide to use a fill color or pattern in the chart area, choose a color or pattern that contrasts with the chart elements that will appear against it.
- To add floating text to the chart area, activate the chart, make sure the formula area of the formula bar is empty, and type in the text you want. You can then drag the text anywhere within the chart area.

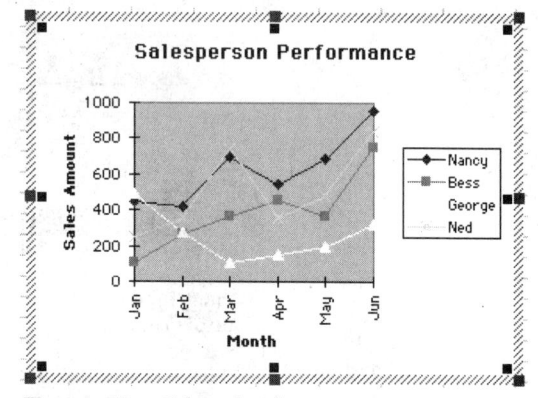

Figure 33a. *Select the chart area...*

Figure 33b. *...then choose Selected Chart Area from the Format menu.*

Editing & Formatting Charts

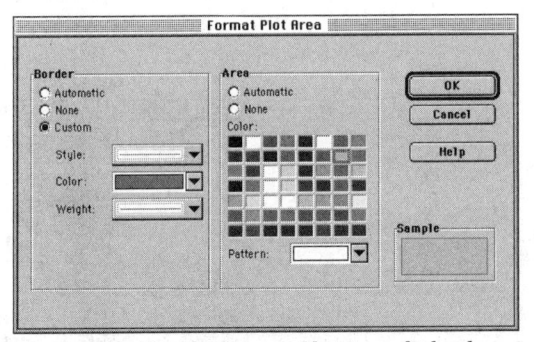

Figure 34. *Use the Format Plot Area dialog box to change the border, color, and pattern of the area between chart axes. For 3-D charts, use the Format Chart Walls dialog box, which is identical (except for title bar name) to this one.*

Figure 35a&b. *Select the plot area on a 2-D chart (top) or select the chart walls on a 3-D chart (bottom)…*

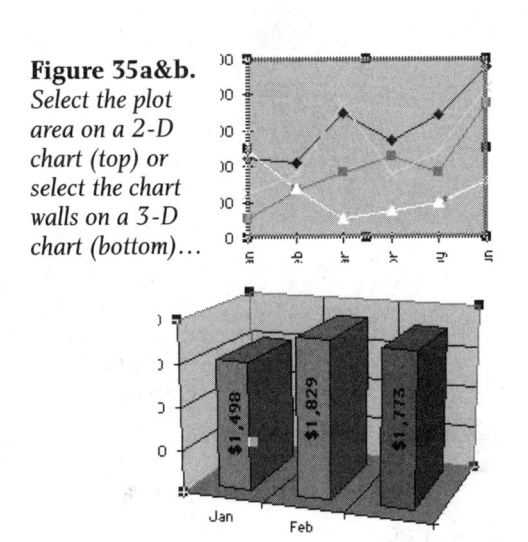

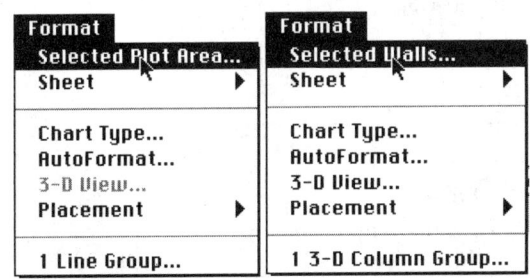

Figure 35c&d. *…then choose Selected Plot Area or Selected Walls from the Format menu.*

About Formatting the Plot Area and Chart Walls

The *plot area* is the area within the axes of the chart. In a 3-D chart, this area is referred to as the *chart walls*.

The Format Plot Area (see **Figure 34**) and Format Chart Walls dialog boxes let you change the border, fill, and pattern for the plot area and chart walls. These two dialog boxes are identical and offer the same options you'll find in the Patterns tab of dialog boxes I tell you about earlier in this chapter and in Chapter 6. If you need additional help using them, check the information I provide there.

To format the plot area or chart walls

1. Select the plot area (see **Figure 35a**) or chart walls (see **Figure 35b**) and choose Selected Plot Area (see **Figure 35c**) or Selected Walls (see **Figure 35d**) from the Format menu.

   or

   Double-click the plot area or a chart wall.

2. In the Format Plot Area (see **Figure 34**) or Format Chart Walls dialog box, make changes in the Borders and Area sections.

3. Click OK or press Return or Enter to accept your changes.

✔ Tip

- If you decide to use a fill color or pattern in the plot area or chart walls, choose a color or pattern that contrasts with the chart elements that will appear against it.

Formatting the Plot Area & Chart Walls

149

Chapter 9

About Formatting a Data Series or Data Point

A *data series* is a group of numbers plotted on a chart. A *data point* is one number plotted on a chart. Some charts, like pie charts, have only one data series. Other charts, like line and column charts, can have multiple data series. Most charts have multiple data points.

The Format Data Series (see **Figure 36**) and Format Data Point (see **Figure 39**) dialog boxes let you change a wide variety of options for a data series or data point. The options offered vary depending on the type and format of the chart. Some of these options are for advanced chartmakers and beyond the scope of this book. Others can be accomplished with other methods discussed elsewhere in this book.

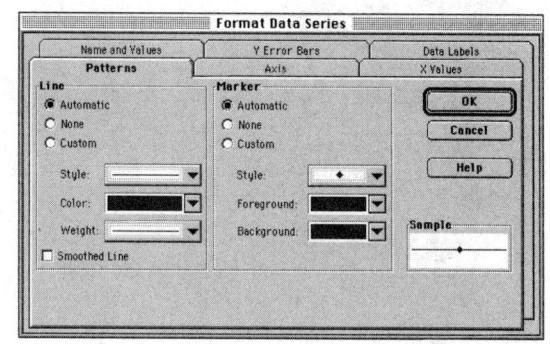

Figure 36. *Use the Format Data Series dialog box to make a wide variety of changes to a data series.*

To change the appearance of lines and markers

1. Select the data series for the line you want to format (see **Figure 37a**) and choose Selected Data Series (see **Figure 37b**) from the Format menu.

   or

   Double-click the data series you want to format.

2. In the Format Data Series dialog box (see **Figure 36**), click the Patterns tab to display its options.

3. Make selections in the Line area to change the Style (shape), Color, and Weight of the line.

4. Make selections in the Marker area to change the Style, Foreground Color, and Background Color of the marker.

5. Click OK or press Return or Enter to accept your changes.

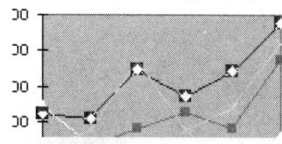

Figure 37a. *Select the data series for the line you want to change…*

Figure 37b. *…then choose Selected Data Series from the Format menu.*

✔ Tip

- If you change the color of a line, choose a color that will stand out against the color of the plot area.

150

Editing & Formatting Charts

Figure 38a. *Select the data point for the bar, column, or pie slice you want to change...*

Figure 38b. *...then choose Selected Data Point from the Format Menu.*

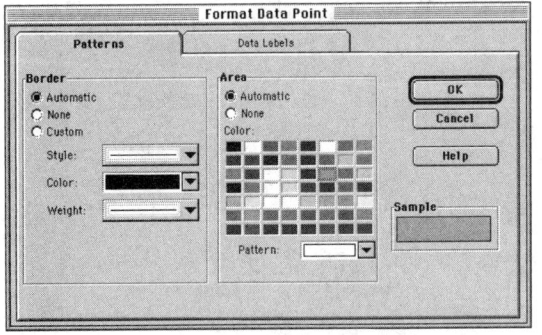

Figure 39. *The Patterns tab of the Format Data Point dialog box lets you change the appearance of a single data point.*

Figure 40a. *Drag a pie piece away from a pie chart...*

Figure 40b. *...for an "exploded" pie chart effect.*

To change the appearance of bars, columns, or pie slices

1. Select the data point for the bar, column, or pie slice you want to format (see **Figure 38a**) and choose Selected Data Point (see **Figure 38b**) from the Format menu.

   or

   Select and then double-click the data point you want to format.

2. In the Format Data Point dialog box (see **Figure 39**), click the Patterns tab to display its options.

3. Make selections in the Border section to change the style, color, and weight of the border.

4. Make selections in the Area section to change the color, pattern, and background color of the bar, column, or pie slice.

5. Click OK or press Return or Enter to accept your changes.

✔ Tip

■ If you change the color of a bar, column, or pie slice, choose a color that will stand out against the color of the plot area or chart walls.

To "explode" a pie chart

1. Select the data point for the pie piece you want to move.

2. Drag the pie piece away from the pie (see **Figure 40a**).

When you release the mouse button, the piece moves away from the pie and the pie gets smaller (see **Figure 40b**).

✔ Tip

■ The farther away you move the pie piece, the smaller the pie gets.

Formatting Bars, Columns, & Pie Slices

Chapter 9

To rotate a 3-D chart

1. Activate the chart you want to rotate (see **Figure 41a**).
2. Choose 3-D View from the Format menu (see **Figure 41b**).
3. In the Format 3-D View dialog box (see **Figure 41c**), click the Elevation and Rotation buttons to change the perspective and rotate the chart.
4. When you're finished making changes, click OK or press Return or Enter to apply them (see **Figure 41d**) and close the dialog box.

Figure 41a. *Start by selecting a 3-D chart...*

Figure 41b. *...choose 3-D View from the Format menu...*

✔ Tips

- You can click the Apply button in the Format 3-D View dialog box (see **Figure 41c**) to get a firsthand look at the modified chart without closing the dialog box. You may have to drag the Format 3-D View dialog box out of the way to see your chart.

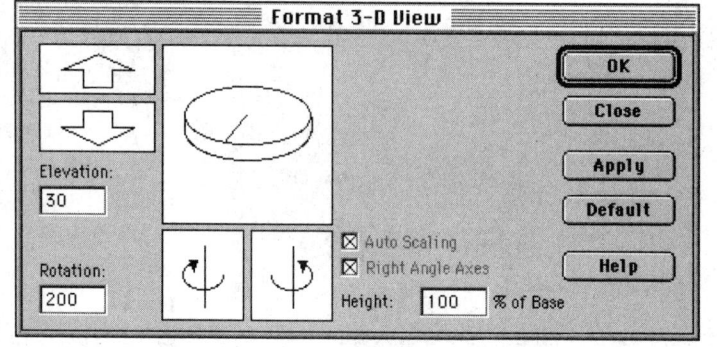

Figure 41c. *...make changes like these in the Format 3-D View dialog box.*

- Some changes in the Format 3-D View dialog box will change the size of the chart.

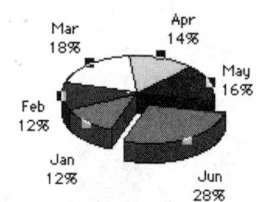

Figure 41d. *...and you'll end up with a modified 3-D chart like this.*

To move a chart item

1. With the chart activated, select the chart item you want to move.
2. Position the mouse pointer on the border of the item, press the mouse button down, and drag the item (see **Figure 42**) to a new position.

   When you release the mouse button, the item moves.

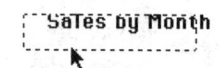

Figure 42. *To move a chart item, simply drag it to a new position.*

152

Editing & Formatting Charts

Figure 43a. *Choose Chart Type from the Format menu.*

To change the chart type

1. Activate the chart you want to change.
2. Choose Chart Type from the Format menu (see **Figure 43a**).
3. In the Chart Type Dialog box (see **Figure 43b**), select a Chart Dimension radio button for the kind of chart you want. Then select the icon representing the chart type and click OK or press Return or Enter.

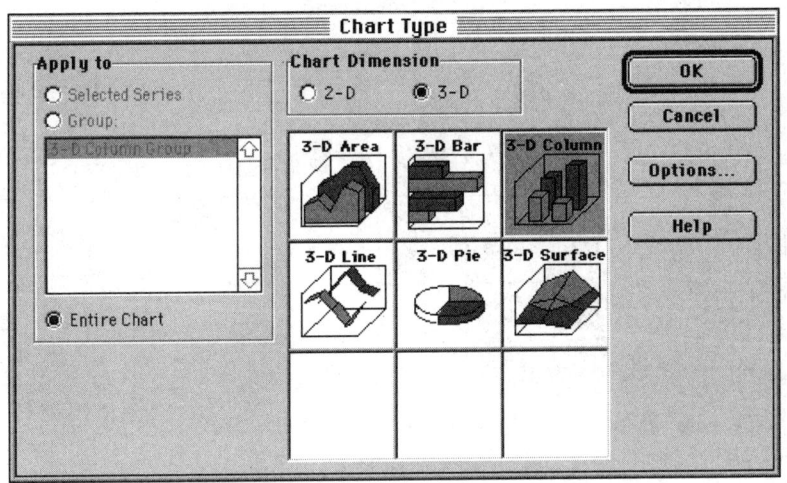

or

1. Activate the chart you want to change.
2. Click the arrow on the right side of the Chart Type button on the Chart toolbar to display a menu of chart types (see **Figure 44**) and choose the one you want.

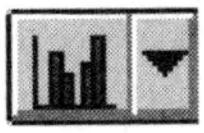

The chart changes immediately to an unformatted chart of the type you chose.

Figure 43b. *Use the Chart Type dialog box to choose the Chart Dimension and new chart type for the selected chart.*

Figure 44. *Or use the Chart Type pop-up menu on the Chart toolbar to select a new chart type.*

✔ Tips

- To change to the default chart type, click the Default Chart button on the Chart toolbar. 
- To apply the chart type illustrated on the Chart Type button on the Chart toolbar, click the button.

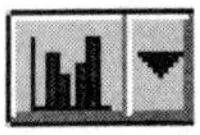

Changing the Chart Type

153

Chapter 9

To Use AutoFormat

1. Activate the chart you want to change.
2. Choose AutoFormat from the Format menu (see **Figure 45a**).
3. In the AutoFormat Dialog box (see **Figure 45b**), select a chart type from the Galleries scrolling list. Then choose a Format by clicking on a format illustration.
4. Click OK or press Return or Enter to apply the format.

Figure 45a. *Choose AutoFormat from the Format dialog box...*

✔ Tip

■ You can use the AutoFormat dialog box to create your own custom formats. Select the User-Defined radio button to display a list of your formats, then click the Customize button. Use the dialog box that appears to add the format of the active chart or delete formats you've already added.

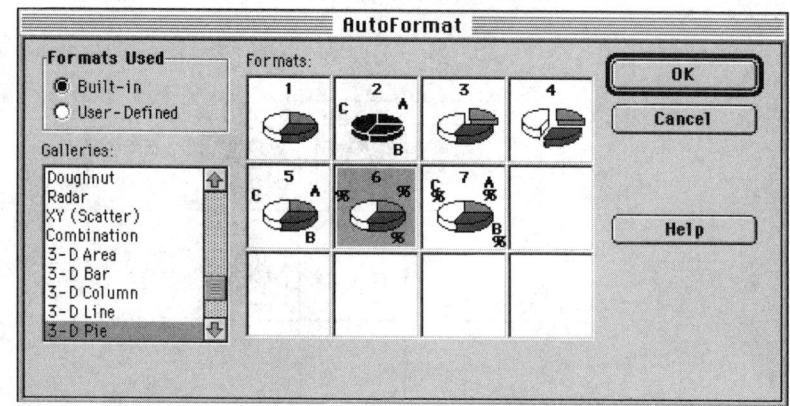

Figure 45b. *...then choose a chart type and format to apply.*

154

PRINTING 10

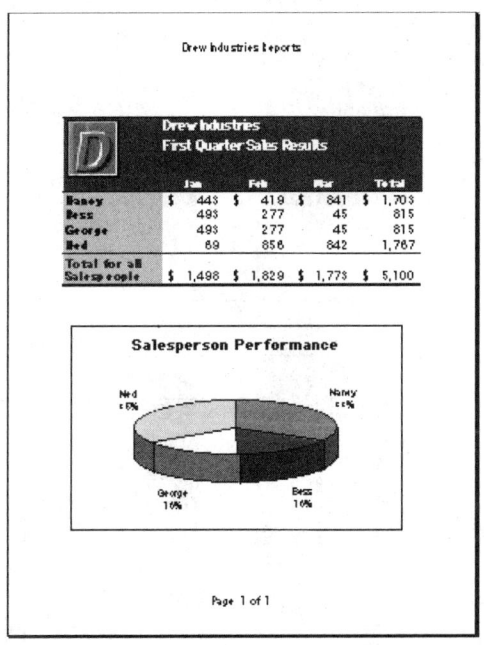

Figure 1. *Print Preview lets you see your reports before you commit them to paper.*

About Printing

In most cases, when you create a worksheet or chart, you'll want to print it. With Excel, you can print all or part of a sheet, multiple sheets, or an entire workbook—all at once. Excel gives you control over page size, margins, headers, footers, page breaks, orientation, scaling, page order, and content. Its Print Preview feature (see **Figure 1**) shows you what your report will look like when printed, so you can avoid wasteful, time consuming reprints.

Printing is basically a four-step process:

1. Choose a printer with Apple's Chooser desk accessory. If you have only one printer, this is something you do once and never worry about again.

2. Use the Page Setup dialog box to set up your report for printing. You can skip this step if you set the report up the last time you printed it and don't need to change the setup.

3. Use the Print Preview feature to take a look at your report before committing it to paper. You can skip this step if you already know what the report will look like.

4. Use the Print command to send the desired number of copies to the printer for printing.

About QuickDraw GX

QuickDraw GX is part of the System 7.5 operating system that changes the way some print-related dialog boxes look and work. If you're using QuickDraw GX on your Macintosh, be sure to check out the special instructions included just for you throughout this chapter.

Chapter 10

About Apple's Chooser

You use Apple's Chooser desk accessory to select a printer driver and a printer. Your selections tell your Macintosh how and where it should print all documents, no matter what application you use.

✔ Tip

- If you only have one printer and you've already printed documents from your Macintosh, you don't need to use the Chooser. Once selected, the printer choice remains set.

Figure 2a. *Choose Chooser from the Apple menu.*

To choose a printer

1. Choose Chooser from the Apple menu (see **Figure 2a**).
2. On the left side of the Chooser window (see **Figure 2b**), click the icon for the printer driver you want to use. If you're not sure which one to pick, check the manual that came with your printer.
3. In the list of printers that appears on the right side of the Chooser window, click the name of the printer to which you want to print.
4. If desired, change other settings.
5. Click the Chooser close box to close its window.
6. If a dialog box like the one in **Figure 2c** appears, click OK or press Return or Enter.

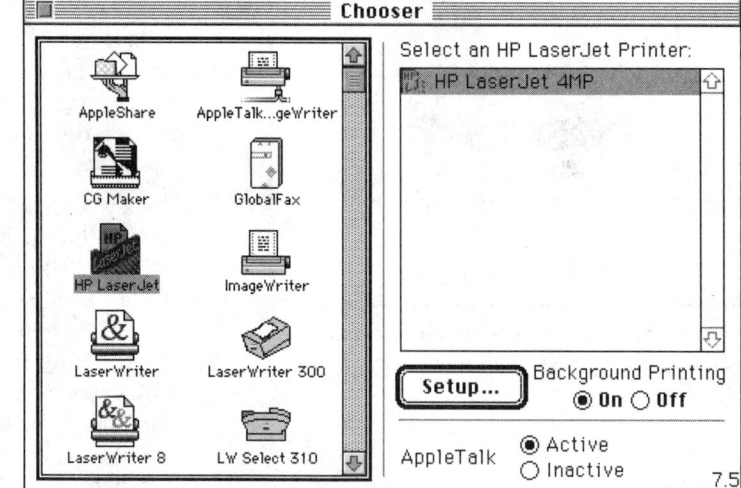

Figure 2b. *Select a printer driver icon and then choose your printer.*

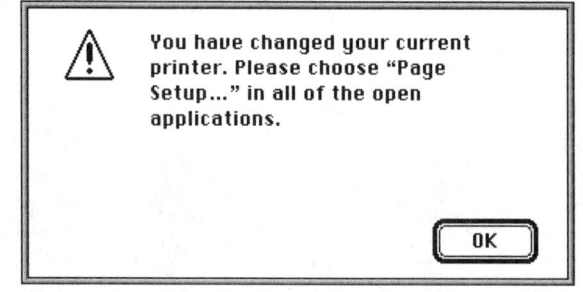

Figure 2c. *If you choose a different printer, your Mac reminds you to check the Page Setup options.*

Choosing a Printer

156

Printing

To choose a printer with QuickDraw GX

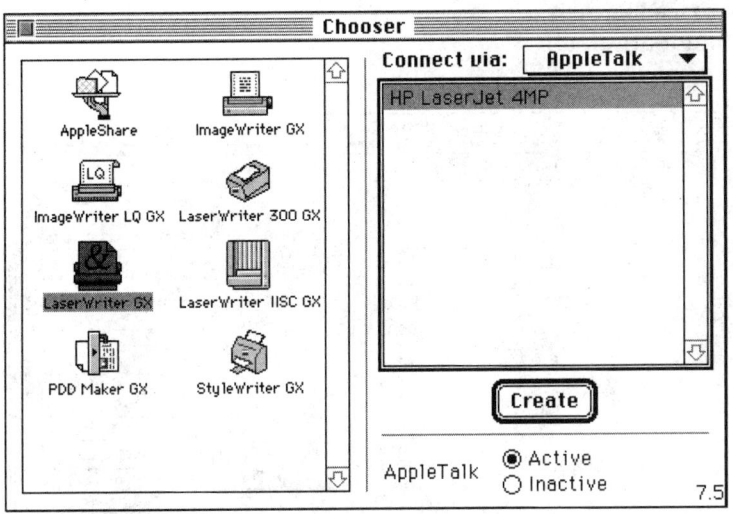

Figure 3a. *The Chooser looks a little different for QuickDraw GX users, but works in much the same way.*

Figure 3b. *If you haven't created a desktop printer, your Mac lets you create one on the spot. Check your* Apple Reference Guide *for information about this QuickDraw GX feature.*

1. Choose Chooser from the Apple menu (see **Figure 2a**).
2. On the left side of the Chooser window (see **Figure 3a**), click the icon for the printer driver you want to use. If you're not sure which one to pick, check the manual that came with your printer.
3. If necessary, choose the correct option from the Connect Via popup menu.
4. In the list of printers that appears on the right side of the Chooser window, click the name of the printer to which you want to print.
5. If desired, change other settings (if they're available).
6. Click the Chooser close box to close its window.
7. If a dialog box like the one in **Figure 3b** appears, click Cancel.

✔ Tip

- If your Macintosh is connected to a network, the Chooser window that appears will look different from the ones in **Figure 2b** and **3a**. After selecting a printer in step 2, you may have to select a zone from a scrolling list before you can choose a printer. If you're not sure which zone or printer to choose, talk to your network administrator.

157

Chapter 10

About the Page Setup dialog box

The Page Setup dialog box (see **Figure 4**) lets you set up a document for printing. Setup options are organized under the following tabs:

- Page (see **Figure 4**) lets you set the orientation, scaling, print quality, and first page number.
- Margins lets you set the page margins, the distance the header and footer should be from the edge of the paper, and the positioning of the document on the paper.

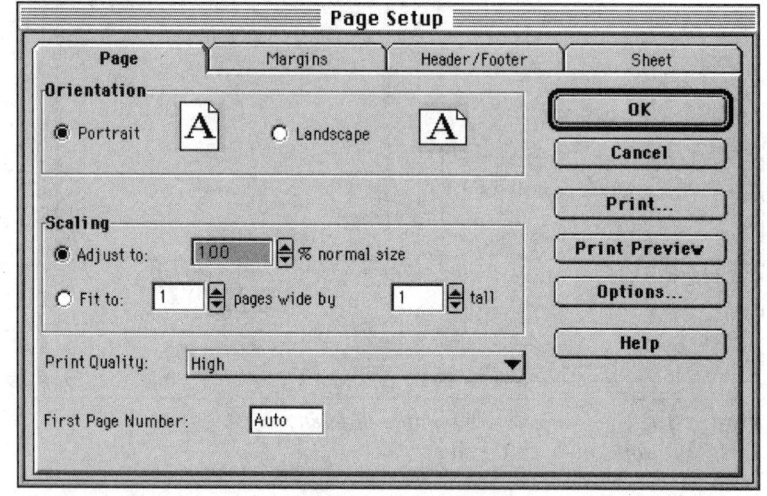

Figure 4. *The Page tab is only one of four tabs in the Page Setup dialog box, which you use to set up your sheets and charts for printing.*

- Header/Footer lets you select a standard header and footer or create custom ones.
- Sheet lets you specify the print area, print titles, items to print, and page order. If a chart sheet is active when you choose Page setup, you'll see a Chart tab (see **Figure 8**) rather than a Sheet tab. Use it to specify the printed chart size and print quality.

✔ Tip

- You may have noticed that this Page Setup dialog box looks very different from the Apple standard. If you want to see the standard Apple Page Setup dialog box (see **Figures 5a** and **5b**) for your printer, click the Options button in the Excel Page Setup dialog box.

158

To set the paper size

1. Choose Page Setup from the File menu (see **Figure 5**).
2. Click the Options button on any tab in the Page Setup dialog box (see **Figure 4**).
3. In the standard Page Setup dialog box that appears (see **Figures 6a** and **6b**), choose a paper size.
4. Click OK (or Format, if you're using QuickDraw GX) or press Return or Enter to dismiss the dialog box.
5. Click OK or press Return or Enter to dismiss Excel's Page Setup dialog box.

To set the page orientation

1. Choose Page Setup from the File menu (see **Figure 5**).
2. If necessary, click the Page tab to display its options (see **Figure 4**).
3. In the Orientation area, select the radio button for Portrait or Landscape.
4. Click OK or press Return or Enter.

Figure 5. *Choose Page Setup from the File menu.*

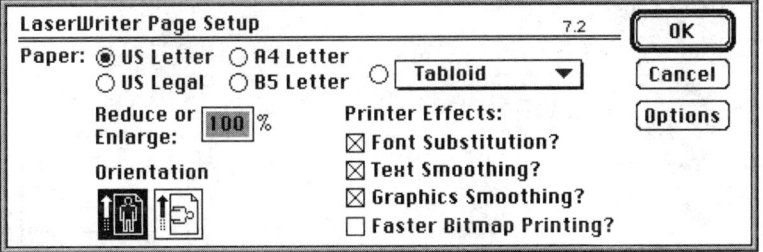

Figures 6a&b. *The standard Apple Page Setup dialog box (above). The QuickDraw GX version of this dialog box (below) looks a bit different.*

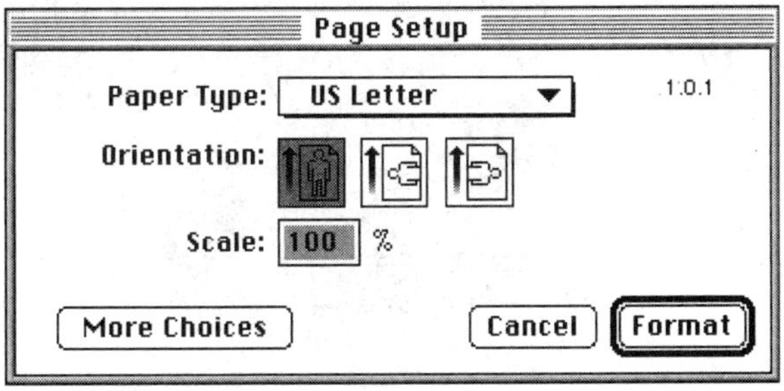

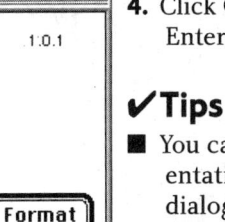

✓Tips

- You can also change the page orientation in the Apple Page Setup dialog box (see **Figures 6a** and **6b**).

- The standard Apple Page Setup dialog box varies in appearance depending on your printer.

To reduce or enlarge a worksheet report

1. Choose Page Setup from the File menu (see **Figure 5**).
2. If necessary, click the Page tab to display its options (see **Figure 4**).
3. To reduce or enlarge a report by a certain percentage, select the Adjust To radio button and enter a percentage in the edit box beside it.

   or

   To force a long report to fit on a certain number of pages, select the Fit To radio button and enter the number of pages you want it to fit on in the edit boxes beside it.
4. Click OK or press Return or Enter.

Figure 7. *The Scaling area on the Page tab is gray when printing a chart sheet.*

✔ Tips

- Both scaling options size your report proportionally, so you don't have to worry about stretched text or charts.
- If you're printing a chart sheet rather than a worksheet, the Scaling area on the Page tab is gray (see **Figure 7**).

To reduce or enlarge a chart

1. Choose Page Setup from the File menu (see **Figure 5**).
2. If necessary, click the Chart tab to display its options (see **Figure 8**).
3. Choose the radio button under Printed Chart Size for the scaling you want. If you choose custom, you'll also have to click the Options button and enter a percentage in the Reduce or Enlarge edit box of the Apple Page Setup dialog box (see **Figures 6a** and **6b**) and click OK there.
4. Click OK or press Return or Enter.

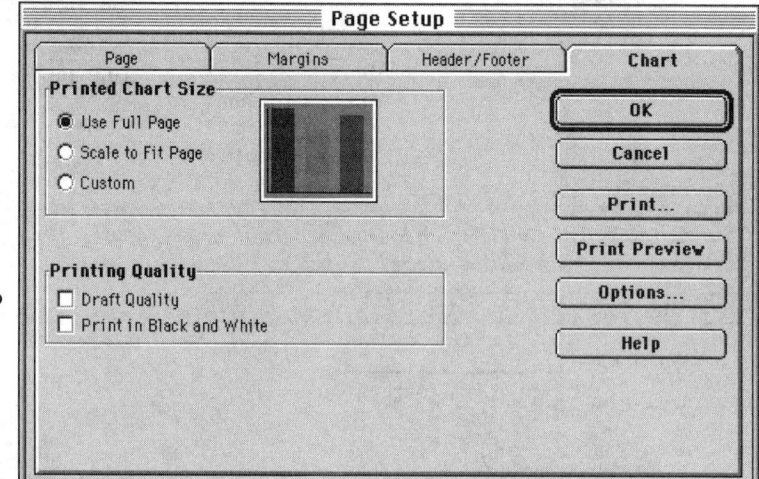

Figure 8. *The Chart tab of the Page Setup dialog box lets you set the size of the printed chart.*

To set margins in the Page Setup dialog box

1. Choose Page Setup from the File menu (see **Figure 5**).
2. If necessary, click the Margins tab to display its options (see **Figure 9**).
3. Enter margin measurements in the Top, Bottom, Left, and Right edit boxes.

   or

   Click the arrows beside the edit boxes to change the values already there.
4. Click OK or press Return or Enter.

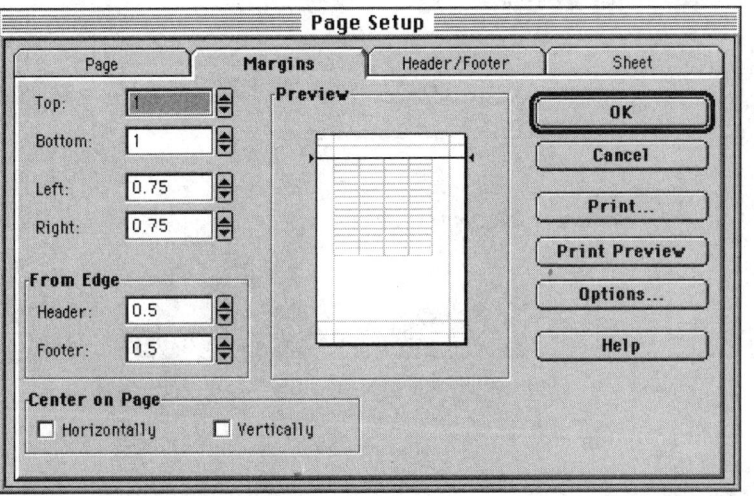

Figure 9. *The Margins tab of the Page Setup dialog box lets you set margins, header and footer locations, and page position.*

Figure 10. *The preview area of the Margins tab when a chart sheet is active.*

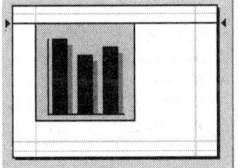

Figure 11. *If you turn on the Horizontally and Vertically check boxes in the Center on Page area, the preview illustration shows the report centered on the page.*

✔ Tips

- If a chart sheet rather than a worksheet is active, the preview area displays a chart (see **Figure 10**).
- You can also set margins in the Print Preview window. I tell you how later in this chapter.
- To center the report horizontally or vertically on the page, turn on the Horizontally and/or Vertically check boxes in the Center on Page area of the Margins tab (see **Figure 9**). The preview area picture changes accordingly (see **Figure 11**).
- Do not set margins to smaller values than the Header and Footer values or Excel will print your report over the header or footer.
- Some printers cannot print close to the edge of the paper. If part of your report is cut off when printed, increase your margins.

Chapter 10

About Page Breaks

When you make changes in the Page Setup dialog box, Excel recalculates page breaks. It displays page breaks as dashed lines between columns and rows (see **Figure 12**).

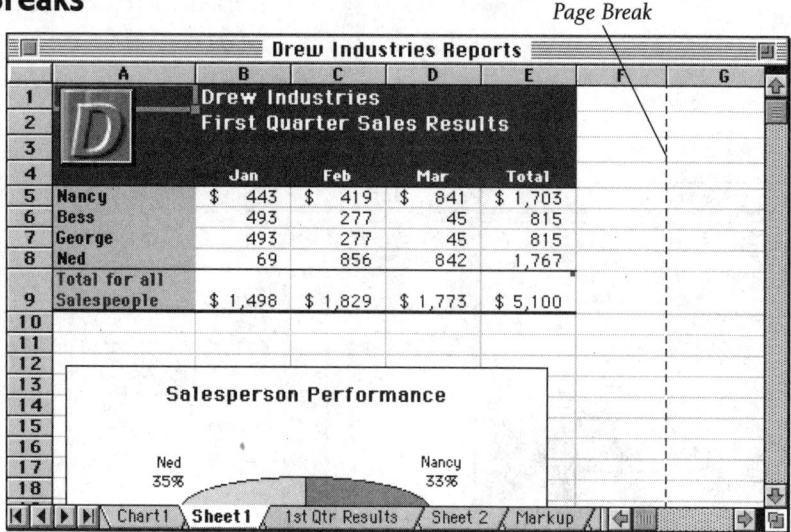

Figure 12. Excel automatically calculates and displays page breaks.

To insert a page break

1. Position the cell pointer in the cell immediately to the right of and immediately below the place you want the break to occur (see **Figure 13a**).
2. Choose Page Break from the Insert menu (see **Figure 13b**).

A manual page break appears to the left of or above the cell pointer (see **Figure 13c**) and any automatic page breaks nearby may disappear.

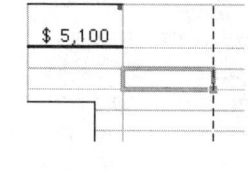

Figure 13a. Position the cell pointer in the cell to the right and below the place where you want the break to occur...

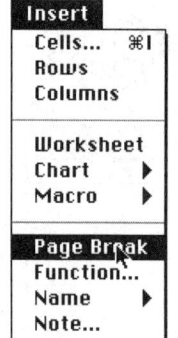

Figure 13b. ...choose Page Break from the Insert menu.

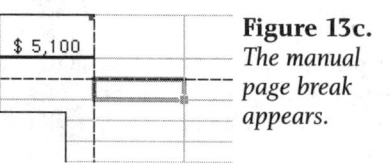

Figure 13c. The manual page break appears.

✔ Tips

- You can insert both a horizontal and a vertical page break at the same time by positioning the insertion point at the intersection of where you want the breaks to occur (see **Figure 13a** and **13c**).
- Excel ignores manual page breaks when you use the Fit To option on the Page tab of the Page Setup dialog box. I tell you about the Fit To feature earlier in this chapter.

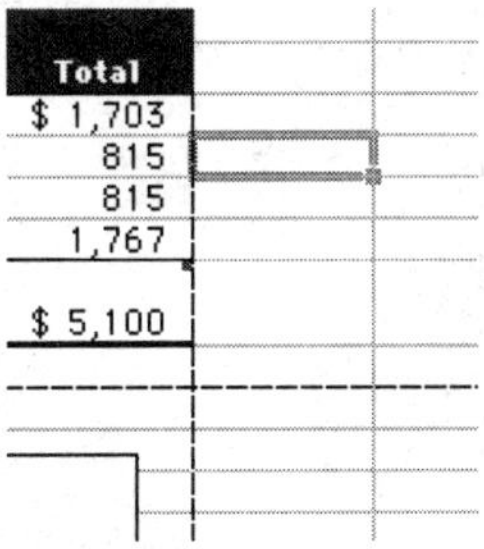

To remove a page break

1. Position the cell pointer in the cell immediately to the right of or immediately below the manual page break (see **Figure 14a**).
2. Choose Remove Page Break from the Insert menu (see **Figure 14b**).

The manual page break disappears and an automatic page break (if required) may appear nearby (see **Figure 14c**).

✔ Tips

- You can use the Remove Page Break command (see **Figure 14b**) to remove manual page breaks only.
- If you try to delete a manual page break and the Remove Page Break command doesn't appear on the Insert menu (see **Figure 14b**), you either have the cell pointer in the wrong position or the page break is an automatic page break.
- You can remove both horizontal and vertical page breaks at the same time by positioning the cell pointer in the cell at the intersection of the two page breaks (see **Figure 13c**).
- To remove all manual page breaks in a worksheet, select the entire worksheet and choose Remove Page Break from the Insert menu (see **Figure 14b**).
- If you have sharp eyes, you can see the difference between a manual and an automatic page break: The manual page break has shorter dashes spaced farther apart. **Figure 14c** shows a manual horizontal page break and an automatic vertical page break.

Figure 14a. *Position the cell pointer to the right of or below the manual page break you want to remove…*

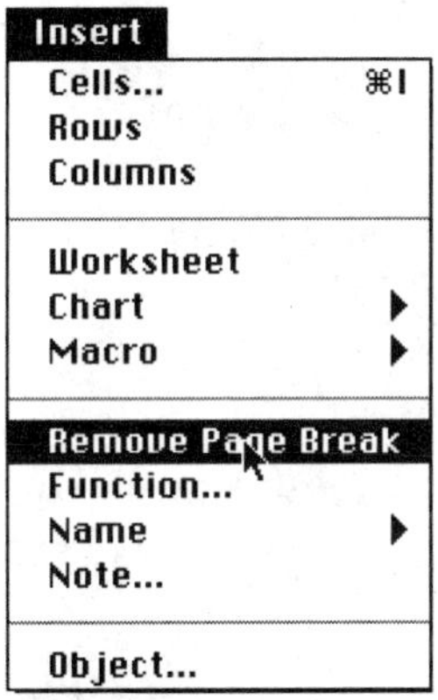

Figure 14b. *…then choose Remove Page Break from the Insert menu.*

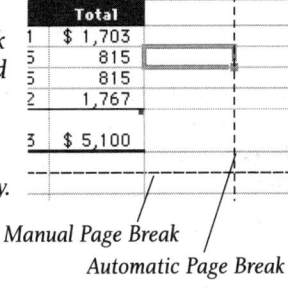

Figure 14c. *The page break disappears and an automatic page break (if necessary) appears nearby.*

Manual Page Break
Automatic Page Break

Chapter 10

About Headers and Footers

A *header* is text that appears at the top of every page. A *footer* is text that appears at the bottom of every page. **Figure 15** shows an example of a page with both a header and footer.

Excel lets you set the distance from the header and the footer to the edge of the paper, as well as the contents of the header and footer.

To set header and footer locations

1. Choose Page Setup from the File menu (see **Figure 5**).
2. If necessary, click the Margins tab to display its options (see **Figure 9**).
3. Enter a value in the Header and Footer edit boxes (see **Figure 16**) to position the header and footer in relation to the edge of the paper.

   or

   Click the little arrows beside the edit boxes to change the values already there.
4. Click OK or press Return or Enter.

✔ Tips

- You can also set header and footer locations in the Print Preview window. I tell you how later in this chapter.
- Do not set the Header and Footer values larger than the margin values or Excel will print your report on top of the header or footer.
- Some printers cannot print close to the edge of the paper. If your header or footer is cut off when printed, increase the values in the Header and Footer edit boxes in step 3 above.

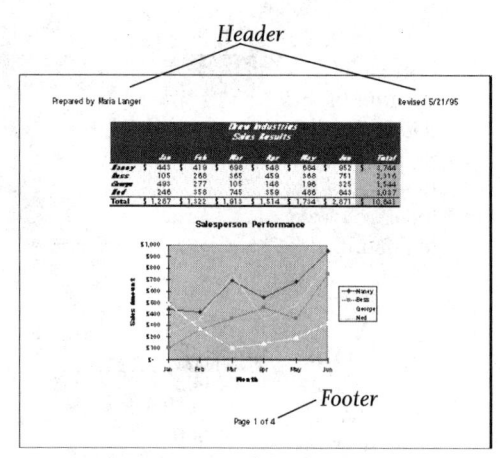

Figure 15. *A page with both a header and a footer.*

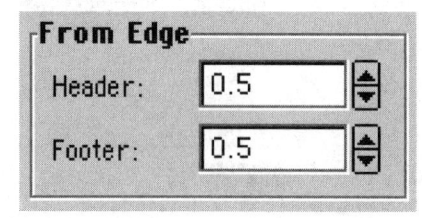

Figure 16. *Enter new values in the Header and Footer edit boxes to specify the distance from the top of the header and the bottom of the footer to the edge of the page.*

To use built-in headers and footers

1. Choose Page Setup from the File menu (see **Figure 5**).
2. If necessary, click the Header/Footer tab to display its options (see **Figure 17**).
3. Choose an option from the Header pop-up menu (see **Figure 18**) to set the header. Choose an option from the Footer pop-up menu to set the footer.
4. Click OK or press Return or Enter.

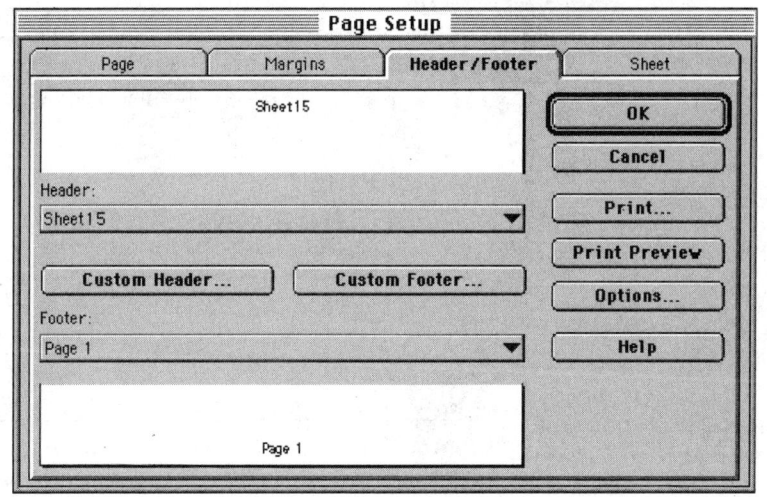

Figure 17. *The Header/Footer tab of the Page Setup dialog box lets you set the contents and formatting of the header and footer.*

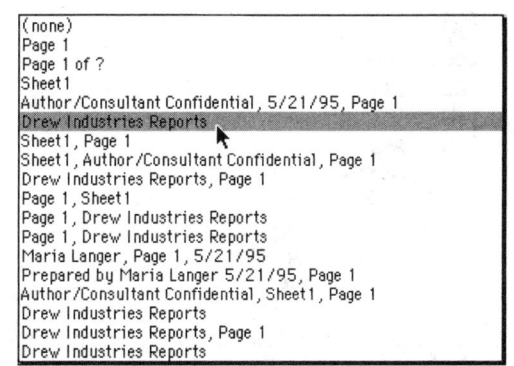

Figure 18. *Excel's built-in headers and footers offer many useful options, some of which include your name and company name (or title, in my case).*

✔ Tips

- The pop-up menu for Footer is identical to the one for Header.
- Excel gets your name and company name from entries you made when you installed Excel. You can change the name by choosing Options from the Tools menu, entering a new User Name in the General tab, and clicking OK. You cannot change the company name without reinstalling Excel.
- To change the formatting of text in the header or footer, you need to use the Custom Header or Custom Footer button in the Header/Footer tab of the Page Setup dialog box. I tell you about that on the next page.

Chapter 10

To create custom headers and footers

1. Choose Page Setup from the File menu (see **Figure 5**).
2. If necessary, click the Header/Footer tab to display its options (see **Figure 17**).
3. Click the Custom Header or Custom Footer button.
4. In the Header (see **Figure 19a**) or Footer dialog box, enter the text or codes you want in the Left Section, Center Section, and Right Section edit boxes. Use the buttons listed in **Table 1** to format selected text or insert codes for dynamic information.
5. Click OK or press Return or Enter.
6. The Page Setup dialog box preview area and Header or Footer pop-up menu reflect your changes (see **Figure 19b**). Click OK or press Return or Enter to accept them.

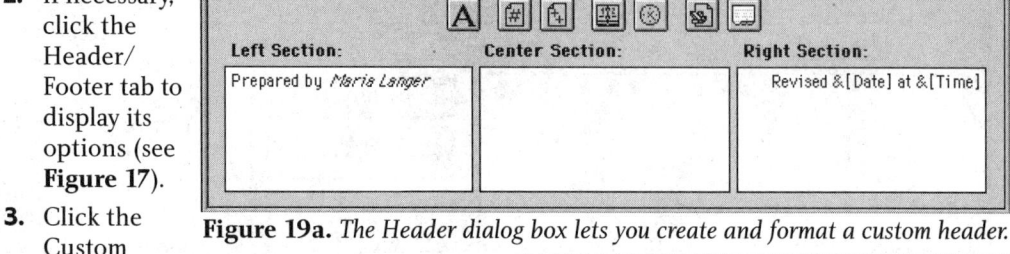

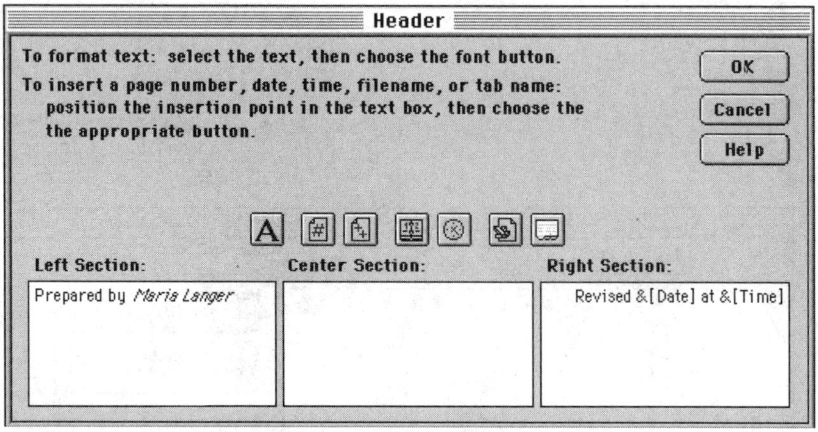

✔ Tips

- The dialog box for Footer is identical to the one for Header.
- To enter an ampersand (&) character in a header or footer, type && where you want it to appear in step 4 above.
- To specify the starting page number to be printed in the header or footer, enter a value in the First Page Number edit box of the Page tab of the Page Setup dialog box (see **Figure 4**).

Figure 19a. *The Header dialog box lets you create and format a custom header.*

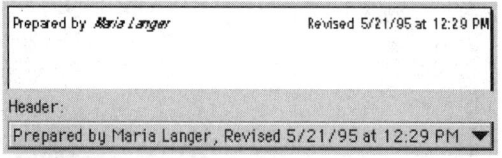

Figure 19b. *The custom header or footer appears in the Page Setup dialog box.*

 A	Use the Font button to format selected text. I tell you about the Font dialog box in Chapter 6.
 #	Use the Page Number button to insert the &[Page] code. This inserts the page number.
 ++	Use the Total Pages button to insert the &[Pages] code. This inserts the total pages number.
 📅	Use the Date button to insert the &[Date] code. This inserts the print date.
 ⏱	Use the Time button to insert the &[Time] code. This inserts the print time.
 📄	Use the Filename button to insert the &[File] code. This inserts the workbook name.
 📋	Use the Sheet Name button to insert the &[Tab] code. This inserts the sheet name.

Table 1. *Use these buttons to insert codes for dynamic information.*

About the Print Area

The *print area* is the portion of a workbook that you want to print. It can be a worksheet range, an entire sheet, multiple sheets, or an entire workbook. You can set the print area in the Page Setup dialog box or select the range(s) just before choosing the Print command. I tell you more about the Print command and Print dialog box later in this chapter.

To set the print area for a worksheet

1. Choose Page Setup from the File menu (see **Figure 5**).
2. If necessary, click the Sheet tab to display its options (see **Figure 20**).
3. To print the entire worksheet or workbook, clear the contents of the Print Area edit box.

    or

    To print only part of a worksheet, enter the cell references for the range you want to print in the Print Area edit box. **Figure 21** shows an example of a properly entered range reference.
4. Click OK or press Return or Enter.

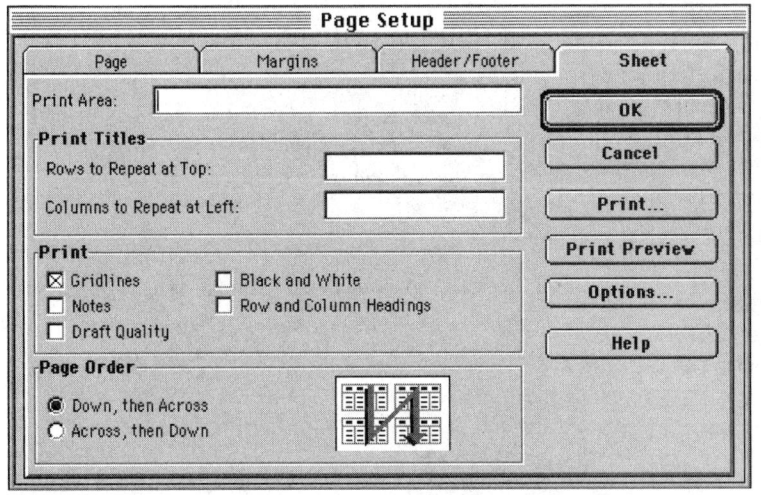

Figure 20. *Use the Sheet tab of the Page Setup dialog box to tell Excel what to print.*

Figure 21. *Enter the cell references for the range you want to print in the Print Area edit box.*

✔ Tips

- If you prefer, for step 3, you can position the insertion point in the Print Area edit box and select cells you want to print in the worksheet window by dragging over them.
- To set multiple non-adjacent print areas, enter the cell references for each range in the Print Area edit box, separated by commas.

Chapter 10

About Print Titles

Print titles are worksheet columns and/or rows that are repeated on every page of the report. This is useful if the print area does not fit on one page and you want to repeat column or row titles on subsequent pages (see **Figures 22a**, **22b**, and **22c**).

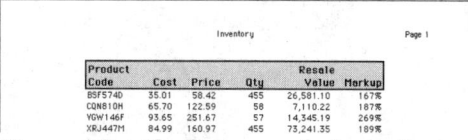

Figure 22a. *The first page of a long report will include column titles as part of the print area…*

To set print titles

1. Choose Page Setup from the File menu (see **Figure 5**).
2. If necessary, click the Sheet tab to display its options (see **Figure 20**).
3. To set column titles to repeat on each page, click in the Rows to Repeat at Top edit box and enter the reference for the rows that contain column titles. **Figure 23** shows an example of a properly entered row reference.

   or

   To set row titles to repeat on each page, click in the Columns to Repeat at Left edit box and enter the reference for the columns that contain row titles.
4. Click OK or press Return or Enter.

Figure 22b. *…but subsequent pages won't.*

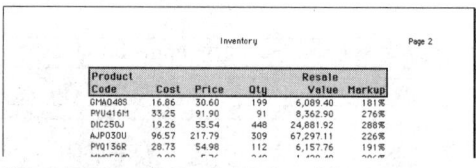

Figure 22c. *By setting print titles, you can include column or row titles on every single page of a report.*

Figure 23. *In this example,* Row 1 *of the worksheet will be printed on every page.*

✔ Tip

- If you prefer, in step 3 above, you can position the insertion point in the appropriate edit box and select the rows or columns in the worksheet window by clicking or dragging over their headings.

About other Print Options

The Sheet tab of the Page Setup dialog box (see **Figure 20**) gives you control over several other print options you might find useful:

- Gridlines, when turned on, prints cell gridlines like those that appear in the worksheet window (see **Figure 24a**). I tell you how to turn off the display of gridlines in the worksheet window in Chapter 14.

- Notes, when turned on, prints cell notes on a separate page at the end of the report (see **Figure 24b**). I tell you about cell notes in Chapter 6.

- Draft Quality, when turned on, prints fewer graphics and omits gridlines (see **Figure 24c**) to speed up printing.

- Black and White, when turned on, converts the Excel elements of the worksheet to black and white (see **Figure 24d**).

- Row and Column Headings, when turned on, prints the row and column headings in the worksheet window (see **Figure 24e**). Don't confuse this with print titles, which I tell you about on the previous page.

- Page Order specifies the print order for the pages of long, wide reports.

✔ Tips

- To print cell notes along with the corresponding cell references, turn on both the Notes and Row and Column Headings check boxes.

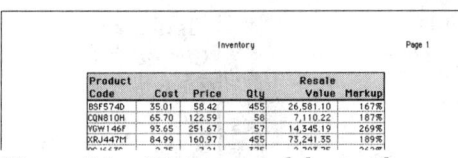

Figure 24a. *Printing a worksheet with Gridlines turned on.*

Figure 24b. *The last page of a report with Notes turned on.*

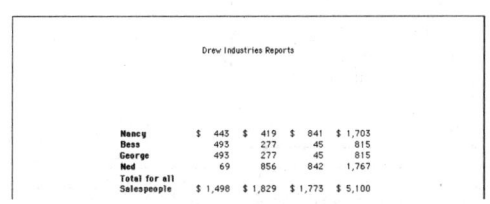

Figure 24c. *Draft Quality turns off most graphic elements—even charts!*

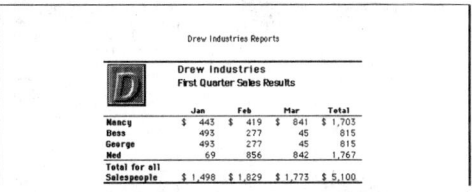

Figure 24d. *Black and White strips the color out of the report when printing. Only the graphic created in Photoshop remains in color or shades of gray.*

Figure 24e. *Printing a worksheet with Row and Column Headings turned on.*

Chapter 10

About Print Preview

Excel's Print Preview feature lets you see what a report will look like before you print it. If a report doesn't look perfect, Page Setup and Margins buttons right inside the Print Preview dialog box let you make adjustments. When you're ready to print, click the Print button.

Figure 25a. *Choose Print Preview from the File menu.*

To preview a report

Choose Print Preview from the File menu (see **Figure 25a**).

or

Click the Print Preview button on the Standard toolbar.

or

Click the Print Preview button in the Page Setup or Print dialog box.

A preview of the current sheet appears (see **Figure 25b**). It reflects all Page Setup dialog box settings.

✔ Tips

- To view the other pages of the report, click the Next or Previous button.
- To zoom in to see report detail, click the Zoom button or click the mouse pointer (a magnifying glass) on the area you want to magnify.
- To open the Print dialog box and print, click the Print button. I tell you about the Print dialog box later in this chapter.
- To change Page Setup dialog box options, click the Setup button.
- To close the Print Preview dialog box, click the Close button.

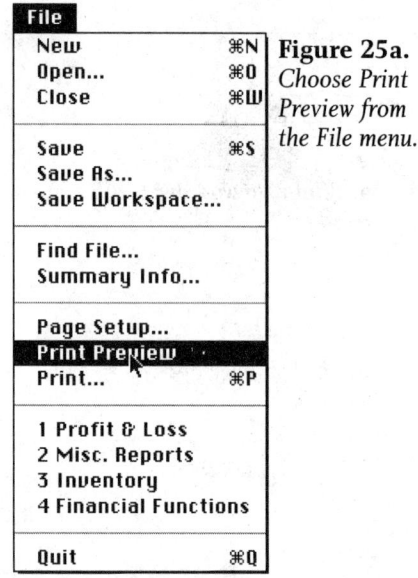

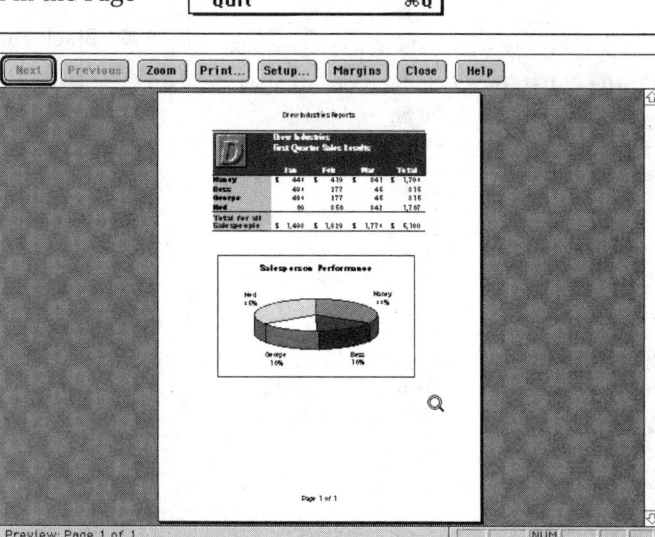

Figure 25b. *The Print Preview dialog box lets you see your report before you print it.*

Using Print Preview

170

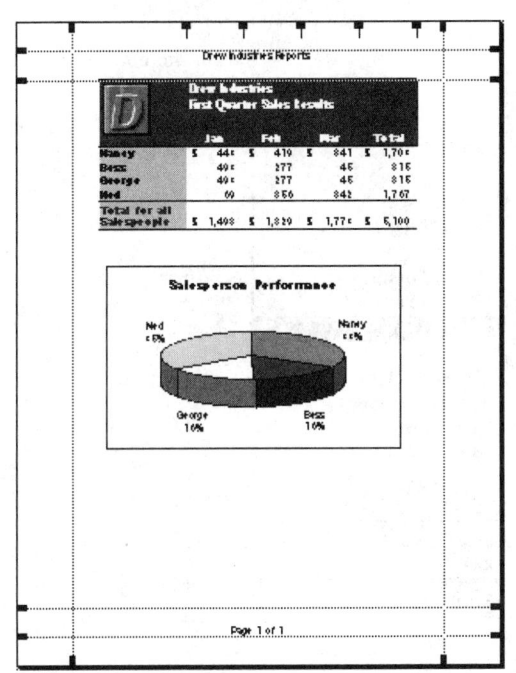

Printing

To change margins, header and footer locations, and column widths in Print Preview

1. In the Print Preview dialog box, click the Margins button.

    Handles for margins, header and footer locations, and column widths appear around the report preview (see **Figure 26a**).

2. Position the mouse pointer over the handle or guideline for the margin, header, footer, or column you want to change. The mouse pointer turns into a line with two arrows coming out of it (see **Figure 26b**).

3. Press down the mouse button and drag to make the change. A measurement for your change appears in the status bar as you drag.

4. Release the mouse button to complete the change. The report reformats automatically.

✔ Tips

- The changes you make by dragging handles in the Print Preview dialog box will be reflected in the appropriate edit boxes of the Page Setup dialog box.

- I tell how to change margins and header and footer locations with the Page Setup dialog box earlier in this chapter. I tell you how to change column widths in the worksheet window or with the Column Width dialog box in Chapter 6.

Figure 26a. *When you click the Margins button, handles for margins, header, footer, and columns appear.*

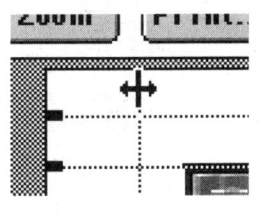

Figure 26b. *Position the mouse pointer over a handle and drag to change the width.*

171

To print a report

1. Choose Print from the File menu (see **Figure 27a**). The Print dialog box appears (see **Figure 27b**).
2. To print more than one copy of the report, enter the number of copies you want in the Copies edit box.
3. To print only certain pages of the report, enter a starting and ending page number in the From and To edit boxes.
4. Select the correct paper source option in the Paper Source area.
5. Select the radio button for what you want to print in the Print area.
6. Click Print or press Return or Enter.

   The report is sent or *spooled* to the printer. A dialog box like the one in **Figure 28** appears while it's being sent. When the dialog box disappears, you can continue working with Excel.

Figure 27a. *Choose Print from the File menu.*

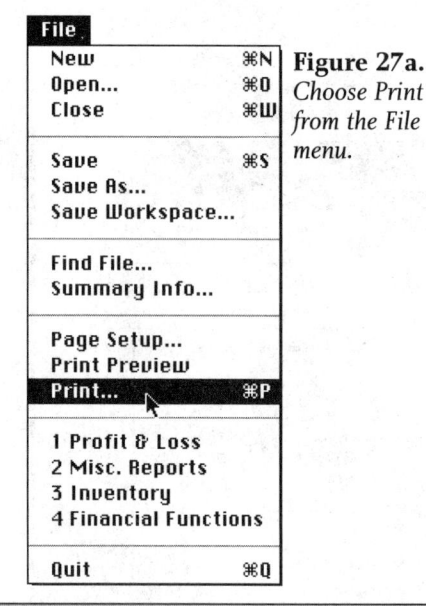

Figure 27b. *The Print dialog box for a LaserWriter printer.*

Figure 28. *A dialog box like this appears while a document is being spooled to the printer for printing.*

Printing

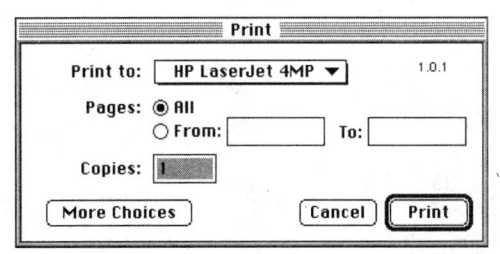

Figure 29a. *The "Fewer Choices" Print dialog box for QuickDraw GX.*

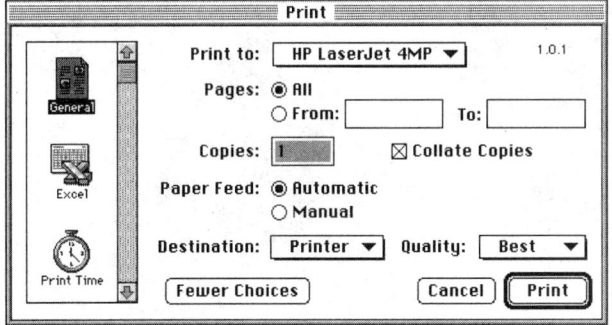

Figure 29b. *The General options in the "More Choices" version of a QuickDraw GX Print dialog box.*

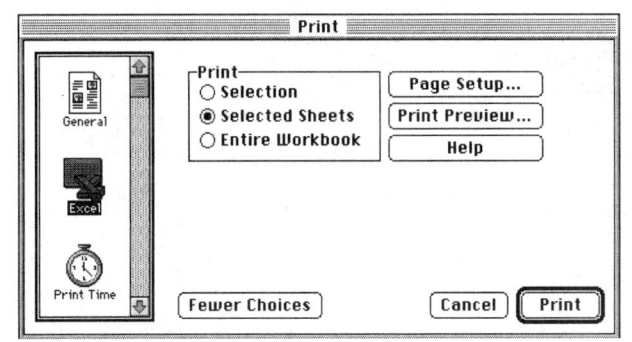

Figure 29c. *The Excel options in the "More Choices" version of a QuickDraw GX Print dialog box.*

To print a report with QuickDraw GX

1. Choose Print from the File menu (see **Figure 27a**). The QuickDraw GX Print dialog box appears (see **Figure 29a**).

2. Select a printer from the Print To pop-up menu.

3. To print only certain pages of the report, enter a starting and ending page number in the From and To edit boxes.

4. To print more than one copy of the report, enter a number in the Copies edit box.

5. To select a paper source, click the More Choices button to expand the Print dialog box. With the General icon selected in the scrolling list (see **Figure 29b**), select the correct paper source option in the Paper Feed area.

6. To tell Excel what you want to print, click the More Choices button to expand the Print dialog box. With the Excel icon selected in the scrolling list (see **Figure 29c**), select the appropriate radio button in the Print area.

7. Click Print or press Return or Enter.

   The report is sent or *spooled* to the printer. A dialog box like the one in **Figure 28** appears while it's being sent. When the dialog box disappears, you can continue working with Excel.

173

✓ Tips

- To print only part of a worksheet without setting a Print Area in the Sheet tab of the Page Setup dialog box, select the range(s) you want to print before choosing Print from the File menu. Then be sure to select the Selection radio button in the Print dialog box (see **Figures 27b** and **29c**).

- To print several sheets in a workbook, select the sheet tabs for the sheets you want to print before choosing Print from the File menu. I tell you how to select multiple sheets in a workbook file in Chapter 4. Then be sure to select the Selected Sheets button in the Print dialog box (see **Figures 27b** and **29c**).

- You can use the Page Setup button in the Print dialog box (see **Figures 27b** and **29c**) to make changes to the Page Setup dialog box options. I tell you about Page Setup options throughout this chapter. When you're finished and click OK in Page Setup, you'll return to the Print dialog box.

- You can use the Print Preview button in the Print dialog box (see **Figures 27b** and **29c**) to take a look at your report before printing it. I tell you about Print Preview earlier in this chapter. When you're finished and click Print, the report prints.

- If you click the Print button on the Standard toolbar, Excel sends the report to the printer without displaying the Print dialog box.

- The appearance of the Print dialog box (see **Figures 27b** and **29b**) varies depending on your printer.

WORKING WITH DATABASES 11

Understanding Databases

About Databases

Excel's database features and functions help make it a flexible tool for creating, maintaining, and reporting data. With Excel, you can use a form to enter data into a list, filter information, sort records, and automatically generate subtotals. You can use Excel's calculating, formatting, charting, and printing features on your database, too.

In Excel, a *database* is any list of information with unique labels in the first row. You don't need to do anything special to identify a database—Excel is smart enough to know one when it sees it. **Figure 1**, for example, shows the first few rows of a list that Excel can recognize as a database.

A database is organized into fields and records. A *field* is a category of information. In **Figure 1**, *Product Code*, *Department*, and *Cost* are the first three fields. A *record* is a collection of fields for one thing. In **Figure 1**, row 2 shows the record for the item with product code *BSF574D* and row 3 shows the record for *CQN810H*.

✔ Tip

- Fields are always in columns while records are aways in rows.

Figure 1. *The first few rows of a list that Excel can automatically recognize as a database.*

	A	B	C	D	E	F	G	H	I
1	Product Code	Department	Cost	Sale Price	Reorder Point	Qty on Hand	Time to Order?	Resale Value	Markup
2	BSF574D	Books	35.01	58.42	170	455		26,581.10	167%
3	CQN810H	Computers	65.70	122.59	170	58	Order Now	7,110.22	187%
4	YGW146F	Vacation Apparel	93.65	251.67	90	57	Order Now	14,345.19	269%
5	XRJ447M	Big & Tall Men's Clothes	84.99	160.97	100	455		73,241.35	189%
6	OGJ663G	Office Supplies	2.75	7.21	160	375		2,703.75	262%
7	LQB586B	Lingerie	34.58	102.37	120	116	Order Now	11,874.92	296%
8	ILC3420	Juniors Clothes	52.45	100.21	130	396		39,683.16	191%

175

Chapter 11

To create a list

1. In a worksheet window, enter unique column titles for each of the fields in your list (see **Figure 2a**). These will be the field names.
2. Beginning with the row immediately after the one containing the column titles, enter the data for each record (see **Figure 2b**). Be sure to put the proper information in each column.

✔ Tips

- Use only one cell for each column title. If the field name is too long to fit in the cell, use the Alignment tab in the Font dialog box to wrap text in the cell (see **Figure 3**). I tell you about alignment options in Chapter 6.
- Do not skip rows when entering information. A blank row indicates the end of the database above it.
- You can format your list any way you like. The formatting will not affect the way Excel recognizes and works with the list data.
- Your list can include formulas. Excel treats the results of the formulas like any other field.

About the Data Form

Excel automatically creates a dialog box with a custom data form (see **Figure 4**) when you choose the Form command from the Data menu. You can use this dialog box to enter, edit, delete, and find records.

Figure 2a. *Begin by entering unique field names in the first row of the list…*

Figure 2b. *…then enter the data, one record per row.*

Figure 3. *Formatting a list doesn't affect the way Excel works with its data.*

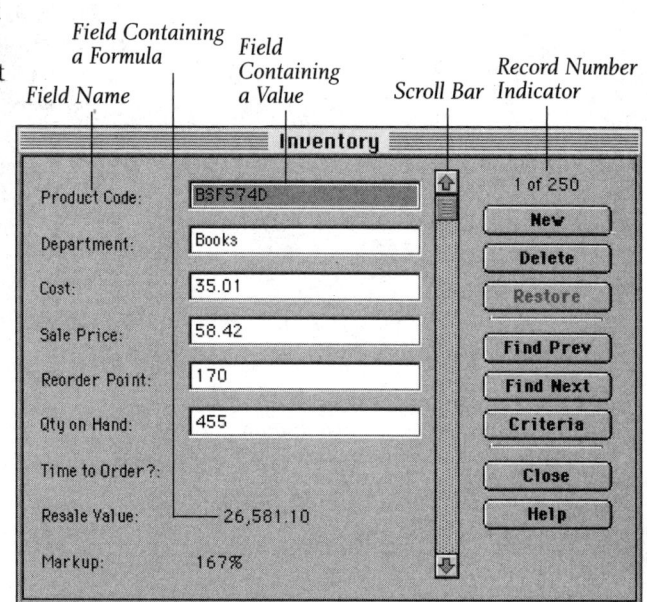

Figure 4. *The data form offers another way to enter, edit, delete, and find records.*

Working with Databases

Figure 5. *Choose Form from the Data menu.*

Click here to see the previous record.

Click here to jump back 10 records.

Click here to jump forward 10 records.

Click here to see the next record.

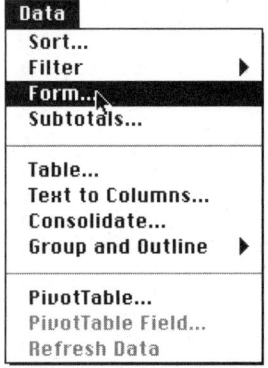

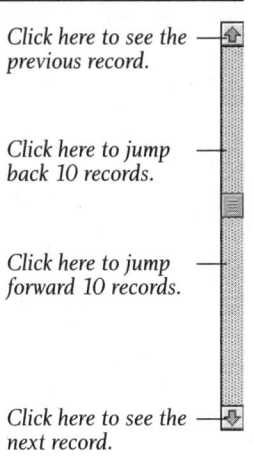

Figure 6. *Use the scroll bar in the data form to browse records.*

To browse records with the data form

1. Position the cellpointer in the list.
2. Choose Form from the Data menu (see **Figure 5**). The data form appears (see **Figure 4**).
3. Use the scroll bar (see **Figure 6**) to browse through the records:
   - To see the next record, click the down arrow on the scroll bar.
   - To see the previous record, click the up arrow on the scroll bar.
   - To jump ahead 10 records, click the scroll bar beneath the scroll box.
   - To jump back 10 records, click the scroll bar above the scroll box.
4. Click the Close button to stop browsing records.

To enter, edit, and delete data with the data form

1. Position the cellpointer in the list.
2. Choose Form from the Data menu (see **Figure 5**). The data form appears (see **Figure 4**).
3. To create a new record, click the New button and enter the information into the empty edit boxes for each field.

   or

   To edit a record, locate the record you want to edit and make changes in the appropriate edit boxes.

   or

   To delete a record, locate the record you want to delete and click the Delete button.
4. Click the Close button to stop entering and editing data. You'll see your changes reflected in the list.

✔ Tips

- Excel records your changes when you move to another record or click the Close button to close the form.
- If a field should contain a formula, Excel automatically carries the formula forward from the previous record and performs the calculation.

177

Chapter 11

To find records with the data form

1. Position the cellpointer in the list.
2. Choose Form from the Data menu (see **Figure 5**). The data form appears (see **Figure 4**).
3. Click the Criteria button. A criteria form appears (see **Figure 7a**).
4. Enter search criteria in the field(s) in which you expect to find a match (see **Figure 7b**).
5. Click the Find Next button to move forward through the list for records that match the criteria or click the Find Prev button to move backward through the list for records that match the criteria. Excel beeps when it reaches the end or beginning of the matches.

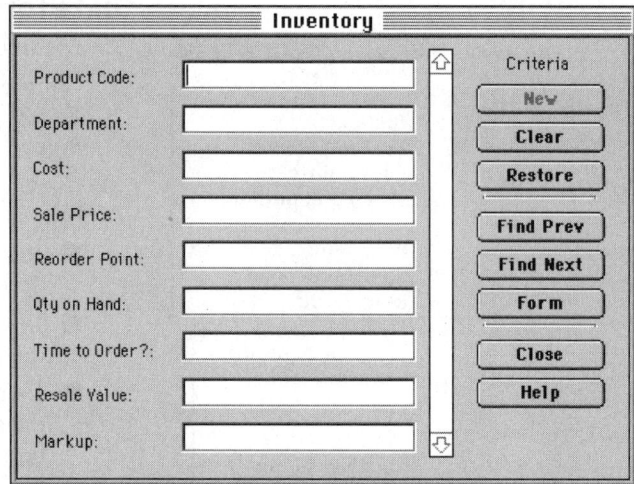

Figure 7a. *The data form turns into a criteria form when you click the Criteria button.*

Figure 7b. *Enter the search criteria in the field(s) in which you expect to find a match.*

✔ Tips

- You can enter criteria in any combination of fields. If you enter criteria into multiple fields, Excel looks for records that match all criteria.
- The more fields you enter data into, the more specific you make the search and the fewer matches you'll find.
- You can use comparison operators (see **Table 1**) and wildcard characters (see **Table 2**) in conjunction with criteria. For example, >100 finds records with values greater than 100 in the field in which the criteria is entered.
- You can also use Excel's AutoFilter feature to quickly locate and display all records that match search criteria. I tell you how next.

Operator	Meaning
=	Equal To
<>	Not Equal To
>	Greater Than
>=	Greater Than or Equal To
<	Less Than
<=	Less Than or Equal To

Table 1. *Comparison operators.*

Character	Meaning
?	Any single character
*	Any group of characters

Table 2. *Wildcard characters.*

Working with Databases

About AutoFilter

The AutoFilter feature puts pop-up menus in the titles of each column (see **Figure 8b**). You can use these menus to choose criteria in the column and display only those records that match the criteria.

To find records with AutoFilter

1. Position the cellpointer in the list.
2. Choose AutoFilter from the Filter submenu under the Data menu (see **Figure 8a**). Excel scans the data and creates pop-up menus for each field (see **Figure 8b**).

Figure 8a. *The Filter submenu under the Data menu offers several filtering options.*

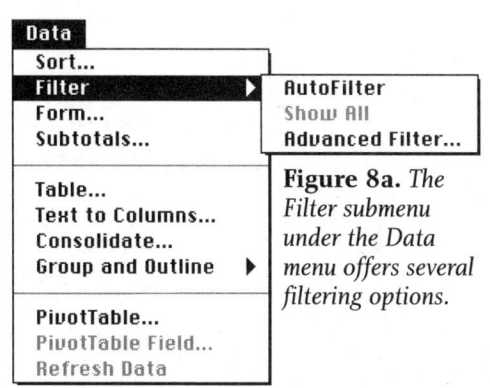

Figure 8b. *The AutoFilter feature creates a pop-up menu for each field.*

Figure 8c. *Choose criteria from a pop-up menu...*

3. Use a pop-up menu to select criteria in a specific field (see **Figure 8c**). When you make your choice, only the records matching the criteria are displayed (see **Figure 8d**).

✔ Tip

- To display all of the records again, choose Show All from the Filter submenu under the Data menu (see **Figure 8a**) or choose (All) from the pop-up list you used to filter the data (see **Figure 8c**).

Figure 8d. *...and Excel displays only the records that match the criteria.*

Using AutoFilter

179

To set a custom AutoFilter

1. Choose (Custom...) from the pop-up menu for the field for which you want to set criteria (see **Figure 8c**).

2. In the Custom AutoFilter dialog box (see **Figure 9**), use the pop-up menus to choose comparison operators and criteria.

3. Select the And or Or radio button to tell Excel whether it should match both criteria (And) or either criteria (Or).

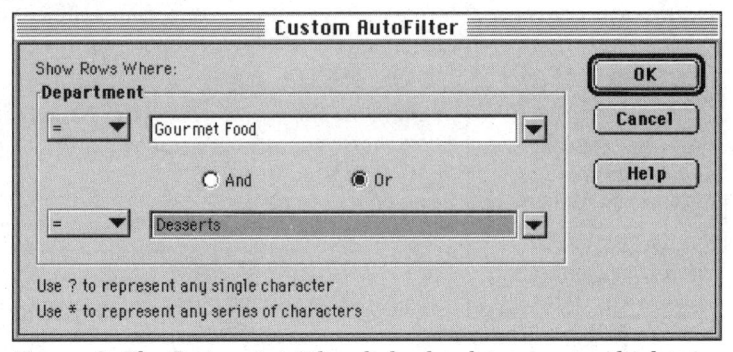

Figure 9. *The Custom AutoFilter dialog box lets you set multiple criteria for a field.*

4. Click OK or press Return or Enter.

   Only the records matching the criteria you set are displayed.

✔ Tips

- If you prefer, in step 2 above, you can type in criteria.
- Criteria can include wildcard characters (see **Table 2**).

To use multiple AutoFilters

Choose filters from the pop-up menus for each of the fields for which you want to set criteria. Excel will display only the records that match all of the filters (see **Figure 10**).

Figure 10. *In this example, three filters were used: Department=Books, Sale Price<100, and Time to Order?=Order Now.*

About Advanced Filters

With advanced filters you can specify even more criteria than with AutoFilters. First set up a criteria range, then use the Advanced Filter dialog box to perform the search.

To use advanced filters

1. Create a criteria range by copying the data labels in the list to a blank area of the worksheet and then entering the criteria in the cells beneath it (see **Figure 11a**).

Figure 11a. *Create a criteria range with field names and values you want to match.*

2. Choose Advanced Filter from the Filter submenu under the Data menu (see **Figure 8a**).

3. In the Advanced Filter dialog box (see **Figure 11b**), select a radio button to specify whether the matches should replace the original list (Filter the List, in-place) or a new list should be created elsewhere (Copy to Another Location).

4. In the List Range edit box, confirm that the correct cell references for your list have been entered.

5. In the Criteria Range edit box, enter the cell references for the range containing your criteria (including the field labels).

6. If you selected the Copy radio button in step 3 above, enter a cell reference for the first cell of the new list in the copy to edit box.

7. Click OK or press Return or Enter.

Excel searches for records that match the criteria and either replaces the original list or creates a new list with the matches (see **Figure 11c**).

Figure 11b. *Then use the Advanced Filter dialog box to tell Excel where the List Range, Criteria Range, and Copy To locations are.*

Figure 11c. *The criteria in Figure 11a yielded these results.*

About Sorting

You can sort lists by any column(s). Excel will quickly put database information in the order you specify.

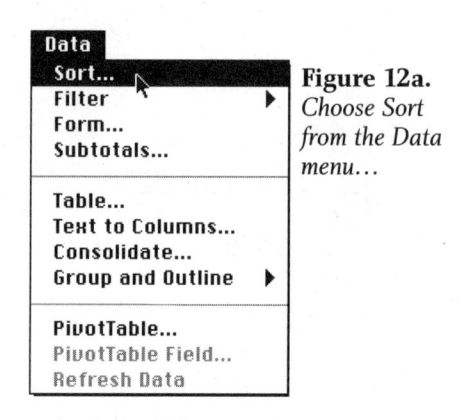

To sort a list

1. Position the cellpointer in the list.
2. Choose Sort from the Data menu (see **Figure 12a**).
3. In the Sort dialog box (see **Figure 12b**), choose a primary sort field from the Sort By pop-up menu (see **Figure 12c**). Then select a radio button to specify whether the sort should be in Ascending (lowest to highest) or Descending (highest to lowest) order.
4. If desired, choose a secondary and tertiary sort field from each of the Then By pop-up menus. Be sure to select a sort order button beside each field.
5. Select a radio button at the bottom of the dialog box to tell Excel whether this list has a Header Row (column titles) or No Header Row.
6. Click OK or press Return or Enter.

   Excel sorts the list as you specified (see **Figure 12d**).

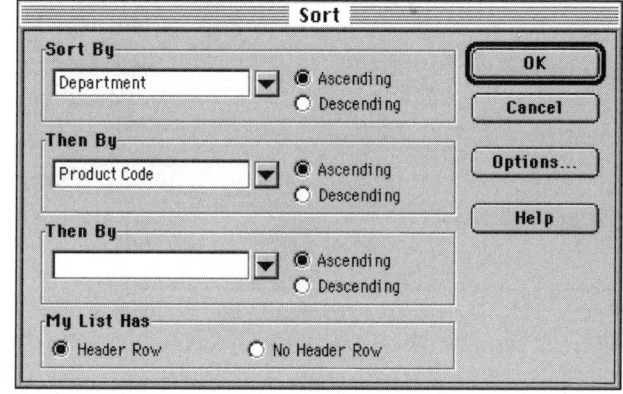

   or

1. Position the cellpointer in the list in the field by which you want to sort.
2. Click the Sort Ascending button to sort from lowest to highest value or the Sort Descending button to sort from highest to lowest value. Both buttons are on the Standard toolbar.

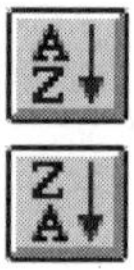

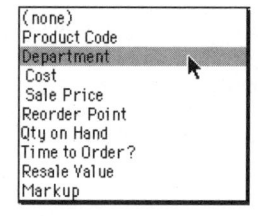

Figure 12a. *Choose Sort from the Data menu...*

Figure 12b. *...choose sort fields in the Sort dialog box...*

Figure 12c. *...by choosing from pop-up menus of field names.*

✔ Tips

- The two Then By fields in the sort dialog box are "tie-breakers" and are only used if the primary sort field has more than one record with the same value.

- If the results of a sort are not what you expected, choose Undo from the Edit menu, press ⌘Z, or click the Undo button on the Standard toolbar to restore the original sort order.

- If you make the wrong selection in the My List Has area at the bottom of the dialog box, you could sort column titles along with the rest of the list. If you see that you've done that, choose Undo from the Edit menu, press ⌘Z, or click the Undo button on the Standard toolbar to restore the original order and try again.

- If you position the cellpointer anywhere in the column by which you want to sort, that column is automatically referenced in the Sort dialog box.

- To sort by more than three columns, sort by the least important columns first, then by the most important ones. For example, to sort a list by *columns A, B, C, D,* and *E,* you'd sort first by *columns D* and *E,* then by columns *A, B,* and *C.*

- In order to use Excel's Subtotal feature, you must first sort the data by the column for which you want subtotals. I tell you about the Subtotal feature next.

Product Code	Department	Cost	Sale Price	Reorder Point	Qty on Hand	Time to Order?	Resale Value	Markup
XFA2360	Big & Tall Men's Clothes	4.09	11.13	110	69	Order Now	767.97	272%
XSK288V	Big & Tall Men's Clothes	19.20	48.82	140	303		14,792.46	254%
KDQ7450	Children's Clothes	24.06	67.14	160	214		14,367.96	279%
KFX312D	Children's Clothes	82.42	211.73	90	431		91,255.63	257%
KTF684J	Children's Clothes	54.19	143.38	170	230		32,977.40	265%
JCU583S	Juniors Clothes	91.36	244.39	10	254		62,075.06	268%
JDG360K	Juniors Clothes	57.41	166.34	90	332		55,224.88	290%
JKI6610	Juniors Clothes	73.01	200.58	110	423		84,845.34	275%
JN0365F	Juniors Clothes	16.82	48.20	140	96	Order Now	4,627.20	287%
JPC105K	Juniors Clothes	92.02	247.19	100	373		92,201.87	269%
WBL354T	Women's Clothes	39.71	109.95	60	469		51,566.55	277%
WCU388F	Women's Clothes	72.06	206.92	170	157	Order Now	32,486.44	287%
WYS571P	Women's Clothes	32.95	87.67	40	493		43,221.31	266%

Figure 12d. *The sort order in Figure 12b yields this report of data filtered from Figure 11c.*

Chapter 11

About Subtotal and the SUBTOTAL Function

Excel's Subtotal feature enters formulas with the SUBTOTAL function in sorted database lists. The SUBTOTAL function (see **Figure 13d**) returns a subtotal for a sorted list. It uses the following syntax:

SUBTOTAL(function_num,ref)

The *function_num* argument is a number that specifies which function to use. **Table 3** shows the valid values. I tell you about most of these functions in Chapter 5. The *ref* argument is the range of cells to subtotal.

To subtotal a list

1. Sort the list by the field(s) for which you want subtotals and position the cellpointer in the list.
2. Choose Subtotals from the Data menu (see **Figure 13a**) to display the Subtotal dialog box (see **Figure 13b**).
3. From the At Each Change In pop-up menu, choose the field to be grouped for subtotaling. This may be the same field you sorted by.
4. Choose a function from the Use Function pop-up menu (see **Figure 13c**).
5. In the Add Subtotal To scrolling list, use the check boxes to choose the field(s) to subtotal.
6. If desired, use the check boxes at the bottom of the dialog box to set other options.
7. Click OK or press Return or Enter.

Excel turns the list into an outline and enters row titles and subtotals (see **Figure 13d**).

✔ Tip

■ To remove subtotals, click the Remove All button in the Subtotal dialog box.

Figure 13a. *Choose Subtotals from the Data menu.*

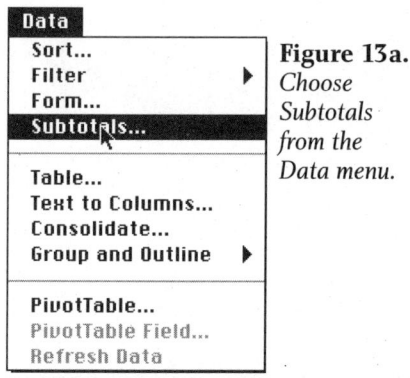

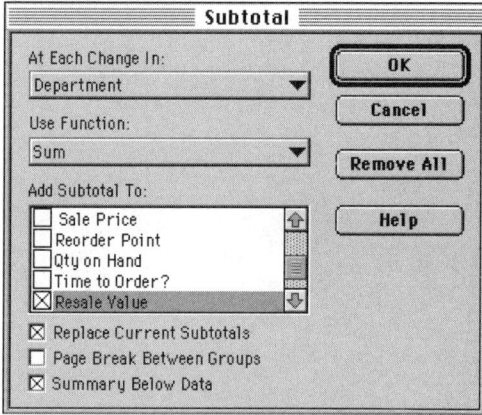

Figure 13b. *The Subtotal dialog box lets you choose the field to group data for, the function, and the field(s) to subtotal.*

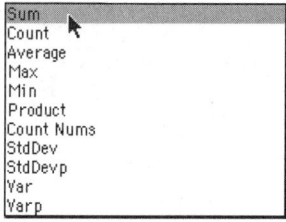

Figure 13c. *The Use Function pop-up menu offers a variety of subtotal functions to choose from.*

Subtotaling Information

About Outlines

Excel's outline feature groups calculated information into different levels. You can then show or hide information based on its level:

- Click a minus sign button to collapse the outline for that section.
- Click a plus sign button to expand the outline for that section.
- Click one of the outline level numbers to collapse or expand the entire outline to that level.

Outline buttons & bars =SUBTOTAL(9,U2:U3)

	Product Code	Department	Resale Value
2	XFA2360	Big & Tall Men's Clothes	767.97
3	XSK288V	Big & Tall Men's Clothes	14,792.46
4		**Big & Tall Men's Clothes Total**	15,560.43
5	KDQ7450	Children's Clothes	14,367.96
6	KFX312D	Children's Clothes	91,255.63
7	KTF684J	Children's Clothes	32,977.40
8		**Children's Clothes Total**	138,600.99
9	JCU583S	Juniors Clothes	62,075.06
10	JDG360K	Juniors Clothes	55,224.88
11	JKI6610	Juniors Clothes	84,845.34
12	JN0365F	Juniors Clothes	4,627.20
13	JPC105K	Juniors Clothes	92,201.87
14		**Juniors Clothes Total**	298,974.35
15	WBL354T	Women's Clothes	51,566.55
16	WCU388F	Women's Clothes	32,486.44
17	WYS571P	Women's Clothes	43,221.31
18		**Women's Clothes Total**	127,274.30
19		**Grand Total**	580,410.67

Figure 13d. *Here's the information sorted in Figure 12d with subtotals. (Some columns are hidden to save space.)*

Figure 14 shows an outline created by the Subtotal command partially collapsed. Note how the outline buttons and bars are set to the left of the data.

Table 3. *Valid function_num values for the SUBTOTAL function.*

Number	Function Name
1	AVERAGE
2	COUNT
3	COUNTA
4	MAX
5	MIN
6	PRODUCT
7	STDEV
8	STDEVP
9	SUM
10	VAR
11	VARP

✔ Tip

- Creating outlines is beyond the scope of this book, but here's a hint to get you started if you decide to explore this feature: Use commands on the Group and Outline submenu under the Data menu to create and clear groups and outlines.

	Product Code	Department	Resale Value
2	XFA2360	Big & Tall Men's Clothes	767.97
3	XSK288V	Big & Tall Men's Clothes	14,792.46
4		**Big & Tall Men's Clothes Total**	15,560.43
8		**Children's Clothes Total**	138,600.99
9	JCU583S	Juniors Clothes	62,075.06
10	JDG360K	Juniors Clothes	55,224.88
11	JKI6610	Juniors Clothes	84,845.34
12	JN0365F	Juniors Clothes	4,627.20
13	JPC105K	Juniors Clothes	92,201.87
14		**Juniors Clothes Total**	298,974.35
18		**Women's Clothes Total**	127,274.30
19		**Grand Total**	580,410.67

Figure 14. *Here's the outline from Figure 13d partially collapsed to hide some of the detail.*

About Database Functions

Excel includes 14 database and list management functions. (SUBTOTAL, which I discussed on the previous page, is one of them.) Here are a few of the most commonly used ones, along with their syntax:

DSUM(*database,field,criteria*)
DAVERAGE(*database,field,criteria*)
DCOUNT(*database,field,criteria*)
DCOUNTA(*database,field,criteria*)
DMAX(*database,field,criteria*)
DMIN(*database,field,criteria*)

The *database* argument is the cell references for a range containing the database or list. The *field* argument is the name of the field you want to summarize. The *criteria* argument is either the data you want to match or a range containing the data you want to match.

Figure 15 shows an example of these database functions in action.

✔ Tips

- Each database function corresponds to a mathematical or statistical function and performs the same kind of calculation—but on records matching criteria only. I tell you about other functions in Chapter 5.

- You can enter database functions with the Function Wizard. I tell you how to use the Function Wizard in Chapter 5.

DSUM	580,410.07	=DSUM(A1:I251,H1,K1:L6)
DAVERAGE	44,646.93	=DAVERAGE(A1:I251,H1,K1:L6)
DCOUNT	13	=DCOUNT(A1:I251,H1,K1:L6)
DCOUNTA	13	=DCOUNTA(A1:I251,H1,K1:L6)
DMAX	92,201.87	=DMAX(A1:I251,H1,K1:L6)
DMIN	767.97	=DMIN(A1:I251,H1,K1:L6)

Figure 15. *These formulas use database functions to summarize information based on criteria. The database is the 250-record list used throughout this chapter. The field is the Department field, which is found in cell H1 of the database. The criteria range is the range illustrated in Figure 11a.*

ADVANCED FORMULA TECHNIQUES 12

About Excel's Advanced Formula Techniques

Excel's advanced formula techniques include:

	A	B	C	D	E	F	G	H
1	Drew Industries							
2	Sales Results							
3								
4		Jan	Feb	Mar	Apr	May	Jun	Total
5	Nancy	443	419	698	548	684	952	3744
6	Bess	105	268	365	459	368	751	2316
7	George	493	277	105	148	196	325	1544
8	Ned	246	358	745	359	486	843	3037
9	Total	1287	1322	1913	1514	1734	2871	10641

Figure 1. *The reference to the selected range would be a lot easier to remember if it had a name like* NancySales *rather than just* B5:G5.

=SUM('1st Qtr Results:4th Qtr Results'!E9)

	A	B
1	Total Sales	$ 24,410
2	Total Costs	9,458
3	Total Profit	$ 14,952

Figure 2. *3-D cell references make it possible to link information between worksheets or workbooks.*

- Names that let you assign easy-to-remember names to cell references (see **Figure 1**). You can then use the names in place of cell references in formulas.
- 3-D cell references that let you write formulas with links to other worksheets and workbooks (see **Figure 2**).
- Consolidations that let you summarize information from several source areas into one destination area (see **Figure 3**), with or without live links.

In Chapter 2, I tell you how to write formulas. In Chapter 3, I tell you how to copy and move formulas and I explain relative and absolute cell references. In Chapter 5, I tell you how to use functions in formulas. In this chapter, I tell you how to take what those chapters cover a step further with advanced formula techniques.

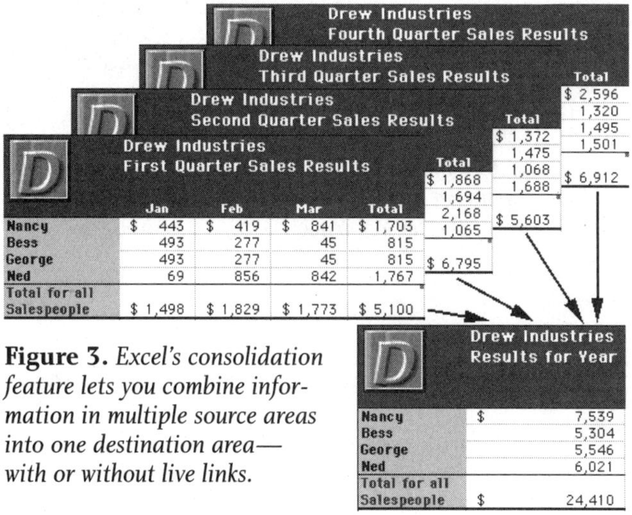

Figure 3. *Excel's consolidation feature lets you combine information in multiple source areas into one destination area—with or without live links.*

✔ Tip

- To get the most out of the information in this chapter, you should have a solid understanding of the information in Chapters 2, 3, and 5.

About Names

The trouble with using cell references in formulas is that they're difficult to remember. To make matters worse, cell references can change if cells above or to the left of them are inserted or deleted.

The Names feature of Excel eliminates both problems by letting you assign easy-to-remember names to cells in your worksheets. The names don't change, no matter how much worksheet editing you do.

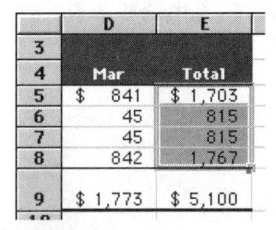

Figure 4a. *Select the cell(s) you want to name.*

Figure 4b. *The Name submenu offers a number of options for working with names.*

✔ Tips

- Names can apply to single cells or cell ranges.
- Names can be up to 255 characters long and can include letters, numbers, periods, question marks, and underscore characters (_). The first character must be a letter. Names cannot contain spaces or "look" like cell references.

To define a name

1. Select the cell(s) you want to name (see **Figure 4a**).
2. Choose Define from the Name submenu under the Insert menu (see **Figure 4b**) or press ⌘L.
3. In the Define Name dialog box (see **Figure 4c**), Excel may suggest a name in the Names in Workbook edit box. You can enter a name you prefer.
4. The cell reference in the Refers To edit box should reflect the range you selected in step 1. You can type in a new range or highlight the contents of the edit box and reselect the cell(s) in the worksheet window.
5. Click OK or press Return or Enter.

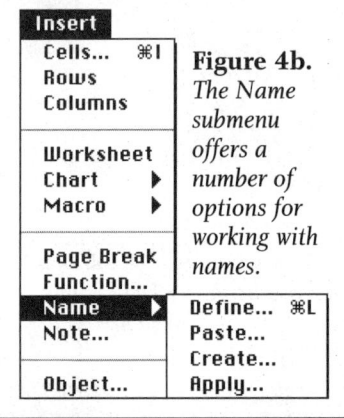

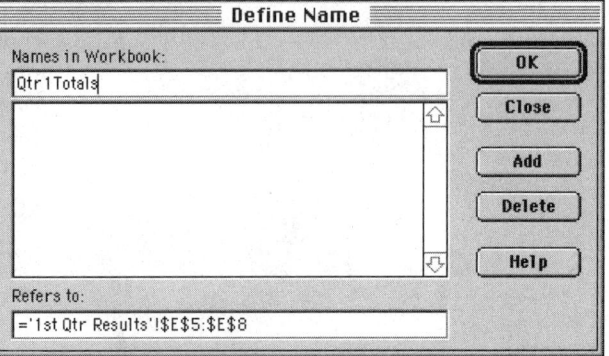

Figure 4c. *Use the Define Name dialog box to set a name for one or more cells. As you can see, the name of the worksheet is part of the cell reference.*

Advanced Formula Techniques

To create a name

1. Select the cells containing the ranges you want to name as well as text in adjoining cells that you want to use as names (see **Figure 5a**).

Figure 5a. *To use the Create Names dialog box, you must first select the cells you want to name as well as adjoining cells with text you want to use as names...*

2. Choose Create from the Name submenu under the Insert menu (see **Figure 4b**).

3. In the Create Names dialog box (see **Figure 5b**), turn on the check box(es) for the cells that contain the text you want to use as names.

Figure 5b. *...then tell Excel which cells contain the text for names.*

4. Click OK or press Return or Enter.

Excel uses the text in the cells you indicated as names for the adjoining cells. You can see the results if you open the Define Names dialog box (see **Figure 5c**).

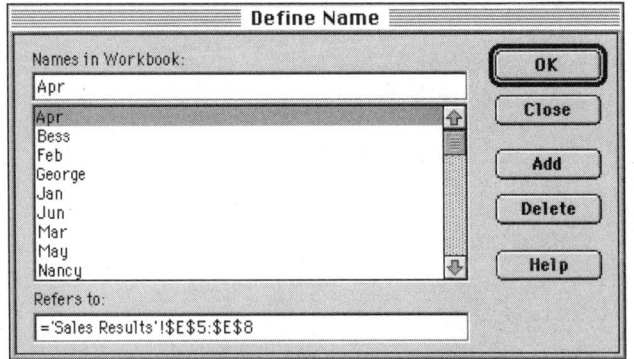

Figure 5c. *Look inside the Define Name dialog box to see how many names were added.*

✔ Tip

- This is a quick way to create a lot of names all at once.

To delete a name

1. Choose Define from the Name submenu under the Insert menu (see **Figure 4b**) or press ⌘L.

2. In the Define Name dialog box (see **Figure 5c**), select the name you want to delete from the scrolling list under Names in Workbook.

3. Click the Delete button.

4. Click OK or press Return or Enter.

✔ Tip

- Deleting a name does not delete the cells to which the name refers.

189

Chapter 12

To enter a name in a formula

1. Position the cellpointer in the cell in which you want to write the formula.
2. Type in the formula, replacing any cell reference with the corresponding name (see **Figure 6**).
3. Press Return or Enter or click the Enter button on the formula bar.

   Excel performs the calculation just as if you'd typed in a cell reference.

Figure 6. *Once a range has been named, it can be used instead of a cell reference in a formula.*

✔ Tips

- You can use the Paste Name command to enter a name for you. Follow the steps above, but when it's time to type in the name, choose Paste from the Name submenu under the Insert menu (see **Figure 4b**). Use the Paste Name dialog box that appears (see **Figure 7**) to select and paste in the name you want. The Paste Name command even works when you use the Function Wizard to write formulas. I tell you about the Function Wizard in Chapter 5.

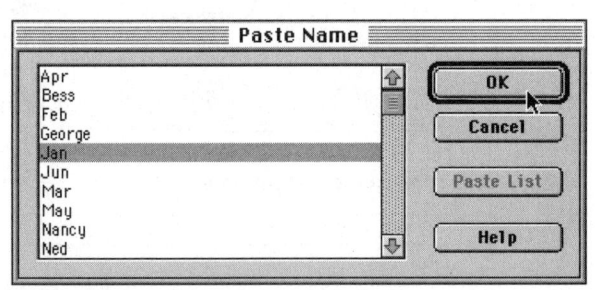

Figure 7. *Use the Paste Name dialog box to select and paste in a name.*

- When you delete a name, Excel responds with a *#NAME?* error in each cell that contains a formula referring to that name (see **Figure 8**). These formulas must be rewritten.

Figure 8. *If you delete a name used in a formula, a #NAME? error results.*

Entering Names in Formulas

190

To apply names to existing formulas

1. Select the cells containing formulas for which you want to apply names. If you want to apply names throughout the worksheet, click any single cell.
2. Choose Apply from the Name submenu under the Insert menu (see **Figure 4b**).
3. In the Apply Names dialog box (see **Figure 9a**), select the names that you want to use in place of the cell reference. To select or deselect a name, click on it.
4. Click OK or press Return or Enter.

Excel rewrites the formulas with the appropriate names from those you selected. **Figure 9b** shows an example of formulas changed by selecting the names for salespeople in **Figure 9a**.

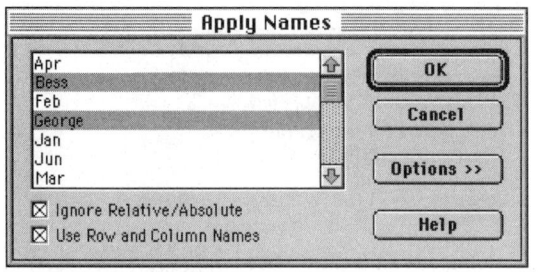

Figure 9a. *Select the names that you want to apply to formulas in your worksheet.*

	A	B	C	D	E	F	G	H
3								
4		Jan	Feb	Mar	Apr	May	Jun	Total
5	Nancy	443	419	698	548	684	952	3744
6	Bess	105	268	365	459	368	751	2316
7	George	493	277	105	148	196	325	1544
8	Ned	246	358	745	359	486	843	3037
9	Total	1287	1322	1913	1514	1734	2871	10641

Before	After
=SUM(B5:G5)	=SUM(Nancy)
=SUM(B6:G6)	=SUM(Bess)
=SUM(B7:G7)	=SUM(George)
=SUM(B8:G8)	=SUM(Ned)

Figure 9b. *Excel applies the names you selected to formulas that reference their ranges.*

✔ Tips

- If only one cell is selected, Excel applies names based on your selection(s) in the Apply Names dialog box, not the selected cell.
- If you turn off the Ignore Relative/Absolute check box in the Apply Names dialog box (see **Figure 9b**), Excel matches the type of reference. I tell you about relative and absolute references in Chapter 3.

Chapter 12

To select named cells

Use the pop-up menu on the left end of the formula bar to choose a name for the cells you want to select (see **Figure 10**).

or

1. Click the cell reference area at the far left end of the formula bar to select it.
2. Type in the name of the cells you want to select (see **Figure 11**).
3. Press Return or Enter.

or

1. Choose Go To from the Edit menu (see **Figure 12a**).

    or

    Press F5 on an extended keyboard.
2. In the Go To dialog box (see **Figure 12b**), select the name of the cells you want to select from the Go To scrolling list.
3. Click OK or press Return or Enter.

✔ Tip

■ When named cells are selected, the name appears in the cell reference area at the far left end of the formula bar.

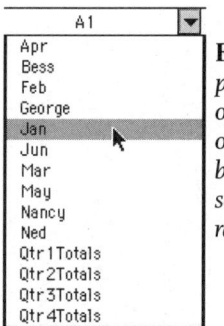

Figure 10. *A pop-up menu on the left end of the formula bar lets you select named ranges quickly.*

Figure 11. *If you prefer, you can type in a name and press Return to select it.*

Figure 12a. *Choose Go To from the Edit menu...*

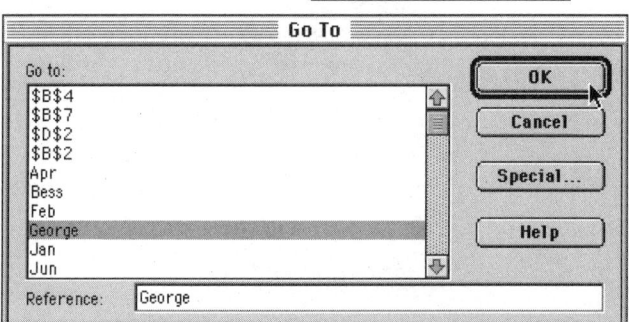

Figure 12b. *...then select the name of the cells you want to select from the Go To scrolling list.*

Advanced Formula Techniques

About 3-D References

3-D cell references let you write formulas that reference cells in other worksheets or workbooks. The links are *live*—when a cell's contents change, the results of formulas in cells that reference it change.

Excel offers several ways to write formulas with 3-D cell references:

- Use cell names. I tell you about cell names in the first part of this chapter. **Figure 13** shows an example.

- Type them in. When you type in a 3-D cell reference, you must include the name of the sheet (in single quotes, if the name contains a space), followed by an exclamation point (!) and cell reference. If the reference is for a cell in another workbook, you must also include the workbook name, in brackets. **Figures 14a**, **14b**, and **14c** show examples.

- Click on them. You'll get the same results as if you had typed the references, but Excel does all the typing for you.

- Use the Paste Special command. The Paste Link button in the Paste Special dialog box lets you paste a link between cells in different sheets of a workbook or different workbooks.

```
=SUM(Nancy,Bess,George,Ned)
```

Figure 13. *This example uses the SUM function to add the contents of the cells named* Nancy, Bess, George, *and* Ned *in the same workbook.*

```
='Results for Year'!$B$9
```

Figure 14a. *This example refers to cell B9 in a worksheet called* Results for Year *in the same workbook.*

```
=SUM('1st Qtr Results:4th Qtr Results1'!E9)
```

Figure 14b. *This example uses the SUM function to add the contents of cell E9 in worksheets starting with* 1st Qtr Results *and ending with* 4th Qtr Results *in the same workbook.*

```
='[Drew Industries Reports]1st Qtr Results'!$E$9
```

Figure 14c. *This example refers to cell E9 in a worksheet called* 1st Qtr Results *in a workbook called* Drew Industries Reports.

✔ Tips

- When you delete a cell, Excel displays a *#REF!* error in any cells that referred to it. The cells containing these errors must be revised to remove the error.

- Do not make references to an unsaved file. If you do and you close the file with the reference before saving (and naming) the file it refers to, Excel won't be able to update the link.

Understanding 3-D References

193

To reference a named cell or range in another worksheet

1. Select the cell in which you want to enter the reference.
2. Type an equal sign (=).
3. If the sheet containing the cells you want to reference is in another workbook, type the name of the workbook (within single quotes, if the name contains a space) followed by an exclamation point (!).
4. Type the name of the cell(s) you want to reference (see **Figures 15a** and **15b**).
5. Press Return or Enter or click the Enter button on the formula bar.

✔ Tip

- If the name you want to reference is in the same workbook, you can paste it in by choosing Paste from the Name submenu under the Insert menu. I tell you how to do this earlier in this chapter.

Figures 15a&b. *Two examples of 3-D references utilizing names. The first example references a name in the same workbook. The second example refers to a name in a different workbook.*

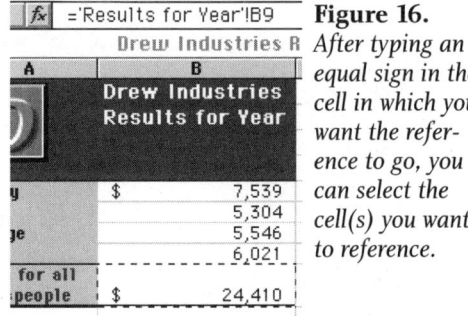

To reference a cell or range in another worksheet by clicking

1. Select the cell in which you want to enter the reference.
2. Type an equal sign (=).
3. If the sheet containing the cells you want to reference is in another workbook, switch to that workbook.
4. Click on the sheet tab for the worksheet containing the cell you want to reference.
5. Select the cell(s) you want to reference (see **Figure 16**).
6. Press Return or Enter or click the Enter button on the formula bar.

Figure 16. *After typing an equal sign in the cell in which you want the reference to go, you can select the cell(s) you want to reference.*

Advanced Formula Techniques

Figure 17a. *Choose Paste Special from the Edit menu...*

Figure 17b. *...then click the Paste Link button in the Paste Special dialog box.*

✔ Tips

- Do not press Enter after using the Paste Special command! Doing so pastes the contents of the Clipboard into the cell, overwriting the link.

- Using the Paste Link button to paste a range of cells creates a special range called an *array*. Each cell in an array shares the same cell reference and cannot be changed unless all cells in the array are changed.

To reference a cell or range in another worksheet by typing

1. Select the cell in which you want to enter the reference.
2. Type an equal sign (=).
3. If the sheet containing the cells you want to reference is in another workbook, type the name of the workbook within brackets ([ ]).
4. Type the name of the sheet followed by an exclamation point (!).
5. Type the cell reference for the cell(s) you want to reference.
6. Press Return or Enter or click the Enter button on the formula bar.

✔ Tip

- If the name of the sheet includes a space character, it must be enclosed within single quotes in the reference. See **Figures 14a**, **14b**, and **14c** for examples.

To reference a cell with the Paste Special command

1. Select the cell you want to reference.
2. Choose Copy from the Edit menu, press ⌘C, or click the Copy button on the Standard toolbar.
3. Switch to the worksheet in which you want to put the reference.
4. Select the cell in which you want the reference to go.
5. Choose Paste Special from the Edit menu (see **Figure 17a**).
6. In the Paste Special dialog box (see **Figure 17b**), click the Paste Link button.

Referencing Cells in other Worksheets

195

To write a formula with 3-D references

1. Select the cell in which you want to enter the formula.
2. Type an equal sign (=).
3. Use any combination of the following techniques until the formula is complete.
   - To enter a function, use the Function Wizard or type in the function. I tell you how to use the Function Wizard in Chapter 5.
   - To enter an operator, type it in. I tell you about using operators in Chapter 2.
   - To enter a cell reference, select the cell(s) you want to reference or type the reference in. If typing the reference, be sure to include single quotes, brackets, and exclamation points as discussed on the previous page.
4. Press Return or Enter or click the Enter button on the formula bar.

To write a formula that sums the same cell on multiple, adjacent sheets

1. Select the cell in which you want to enter the formula.
2. Type *=SUM(* (see **Figure 18a**).
3. If the cells you want to add are in another workbook, switch to that workbook.
4. Click the sheet tab for the first worksheet containing the cell you want to sum.

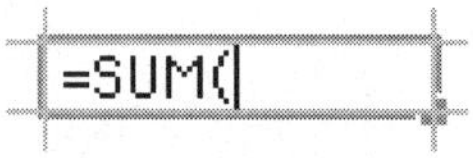

Figure 18a. *Type the beginning of a formula with the SUM function...*

Advanced Formula Techniques

Figure 18b. ...*select all of the tabs for sheets containing the cell you want to sum*...

`=SUM('1st Qtr Results:4th Qtr Results'!`

Figure 18c. ...*so the sheet names are appended as a range in the formula bar*...

Figure 18d. ...*then click on the cell you want to add*...

`=SUM('1st Qtr Results:4th Qtr Results'!E9`

Figure 18e. ...*so that its reference is appended to the formula in the formula bar.*

5. Hold down the Shift key and click on the sheet tab for the last sheet containing the cell you want to sum. All tabs from the first to the last become selected (see **Figure 18b**). The formula in the formula bar looks something like the one in **Figure 18c**.

6. Click the cell you want to sum (see **Figure 18d**). The cell reference is added to the formula (see **Figure 18e**).

7. Type).

8. Press Return or Enter or click the Enter button on the formula bar.

✔ Tips

- Use this technique to link cells of identically arranged worksheets. This results in a "3-D worksheet" effect.

- Although you can use this technique to consolidate data, the Consolidate command, which I begin discussing on the next page, automates consolidations with or without links.

About Opening Worksheets with Links

When you open a worksheet that has a link to another workbook file, a dialog box like the one in **Figure 19** appears.

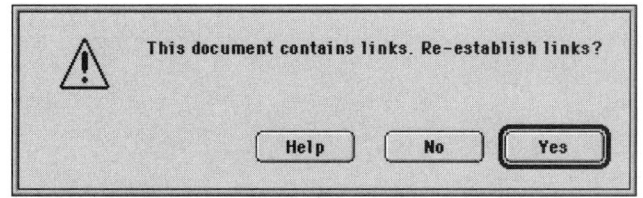

Figure 19. *This dialog box appears if you open a workbook that contains links to another workbook.*

- If you click Yes, Excel checks the other file and updates linked information. If Excel can't find the other workbook, it displays a standard Open dialog box so you can find it.

- If you click No, Excel does not check the data in the other file.

Writing Formulas with 3-D References

197

Chapter 12

About Consolidations

The Consolidate command lets you combine data from multiple sources. Excel lets you do this in two ways:

- Consolidate based on the arrangement of data. This is useful when data occupies the same number of cells in the same arrangement in multiple locations (see **Figure 3**).
- Consolidate based on identifying labels or categories. This is useful when the arrangement of data varies from one source to the next.

Excel can even create links to the source information so the consolidation changes automatically when linked data changes.

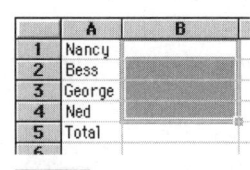

Figure 20a. Select the cells in which you want the consolidated data to go…

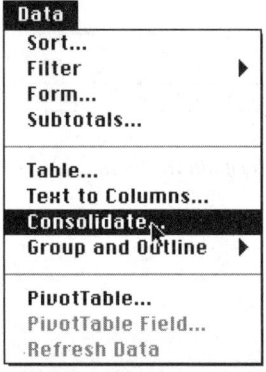

Figure 20b. …and choose Consolidate from the Data menu.

To consolidate based on the arrangement of data

1. Select the cell(s) where you want the consolidated information to go (see **Figure 20a**).
2. Choose Consolidate from the Data menu (see **Figure 20b**).
3. In the Consolidate dialog box (see **Figure 20c**), choose a function from the Function pop-up menu.
4. Switch to the worksheet containing the first cell(s) to be included in the consolidation. The reference is entered into the Reference edit box.
5. Select the cell(s) you want to include in the consolidation (see **Figure 20d**). The reference is entered into the Reference edit box.
6. Click Add.

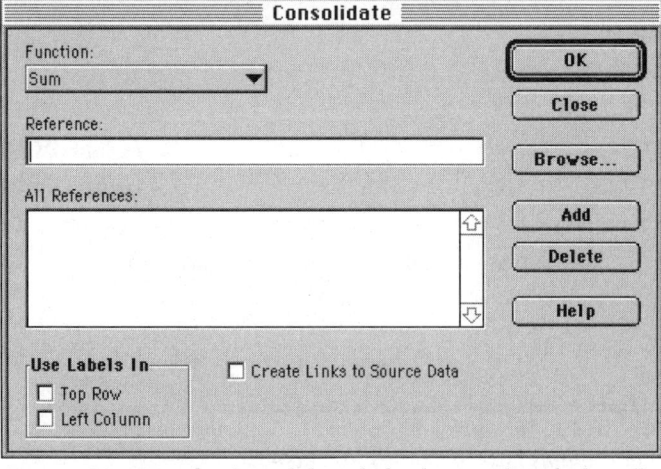

Figure 20c. Use the Consolidate dialog box to identify the cells you want to combine.

Figure 20d. Enter references for cells in the Consolidate dialog box by selecting them.

Consolidating Based on Data Arrangement

Advanced Formula Techniques

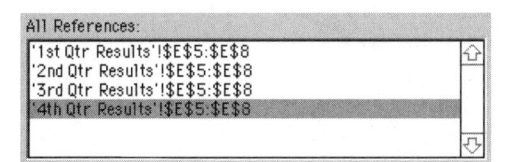

```
All References:
'1st Qtr Results'!$E$5:$E$8
'2nd Qtr Results'!$E$5:$E$8
'3rd Qtr Results'!$E$5:$E$8
'4th Qtr Results'!$E$5:$E$8
```

Figure 20e. *The cells you want to consolidate are listed in the All References area of the Consolidate dialog box.*

Figure 20f. *Excel combines the data in the cell(s) you originally selected.*

	A	B
5	Nancy	$ 7,539
10	Bess	5,304
15	George	5,546
20	Ned	6,021

7. Repeat steps 4, 5, and 6 for all cells you want to include in the consolidation. When you're finished, the All References area of the Consolidate dialog box might look something like **Figure 20e**.

8. To create links between the source data and destination cell(s), turn on the Create Links to Source Data check box.

9. Click OK or press Return or Enter.

   Excel consolidates the information in the originally selected cell(s) (see **Figure 20f**).

✔ Tips

- In order for this technique to work, each source range must have the same number of cells with data arranged in the same way.
- If the Consolidate dialog box contains references when you open it, you can clear them by selecting each one and clicking the Delete button.
- If you turn on the Create Links to Source Data check box, Excel creates an outline with links to all source cells (see **Figure 20f**). You can expand or collapse the outline by clicking the outline buttons. I tell you more about outlines in Chapter 11.

Consolidating Based on Data Arrangement

199

Chapter 12

Consolidating Based on Labels

To consolidate based on labels

1. Select the cell(s) in which you want the consolidated information to go. As shown in **Figure 21a**, you can select just a single starting cell.
2. Choose Consolidate from the Data menu (see **Figure 20b**).
3. In the Consolidate dialog box (see **Figure 20c**), choose a function from the Function pop-up menu.
4. Switch to the worksheet containing the first cell(s) to be included in the consolidation. The reference is entered into the Reference edit box.
5. Select the cell(s) you want to include in the consolidation, including any text that identifies data (see **Figure 21b**). The text must be in cells adjacent to the data. The reference is entered into the Reference edit box.
6. Click Add.
7. Repeat steps 4, 5, and 6 for all cells you want to include in the consolidation. **Figures 21c** and **21d** show the other two ranges included for the example. When you're finished, the Consolidate dialog box might look something like **Figure 21e**.
8. Turn on the appropriate check box(es) in the Use Labels In area to tell Excel where identifying labels for the data are.
9. Click OK or press Return or Enter.

   Excel consolidates the information in the originally selected cell(s) (see **Figure 21f**).

Figure 21a. *Select the destination cell(s).*

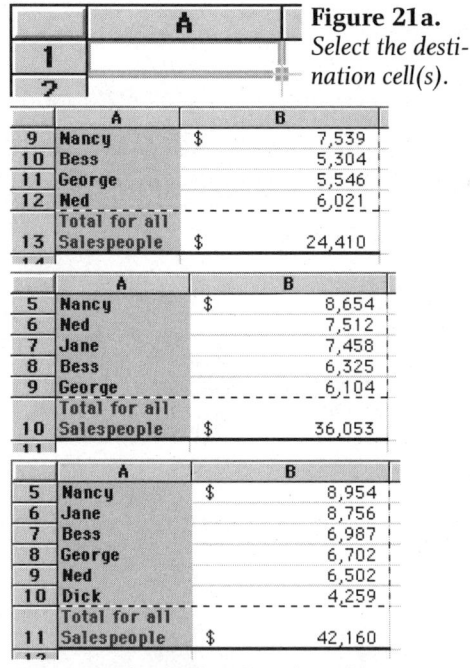

Figure 21b,c,&d. *Select the cell(s) you want to include in the consolidation.*

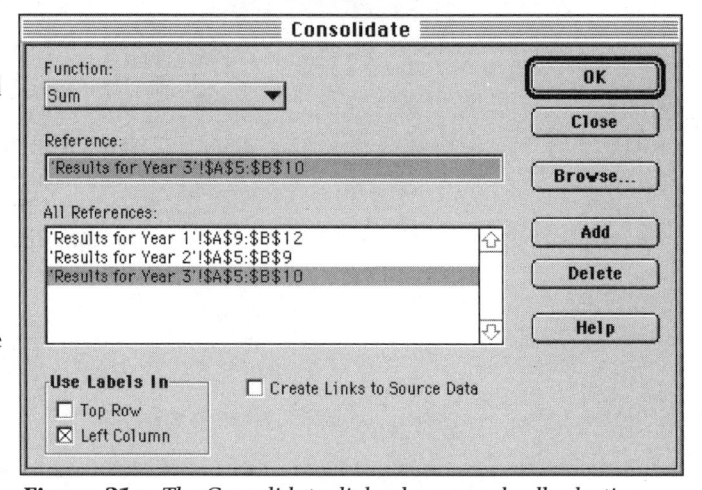

Figure 21e. *The Consolidate dialog box records all selections.*

Figure 21f. *The final consolidation accounts for all data.*

200

ADD-INS & MACROS   13

About Add-ins

An add-in is a special kind of file that, when installed, adds features to Excel. Excel comes with more than a dozen add-ins.

While many add-ins provide advanced features for Excel "power users," some add-ins provide basic features that any Excel user can benefit from. In this chapter, I tell you about three add-ins I think are useful: AutoSave, View Manager, and Report Manager.

Figure 1a. *Choose Add-Ins from the Tools menu.*

✔ Tips

- Once installed, an add-in is fully integrated with the Excel program. It may add a menu command to one of Excel's menus or a function to the Function Wizard dialog box.

- The add-ins available for installation and use depend on the way Excel was installed on your Macintosh. For example, if you performed a "Typical" installation, only the Crosstab sheet function add-in will be available. You can see what add-ins are available by choosing Add-Ins from the Tools menu (see **Figure 1a**) and checking the Add-Ins Available scrolling list (see **Figure 1b**). If the add-in you want to use is not one of those listed, you'll have to use Excel's Setup Program to add it. I tell you how on the next page.

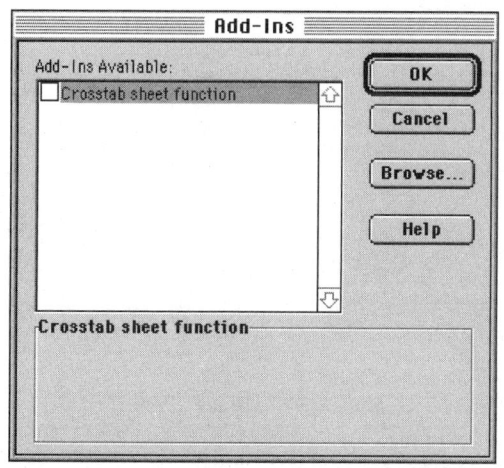

Figure 1b. *The Add-Ins dialog box displays a list of all available add-ins.*

Understanding Add-ins

201

Chapter 13

To add add-in files with Setup

1. If Excel is running, choose Quit from the File menu.
2. In the Finder, locate the Microsoft Excel Setup icon (it should be in the Microsoft Excel 5 folder) or the Microsoft Office Setup icon (it should be in the Microsoft Office folder) and double-click it. This launches the Setup program.
3. In the main Setup window (see **Figure 2a**), click the Add/Remove button.
4. In the scrolling list on the left side of the Maintenance Installation window (see **Figure 2b**), click the triangle beside the Microsoft Excel and Add-ins options to display their sub-items. Turn on only the check boxes for the add-ins you want to use. (You may have to turn check boxes off.)
5. Click Continue.
6. Insert disks as prompted by the Setup program (**Figure 2c**).
7. When the Successful Installation dialog box appears, click the Quit or Restart button. (The button that appears depends on what add-ins you added.)

The add-ins you added will now appear in the Add-Ins dialog box in Excel (see **Figure 3**).

Figure 2a. *The main Setup window lets you tell Setup what you want to do.*

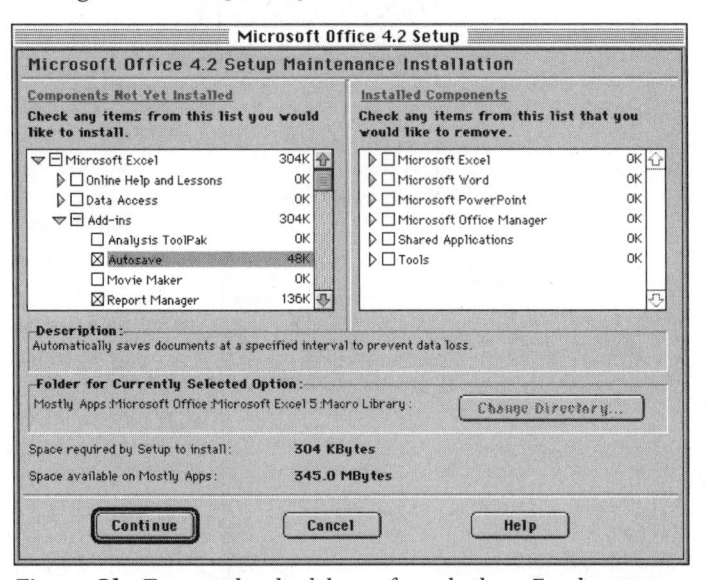

Figure 2b. *Turn on the check boxes for only those Excel components you want to install.*

Figure 2c. *Insert disks as prompted.*

Add-ins & Macros

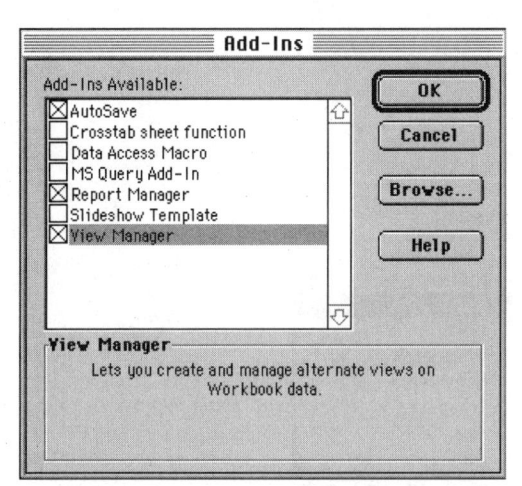

Figure 3. *Turn on the check box(es) for add-in(s) you want to install and turn off the check box(es) for add-in(s) you want to remove.*

To install add-ins

1. Choose Add-Ins from the Tools menu (see **Figure 1a**).
2. In the Add-Ins dialog box (see **Figure 3**), turn on the check box(es) for the add-in(s) you want to install.
3. Click OK or press Return or Enter.

✔ Tips

- If you're not sure what an add-in does, in step 2, click the add-in name to select it. The name and a description appears at the bottom of the dialog box (see **Figure 3**).
- Add-ins remain installed until you remove them.

To remove add-ins

1. Choose Add-Ins from the Tools menu (see **Figure 1a**).
2. In the Add-Ins dialog box (see **Figure 3**), turn off the check box(es) for the add-in(s) you want to remove.
3. Click OK or press Return or Enter.

✔ Tips

- Add-ins you remove are not disabled until you quit Excel. Once removed, they remain removed until you install them again.
- The more add-ins you install, the more RAM Excel requires to operate.

Installing and Removing Add-ins

Chapter 13

Using AutoSave

About AutoSave

The AutoSave add-in, when installed and activated, automatically saves your work at a time interval you specify. This is especially useful for people who can't remember to save their Excel documents periodically as they work.

To use AutoSave

1. Install the AutoSave add-in as discussed on the previous page.
2. Pull down the Tools menu. You'll see a new command named AutoSave (see **Figure 4a**). A check mark beside it indicates that it is turned on. Choose the AutoSave command to configure the add-in.
3. In the AutoSave dialog box (see **Figure 4b**), make sure the check box beside Automatic Save is turned on. Then enter the number of minutes you want Excel to wait before each save in the Minutes edit box beside it.
4. Under Save Options, select the appropriate radio button to tell Excel whether it should save just the active workbook or all open workbooks.
5. If you want Excel to display a dialog box like the one in **Figure 4c** before it saves a workbook, turn on the check box beside Prompt Before Saving.
6. Click OK or press Return or Enter to accept your settings.

✔ Tip

- The settings you enter in the AutoSave dialog box (see **Figure 4b**) remain in effect until you change them or remove the AutoSave add-in.

Figure 4a. *The AutoSave add-in puts an AutoSave command under the Tools menu when installed.*

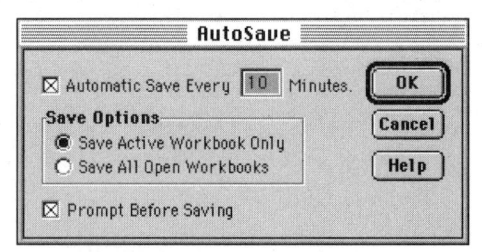

Figure 4b. *The AutoSave dialog box lets you set options for the automatic saving of workbooks.*

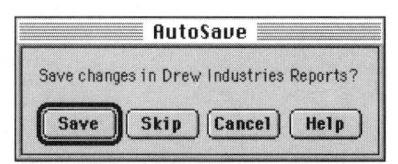

Figure 4c. *If you want to, you can have Excel display a dialog box like this before it automatically saves a workbook.*

Add-ins & Macros

Figure 5a. *Create a view you'd like to save…*

About View Manager

The View Manager add-in lets you create several *views* of a workbook file. A view includes the window size and position, the active cell, the zoom percentage, and most Page Setup and Options dialog box settings. Once you've set up a view, you can choose it from a dialog box to see it quickly.

Figure 5b. *…choose View Manager from the View menu…*

✔ Tip

- Views are stored for each sheet in a workbook. That means the View Manager dialog box will only display the views for the active sheet.

To add a view with View Manager

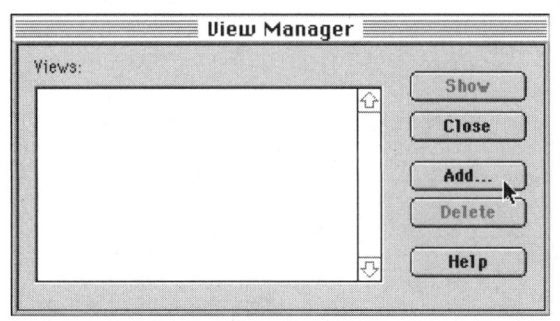

Figure 5c. *…click Add in the View Manager dialog box…*

1. Install the View Manager add-in as discussed earlier in this chapter.
2. Create the view you want to save. **Figure 5a** shows an example.
3. Choose View Manager from the View menu (see **Figure 5b**). (This command only appears when the View Manager add-in is installed.)
4. In the View Manager dialog box (see **Figure 5c**), click the Add button.
5. In the Add View dialog box (see **Figure 5d**), enter a name for the view in the Name edit box.
6. Turn on the appropriate check boxes if you want the view to include all current Print Settings and Hidden Rows & Columns.
7. Click OK or press Return or Enter.
8. Repeat steps 2 through 7 for all of the views you want to create.

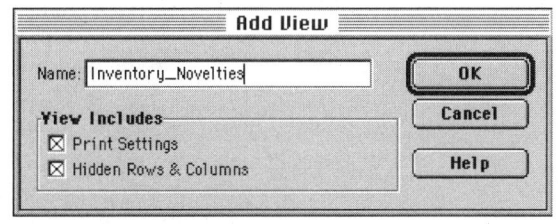

Figure 5d. *…then enter a name and set options for the view and click OK.*

Adding Views with View Manager

205

Chapter 13

To switch to a view with View Manager

1. Switch to the sheet containing the view you want to see.
2. Choose View Manager from the View menu (see **Figure 5a**).
3. In the View Manager dialog box (see **Figure 6**), select the view you want to see from the Views scrolling list.
4. Click Show or press Return or Enter.

   Excel changes the sheet so it looks just like it did when you created the view.

To delete a view

1. Switch to the sheet containing the view you want to delete.
2. Choose View Manager from the View menu (see **Figure 5a**).
3. In the View Manager dialog box (see **Figure 6**), select the view you want to delete from the Views scrolling list.
4. Click Delete.
5. In the confirmation dialog box that appears (see **Figure 7**), click OK.
6. Repeat steps 3 through 5 for each view you want to delete.
7. Click Close to dismiss the View Manager dialog box.

Figure 6. *To see or delete a view, select the name of the view in the View Manager dialog box, then click Show or Delete.*

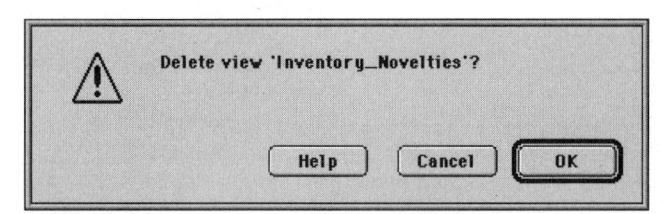

Figure 7. *Excel lets you confirm that you really do want to delete a view.*

✔ Tip

- Deleting a view does not delete the information contained in the view. It simply removes the reference to the information from the View Manager.

206

Add-ins & Macros

Figure 8a. *Choose Print Report from the File menu...*

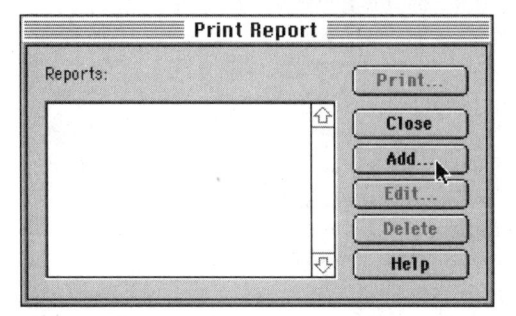

Figure 8b. *...click Add in the Print Report dialog box...*

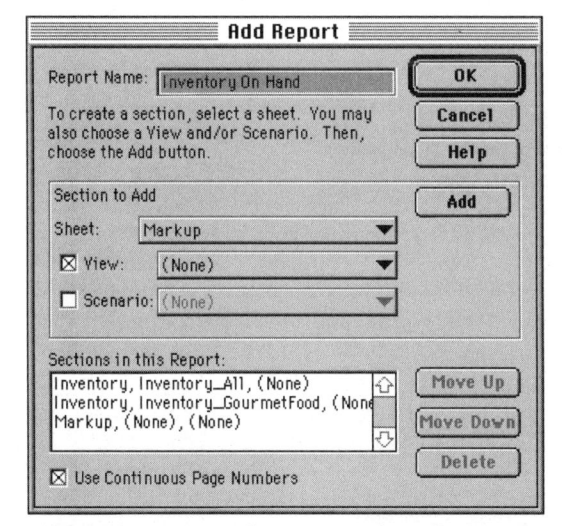

Figure 8c. *...name the report and use the pop-up menus and Add button to add sections to it.*

About Report Manager

With the Report Manager add-in, you can automate the printing of reports. Set up reports with sections that include different sheets, views, and scenarios, then choose a report when it's time to print.

✔ Tips

- To get the most out of Report Manager, use View Manager to set up views that include Page Setup options for report sections you want to print.
- Excel's Scenarios feature changes cell contents as you specify to show different results. To explore this advanced feature on your own, choose Scenarios from the Tools menu.

To add a report with Report Manager

1. Install the Report Manager add-in as discussed earlier in this chapter.
2. Choose Print Report from the File menu (see **Figure 8a**). (This command only appears when the Report Manager add-in is installed.)
3. In the Print Report dialog box (see **Figure 8b**), click the Add button.
4. In the Add Report dialog box (see **Figure 8c**), enter a name for the report in the Report Name edit box.
5. Use the pop-up menus in the Section to Add area to select the Sheet, View, and Scenario for a report section. Then click Add. The information is added to the Sections in this Report scrolling list (see **Figure 8c**).
6. Repeat step 5 for each section of the report.
7. If desired, turn on the Use Continuous Page Numbers check box.
8. Click OK or press Return or Enter.

Adding Reports with Report Manager

207

Chapter 13

To print a report with Report Manager

1. Choose Print Report from the File menu (see **Figure 8a**).
2. In the Print Report dialog box (see **Figure 9a**), select the report you want to print from the Reports scrolling list.
3. Click Print or press Return or Enter.
4. A tiny Print dialog box like the one in **Figure 9b** appears. Enter the number of copies you want to print and click OK or press Return or Enter.

   Excel begins sending report sections to the printer. The mouse pointer turns into a watch cursor while it works. When the watch cursor turns back into a regular Excel pointer, you can continue working with Excel.

Figure 9a. *Select the report you want to print from the Reports scrolling list.*

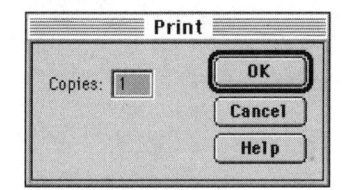

Figure 9b. *Enter the number of copies you want to print and click OK.*

To delete a report

1. Choose Print Report from the File menu (see **Figure 8a**).
2. In the Print Report dialog box (see **Figure 9a**), select the report you want to delete from the Reports scrolling list.
3. Click Delete.
4. In the confirmation dialog box that appears (see **Figure 10**), click OK.
5. Repeat steps 2 through 4 for each view you want to delete.
6. Click Close to dismiss the Print Report dialog box.

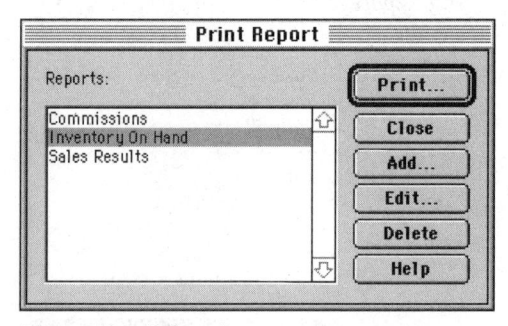

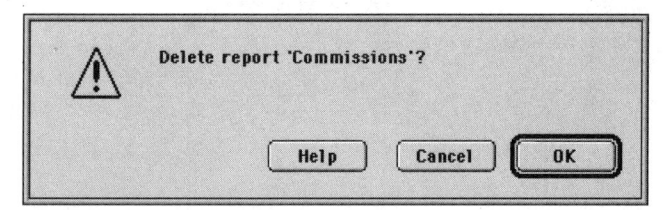

Figure 10. *Excel lets you confirm that you really do want to delete the report.*

✔ Tip

- Deleting a report does not delete sheet data. It simply removes the report information from the Report Manager.

208

About Macros

A macro is a series of commands that Excel can perform automatically. You can create simple macros to automate repetitive tasks, like entering data or formatting cells.

Although macros are stored as Visual Basic modules, you don't need to be a Visual Basic programmer to create them. Excel's Macro Recorder will record your keystrokes, menu choices, and dialog box settings as you make them and will write the programming code for you. This makes macros useful for all Excel users, even raw beginners.

To record a macro with the Macro Recorder

1. Choose Record New Macro from the Record Macro submenu under the Tools menu (see **Figure 11a**).

2. In the Record New Macro dialog box (see **Figure 11b**), enter a name for the macro in the Macro Name edit box. If desired, you can also edit the description automatically entered in the Description edit box.

3. Click OK.

4. Perform all the steps you want to include in your macro. Excel records them all—even the mistakes—so be careful!

5. When you're finished recording macro steps, click the Stop button on the tiny Stop toolbar (see **Figure 11c**).

Figure 11a. *Choose Record New Macro from the Record Macro submenu under the Tools menu...*

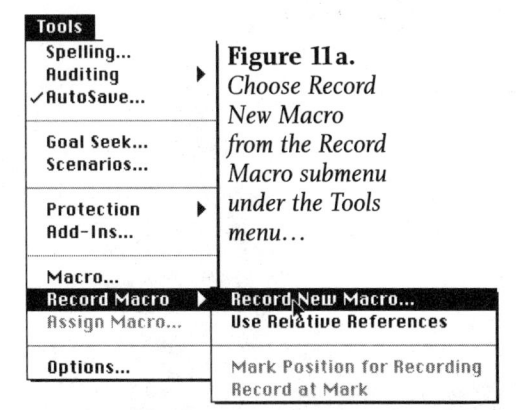

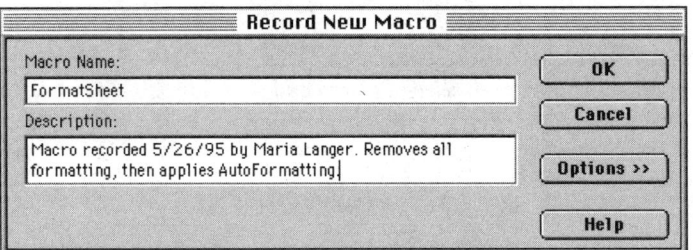

Figure 11b. *...enter a macro name and description in the Record New Macro dialog box, and click OK.*

Figure 11c. *When you're finished recording your macro, click the Stop Macro button on the Stop Macro toolbar.*

Chapter 13

To run a macro

1. Choose Macro from the Tools menu (see **Figure 12a**).
2. In the Macro dialog box (see **Figure 12b**), select the macro you want to run from the scrolling list.
3. Click Run.

   Excel performs each macro step, just the way you recorded it.

✔ Tips

- Save your workbook before running a macro for the first time. You may be surprised by the results and need to revert the file to the way it was before you ran the macro.

- Excel stores each macro in a module sheet at the end of the workbook. View a macro by clicking the tab for its sheet (see **Figure 13**). You can edit a module to change the way it works.

- More advanced uses of macros include the creation of custom functions and applications that work within Excel. Add-ins, which I discuss earlier in this chapter, are just complex macros.

Figure 12a. *Choose Macro from the Tools menu...*

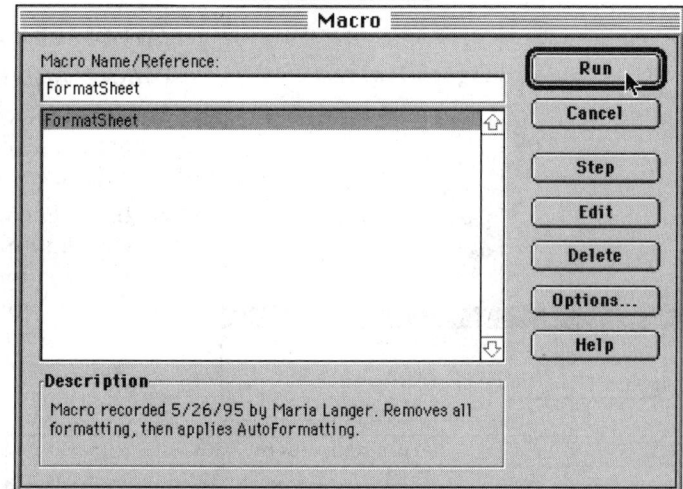

Figure 12b. *...then select a macro and click Run.*

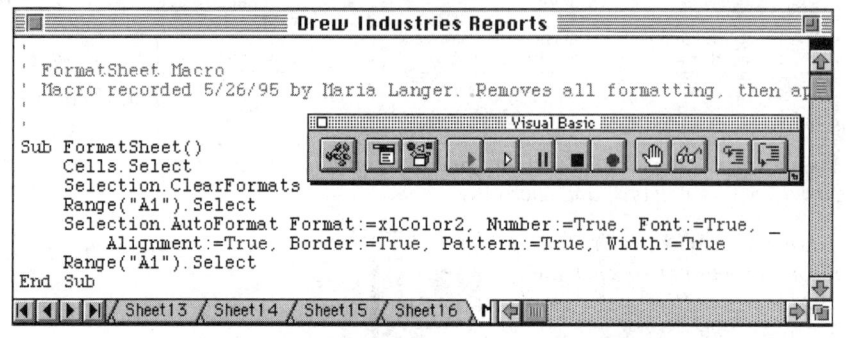

Figure 13. *This Visual Basic Module sheet changes cell formatting.*

210

CUSTOMIZING EXCEL 14

About Customization

Excel offers a number of ways to customize the way it looks and works:

- Changing general options like your name, the default font, and whether Excel should display a list of recently opened files on the File menu.

- Modifying editing options to enable or disable editing features.

- Changing display options to show or hide gridlines, column and row headings, formulas, and other elements (see **Figure 1**).

Figure 1. *In this example, display options were changed to hide gridlines and sheet tabs and display formulas instead of values.*

- Turning automatic recalculation on or off.

- Creating custom AutoFill lists (see **Figures 2a** and **2b**).

Figure 2a&b. *With a custom list, you can use the fill handle to enter any list of data.*

- Customizing existing toolbars or creating your own from scratch (see **Figure 3**).

In this chapter, I tell you how to make all of these customization changes so Excel looks and works the way you want it to.

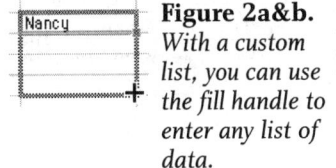

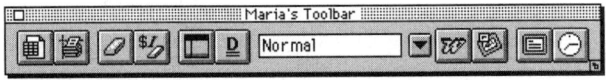

Figure 3. *You can create a custom toolbar with buttons for commands you like to keep handy.*

Understanding Customization

211

Chapter 14

Changing General Options

About General Options

The options available under the General tab of the Options dialog box (see **Figure 4b**), control basic Excel settings. Here's a list of the ones you'll find most useful:

- Recently Used File List displays a list of the four most recently opened files under the File menu.

- Prompt for Summary Info displays the Summary Info dialog box the first time you save a file.

- Sheets in New Workbook lets you change the default number of worksheets in new workbooks you create.

- Standard Font and Size let you change the default font and font size used in worksheets.

- User Name lets you change the default user name that appears in various places when you work with Excel.

To change General options

1. Choose Options from the Tools menu (see **Figure 4a**).

2. In the Options dialog box, click the General tab to display its options (see **Figure 4b**).

3. Make changes as desired to options.

4. Click OK or press Return or Enter to accept your changes.

Figure 4a. *To display the Options dialog box, choose Options from the Tools menu.*

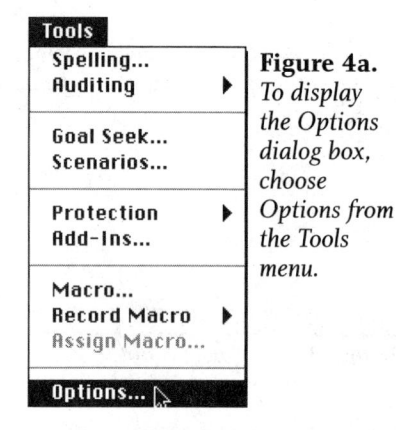

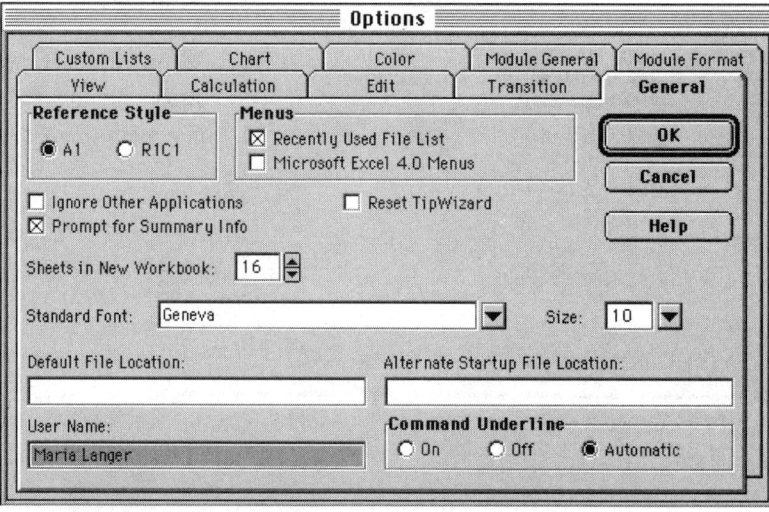

Figure 4b. *The General tab of the Options dialog box.*

212

Customizing Excel

About Editing Options

The options available under the Edit tab of the Options dialog box (see **Figure 5**), let you turn certain editing features on or off. Here's what each option does:

- Edit Directly in Cell controls whether you can edit the contents of a cell by double-clicking it.

- Allow Cell Drag and Drop controls whether you can move or copy cells by dragging them to another location.

- Alert before Overwriting Cells controls whether Excel warns you about overwriting a cell's contents when you drag another cell on top of it.

- Move Selection after Return controls whether Excel moves the cell pointer to the next cell when you press Return.

- Fixed Decimal lets you set a fixed number of decimal places for all numbers that are entered or calculated.

- Cut, Copy, and Sort Objects with Cells controls whether objects stay with cells when you cut, copy, or sort the cells.

- Ask to Update Automatic Links controls whether Excel asks you about updating links to other documents when you open a document with links.

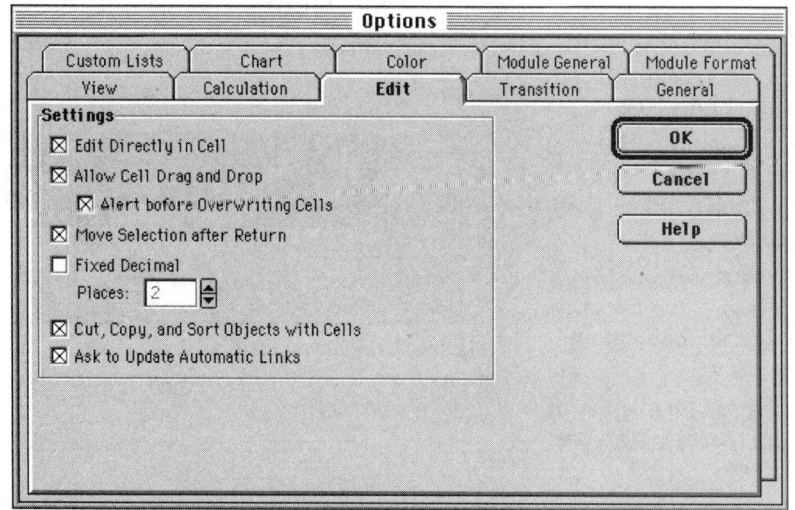

Figure 5. *The Edit tab of the Options dialog box.*

To change Editing options

1. Choose Options from the Tools menu (see **Figure 4a**).
2. In the Options dialog box, click the Edit tab to display its options (see **Figure 5**).
3. Make changes as desired to options.
4. Click OK or press Return or Enter to accept your changes.

213

Chapter 14

About View Options

The options available under the View tab of the Options dialog box (see **Figure 9**), control what is displayed in Excel windows. Here's what each option does:

- The four Show options let you toggle the display of the Formula Bar, Status Bar, Note Indicator, and Info Window (see **Figure 6**).
- The Objects radio buttons specify how Excel displays objects. Placeholders show only boxes the size of the objects that would appear (see **Figure 7**).
- Automatic Page Breaks lets you toggle the display of dashed lines at automatic page breaks.
- Formulas lets you switch between displaying formula results (the default) in cells or formulas (see **Figure 1**).
- Gridlines lets you toggle the display of gridlines (see **Figure 1**). The Color pop-up menu (see **Figure 8**) lets you select a gridline color.
- Row & Column Headers toggles the display of the letters and numbers that appear at the top of each column and the left side of each row.
- Outline Symbols toggles the display of outline buttons and bars when an outline appears on screen.
- Zero Values toggles the display of 0s in cells. When turned off, any cell containing the value 0 appears empty.
- Horizontal Scroll Bar and Vertical Scroll Bar toggle the display of scroll bars on the right side or bottom of the window.
- Sheet Tabs toggles the display of sheet tabs at the bottom of the window (see **Figure 1**).

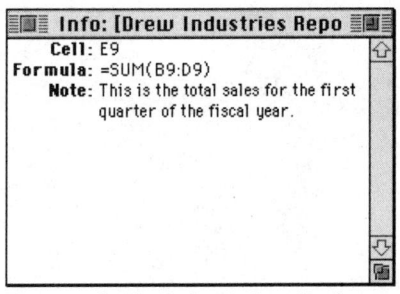

Figure 6. *The Info window displays the cell reference, contents, and note for the active cell.*

Figure 7. *When you display placeholders rather than actual objects, only gray boxes are displayed on screen.*

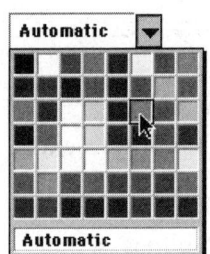

Figure 8. *Change the color of the gridlines with the Color pop-up menu.*

Customizing Excel

✔ Tips

- Displaying only placeholders in a worksheet containing graphics can speed up the scrolling and displaying of windows by reducing the amount of detail that must be drawn on screen.
- To help troubleshoot a complex worksheet, use the View options to display formulas and check your cell references.
- When you print a worksheet that has formulas displayed, the formulas print.

To change View options

1. Choose Options from the Tools menu (see **Figure 4a**).
2. In the Options dialog box, click the View tab to display its options (see **Figure 9**).
3. Make changes as desired to options.
4. Click OK or press Return or Enter to accept your changes.

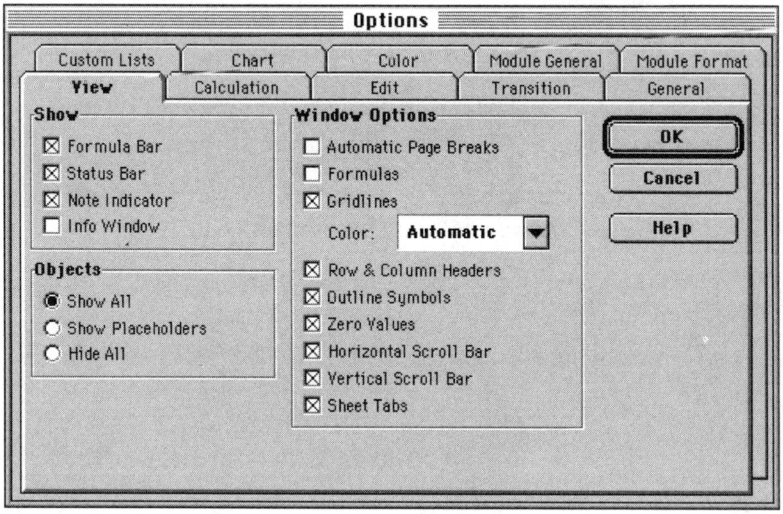

Figure 9. *The View tab of the Options dialog box.*

215

Chapter 14

Changing Calculation Options

About Calculation Options

The options available under the Calculation tab of the Options dialog box (see **Figure 10**) control the way Excel calculates formulas. Of these options, the Calculation area radio buttons, which set calculation frequency, are the most useful:

- Automatic, which is the default, tells Excel to recalculate each time you enter or change information.

- Automatic Except Tables calculates all formulas automatically except those in data tables.

- Manual calculates only when you click the Calculate Now button in the Options dialog box or press ⌘=. When you select Manual, you can turn on the Recalculate before Save check box to ensure that worksheets are completely recalculated before being saved.

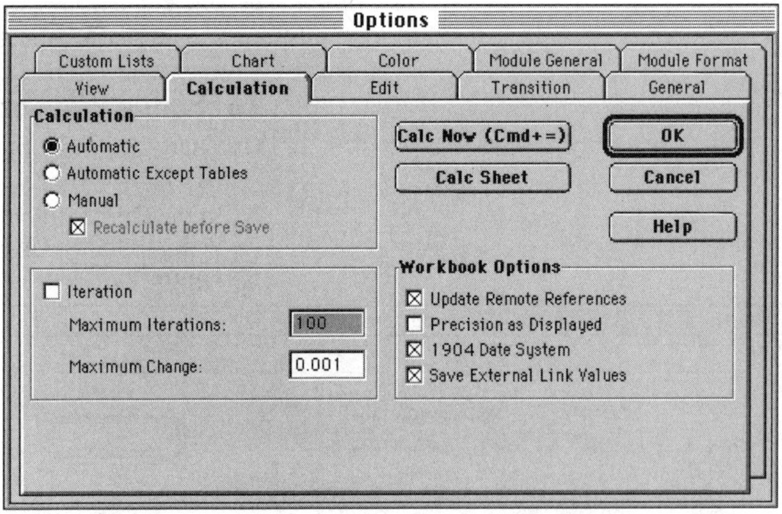

Figure 10. *The Calculation tab of the Options dialog box.*

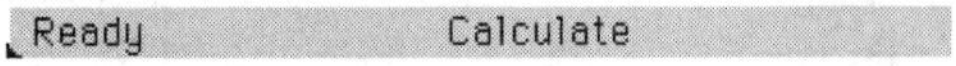

Figure 11. *If you set Calculation to Manual, Excel reminds you to recalculate by putting the word* Calculate *in the status bar.*

✔ Tips

- If a worksheet has not been calculated but needs to be, a Calculate reminder message appears in the status bar at the bottom of the screen (see **Figure 11**).

- If your worksheet is long and complex, selecting Manual calculation could make it faster to work with by reducing the frequency of recalculations.

To change Calculation options

1. Choose Options from the Tools menu (see **Figure 4a**).

2. In the Options dialog box, click the Calculation tab to display its options (see **Figure 10**).

3. Make changes as desired to options.

4. Click OK or press Return or Enter to accept your changes.

Customizing Excel

About Custom Lists

The custom list feature of Excel lets you create your own lists of information to be entered with the AutoFill handle (see **Figures 2a** and **2b**) or Series command. (I discuss AutoFill and the Series command in Chapter 3.) This can considerably speed up data entry when you're creating a worksheet.

To create a custom list

1. Choose Options from the Tools menu (see **Figure 4a**).
2. In the Options dialog box, click the Custom Lists tab to display its options (see **Figure 12**).
3. With *NEW LIST* selected in the Custom Lists scrolling list, enter each value you want in your list in the List Entries scrolling list. Be sure to press Return after each entry to separate them.
4. Click the Add button.
5. Repeat steps 2 through 4 for each list you want to create.
6. Click OK.

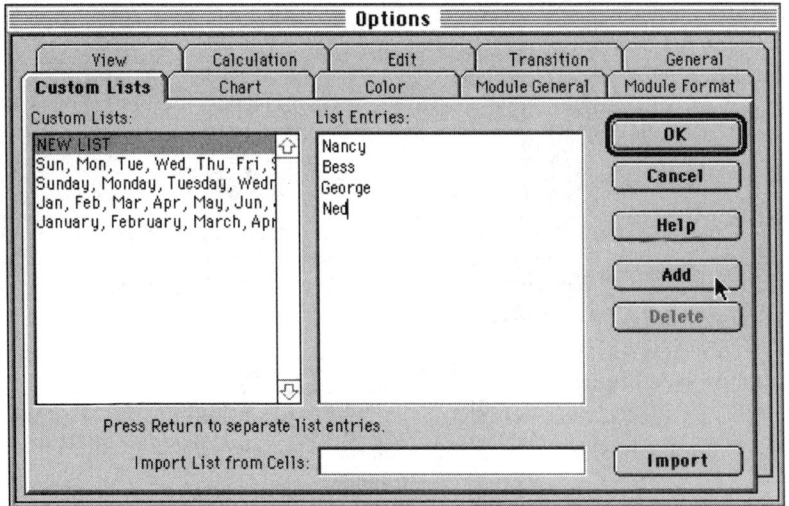

Figure 12. *The Custom Lists tab of the Options dialog box.*

✔ Tips

- If the list has already been entered into a worksheet, enter the cell references for the cells containing the list in the Import List from Cells edit box in step 3. Then click Import instead of Add in step 4.
- To delete a custom list, select it from the Custom Lists scrolling list and click the Delete button. Then click OK in the confirmation dialog box that appears.

217

Chapter 14

About Toolbars

Excel has a variety of toolbars, each with its own collection of buttons. You can show or hide toolbars, change the way their buttons look, move them around your screen, and customize them.

Figure 13a. *Choose Toolbars from the View menu.*

To show or hide toolbars

1. Choose Toolbars from the View menu (see **Figure 13a**).
2. In the Toolbars dialog box (see **Figure 13b**), turn on the check box for the name of a toolbar you want to show or turn off the check box for the name of a toolbar you want to hide.
3. Click OK or press Return or Enter.

or

1. Position the mouse pointer on any part of the toolbar.
2. Hold down the Control key while pressing the mouse button down to display the Toolbars shortcut menu (see **Figure 14**).
3. Choose the toolbar you want to show or hide.

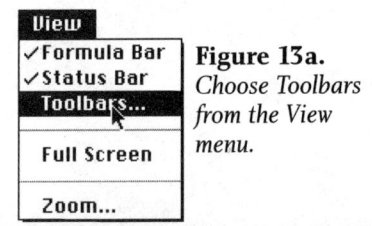

Figure 13b. *Use the Toolbars dialog box to show, hide, customize, or create new toolbars.*

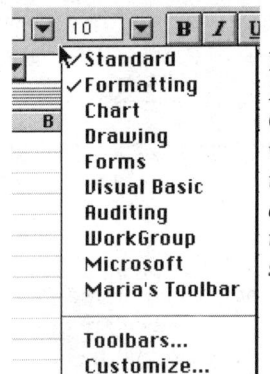

Figure 14. *Hold down the Control key while clicking in the gray toolbar area to display the Toolbar shortcut menu.*

✔ Tips

- If a toolbar is floating, you can hide it by clicking its close box. I tell you about floating toolbars on the next page.
- Turn on the Large Buttons check box in the Toolbars dialog box to increase the size of the buttons (see **Figure 15**).
- Toggle the ToolTips feature on or off by clicking the Show ToolTips check box in the Toolbars dialog box.

Figure 15. *A standard size button and a large button, shown at actual size.*

Showing & Hiding Toolbars

218

Customizing Excel

Figure 16. *A floating toolbar appears on top of a window and can be moved or resized.*

Figure 17a. *Position the mouse pointer on the toolbar's size box...*

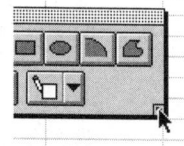

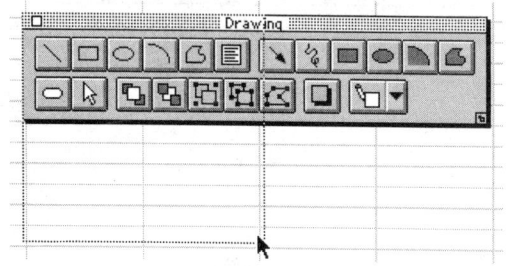

Figure 17b. *...press the mouse button down and drag.*

Figure 17c. *When you release the mouse button, the toolbar is resized and reshaped.*

Docked vs. floating toolbars

Toolbars can be *docked* or *floating*. Docked toolbars appear along the edge of the window, like the Standard and Formatting toolbars. Floating toolbars appear in separate, moveable windows on top of the main window (see **Figure 16**). Floating toolbars can be moved or resized.

To move a toolbar

1. Position the mouse pointer on any part of the toolbar that is not a button.
2. Press your mouse button down, and drag.

✔ Tips

- If the toolbar is docked, you can move it anywhere within the window to float it.
- If the toolbar is floating, you can move it against any side of the window to dock it.

To resize a floating toolbar

1. Position the mouse pointer on the toolbar's size box (see **Figure 17a**).
2. Press the mouse button down and drag to change its size and shape (see **Figure 17b**). You'll find that you're restricted to sizes that display all of the buttons.
3. When you release the mouse button, the toolbar resizes and reshapes itself (see **Figure 17c**).

Moving & Resizing Toolbars

Chapter 14

To customize a toolbar

1. Choose Toolbars from the View menu (see **Figure 13a**).

2. In the Toolbars dialog box (see **Figure 13b**), make sure the check box beside the toolbar you want to customize is turned on. (The toolbar must be displayed to customize it.) Then click the Customize button.

3. To add a button to a toolbar, in the Customize dialog box (see **Figure 18**), select a toolbar button category from the Categories scrolling list. Then drag the button you want to add to the toolbar from the Buttons area of the dialog box to the toolbar. When you release the button, it's added to the toolbar.

4. To remove a button from a toolbar, drag the button off of the toolbar. When you release it, it disappears.

5. To change a toolbar button's position, drag it to a new position on the toolbar.

6. When you're finished making changes to the toolbar(s), click the Close button or press Return or Enter.

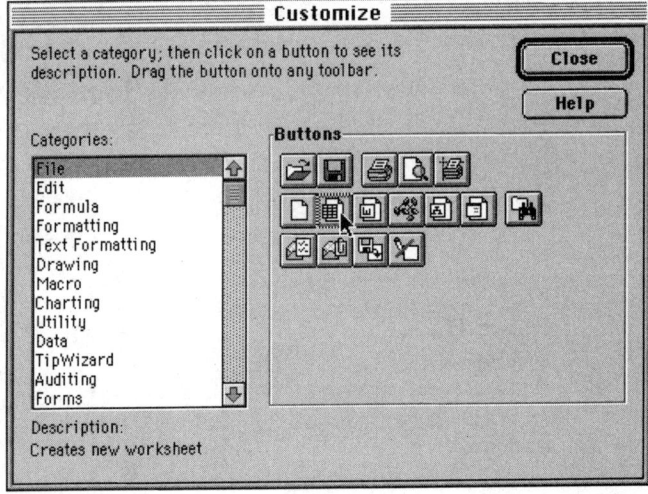

Figure 18. *Use the Customize dialog box to add or remove toolbar buttons.*

✔ Tip

- To find out what a button does, click it while the Customize dialog box is open. A description of the button appears at the bottom of the dialog box (see **Figure 18**).

Customizing Excel

To reset a toolbar

1. Choose Toolbars from the View menu (see **Figure 13a**).
2. In the Toolbars dialog box (see **Figure 13b**), select the toolbar you want to reset from the Toolbars scrolling list.
3. Click Reset. The toolbar is restored to its "factory defaults."

✔ Tip

- You can only reset Excel's toolbars, not ones you create from scratch.

To create a toolbar

1. Choose Toolbars from the View menu (see **Figure 13a**).
2. In the Toolbars dialog box (see **Figure 13b**), type the name of your new toolbar in the Toolbar Name edit box (see **Figure 19a**).
3. Click New. A tiny, empty, floating toolbar appears (see **Figure 19b**).
4. In the Customize dialog box (see **Figure 18**), select a toolbar button category from the Categories scrolling list. Then drag the button you want to add to the toolbar from the Buttons area of the dialog box to the toolbar. When you release the button, it's added to the toolbar (see **Figure 19c**).
5. Repeat step 4 until the toolbar contains all of the buttons you want.
6. Click the Close button in the Customize dialog box or press Return or Enter.

Figure 19a. *Enter a name for the toolbar you want to create.*

Figure 19b. *A newborn toolbar.*

Figure 19c. *Drag buttons onto the toolbar to build it.*

✔ Tips

- Once a toolbar has been created, it appears in the Toolbars scrolling list inside the Toolbars dialog box (see **Figure 13b**) and on the Toolbars shortcut menu (see **Figure 14**).
- You customize a toolbar that you created from scratch just as you would customize any other toolbar.

Resetting & Creating Toolbars

221

Chapter 14

To delete a toolbar

1. Choose Toolbars from the View menu (see **Figure 13a**).
2. In the Toolbars dialog box (see **Figure 13b**), select the toolbar you want to delete from the Toolbars scrolling list.
3. Click Delete.
4. In the confirmation dialog box that appears (see **Figure 20**), click OK.

✔ Tip

- You can only delete toolbars you created. Excel's built-in toolbars cannot be deleted.

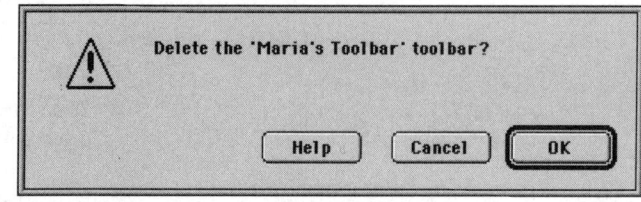

Figure 20. *Excel asks you to confirm that you really do want to delete the toolbar.*

SHORTCUT KEYS A

About Shortcut Keys

This appendix provides a list of shortcut keys for Excel menu commands and tasks. To use a shortcut key, hold down the modifier key(s) while pressing the shortcut key. Using shortcut keys is discussed in Chapter 1.

Modifier Keys

⌘	Command Key
⇧	Shift Key
⌥	Option Key
⌃	Control Key
Left	Left Arrow
Right	Right Arrow
Up	Up Arrow
Down	Down Arrow

File Menu Commands

⌘N	New
⌘O	Open
⌘F12	Open
⌘W	Close
⌘F4	Close
⌘S	Save
⇧F12	Save
F12	Save As
⌘P	Print
⌘⇧F12	Print
⌘Q	Quit

File

New	⌘N
Open...	⌘O
Close	⌘W
Save	⌘S
Save As...	
Save Workspace...	
Find File...	
Summary Info...	
Page Setup...	
Print Preview	
Print...	⌘P
1 Misc. Reports	
2 Inventory	
3 Financial Functions	
4 Drew Industries Financials	
Quit	⌘Q

223

Appendix A

Edit Menu Commands

⌘Z	Undo
F1	Undo
⌘Y	Repeat
⌘X	Cut
F2	Cut
⌘C	Copy
F3	Copy
⌘V	Paste
F4	Paste
⌘⇧V	Paste Special
⌘⇧C	Copy Picture
⌘D	Fill Down
⌘R	Fill Right
⌘B	Clear Contents (worksheet)
Del	Clear Contents (worksheet)
⌘B	Clear All (chart sheet)
Del	Clear All (chart sheet)
⌘K	Delete (row, column, or cells)
⌘F	Find
⌘H	Replace
⌥G	Go To
F5	Go To

View Menu Commands

| ⌘7 | Toggles Standard Toolbar |

Insert Menu Commands

⌘I	Cells
⇧F11	Worksheet
F11	Chart Sheet
⌘F11	MS Excel 4.0 Macro Sheet
⇧F3	Function
⌘L	Define Name
⌘F3	Define Name
⌘⇧F3	Create Names
⌘⇧N	Note
⇧F2	Note

224

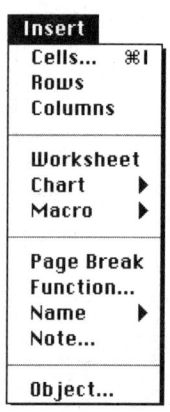

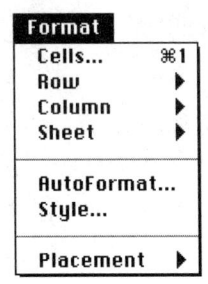

Format Menu Commands

⌘1	Cells
⌃⇧~	Apply General Number Format
⌃⇧$	Apply Currency Style
⌃⇧%	Apply Percent Style
⌃⇧!	Apply Comma Style
⌃⇧^	Apply Exponential Number Format
⌃⇧#	Apply Date Format
⌃⇧@	Apply Time Format
⌘⇧P	Apply Plain Text
⌘⇧B	Toggle Bold
⌘⇧I	Toggle Italic
⌘⇧U	Toggle Underline
⌘⇧_	Toggle Strikethrough
⌘⇧D	Toggle Outline Style
⌘⇧W	Toggle Shadow
⌘⌥Left	Toggle Left Border
⌘⌥Right	Toggle Right Border
⌘⌥Up	Toggle Top Border
⌘⌥Down	Toggle Bottom Border
⌘⌥0	Apply Outline Border
⌘⌥-	Remove All Borders
⌃9	Hide Rows
⌃⇧(	Unhide Rows
⌃0	Hide Columns
⌃⇧)	Unhide Columns
⌘⇧L	Style

Appendix A

Tools Menu Commands

F7	Spelling
⌘F2	Toggle Info Window
⌘⇧=	Calculate Now (All Sheets)
F9	Calculate Now (All Sheets)
⇧F9	Calculate Now (Active Sheet)
⌘6	Toggles Object Display
⌘`	Toggles Formula Display

Data Menu Commands

| ⌘⇧K | Group |
| ⌘⇧J | Ungroup |

Window Menu Commands

⌘F6	Next Window
⌘M	Next Window
⌥Tab	Next Window
⌘⇧F6	Previous Window
⌘⇧M	Previous Window
⌥⇧Tab	Previous Window
F6	Next Pane
⇧F6	Previous Pane

Help Commands

Help	Help Contents
⌘/	Help Contents
⇧Help	Context Sensitive Help
⇧F1	Context Sensitive Help

Application Menu Commands

| ⌘Tab | Activates QuickSwitch (if Microsoft Office Manager is installed and QuickSwitch is enabled) |

Tools
Spelling...
Auditing ▶

Goal Seek...
Scenarios...

Protection ▶
Add-Ins...

Macro...
Record Macro ▶
Assign Macro...

Options...

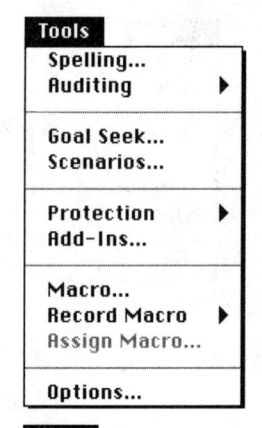

Data
Sort...
Filter ▶
Form...
Subtotals...

Table...
Text to Columns...
Consolidate...
Group and Outline ▶

PivotTable...
PivotTable Field...
Refresh Data

Window
New Window
Arrange...
Hide
Unhide...

Split
Freeze Panes
Show Clipboard

✓1 Financial Functions
2 Drew Industries Financials
3 Drawing Examples
4 Workbook1

Shortcut Keys

Movement Keys

Home	Moves to beginning of row
⌘Home	Moves to cell A1
⌘End	Moves to last cell in worksheet containing data
Up	Moves one cell up
Down	Moves one cell down
Left	Moves one cell left
Right	Moves one cell right
Page Up	Moves one screen up
Page Down	Moves one screen down
⌥Page Up	Moves one screen left
⌥Page Down	Moves one screen right
⌘Page Up	Moves to previous sheet
⌘Page Down	Moves to next sheet
⌘Up	Moves to top edge of data region
⌘Down	Moves to bottom edge of data region
⌘Left	Moves to left edge of data region
⌘Right	Moves to right edge of data region
Tab	Moves through unlocked cells in protected worksheet
⌘Delete	Moves to display active cell
Return	Moves from top to bottom in selection
⇧Return	Moves from bottom to top in selection
Tab	Moves from left to right in selection
⇧Tab	Moves from right to left in selection
⌘⇧A	Moves clockwise to next corner of selection
⌥Left	Moves to previous workbook tab
⌥Right	Moves to next workbook tab

Selection Keys

⌘A	Selects entire worksheet
⌘A	With an object selected, selects all objects on sheet
⌘⇧Spacebar	Selects entire worksheet
⌘⇧Spacebar	With an object selected, selects all objects on sheet
⌘Spacebar	Selects entire column
⇧Spacebar	Selects entire row
⇧Home	Extends selection to beginning of row
⇧Page Up	Extends selection up one screen
⇧Page Down	Extends selection down one screen
⌘⇧End	Extends selection to last cell in worksheet
⇧Delete	Collapses selection to active cell
⌥⇧*	Selects the current region
⌘⇧O	Selects cells that contain a note
⌥/	Selects the current cell's array
⌘[	Selects cells directly referred to by formulas in the selection
⌘⇧{	Selects cells directly or indirectly referred to by formulas in the selection
⌘]	Selects cells with formulas that refer directly to the active cell
⌘⇧}	Selects cells with formulas that refer directly or indirectly to the active cell

227

Appendix A

Data Entry & Editing Keys

⌘U	Activates the active cell
=	Starts a formula
⌘T	Toggles cell references between relative, absolute, and mixed
⌘-	Enters the date
⌘;	Enters the time
⌘⇧"	Copies the value in the cell above the current cell to the current cell
⌘'	Copies the formula in the cell above the current cell to the current cell
⌃A	After typing a valid function name in a formula, displays the function wizard
⌃⇧A	After typing a valid function name in a formula, inserts argument names for function
⌘⇧T	Inserts AutoSum formula
Delete	Activates and clears the selected cell
Delete	Deletes previous character in the active cell
Del	Clears the selection
Del	Deletes the next character in the active cell
⌃⌥Del	Deletes text to the end of the line
Enter	Completes an entry
Return	Completes an entry and moves to the next cell in the column or range
Tab	Completes an entry and moves to the next cell in the row or range
⇧Tab	Completes an entry and moves to the previous cell in the row or range
⌘.	Cancels an entry
Esc	Cancels an entry

Dialog Box Keys

⌃Tab	Selects next tab
⌘Page Down	Selects next tab
⌃⇧Tab	Selects previous tab
⌘Page up	Selects previous tab
letter key	Moves to the next item beginning with that letter in an active list
⌘letter key	Selects the item beginning with that underlined letter
⌥Down	Displays an active pop-up list
Esc	Collapses a displayed pop-up list
Return	"Clicks" the default button
Enter	"Clicks" the default button
Esc	"Clicks" the Cancel button
⌘.	"Clicks" the Cancel button

Edit Box Keys

Home	Moves to the beginning of the entry
End	Moves to the end of the entry
⇧Home	Selects from the insertion point to the beginning of the entry
⇧End	Selects from the insertion point to the end of the entry
⇧Left	Selects the character to the left of the insertion point
⇧Right	Selects the character to the right of the insertion point.

TOOLBARS B

About Toolbars

Excel has many toolbars, some of which appear automatically as you work. I tell you how to use toolbars in Chapter 1 and how to customize them in Chapter 14. I tell you about toolbar buttons thoughout this book. In this appendix, I illustrate and label the four toolbars you'll see most often.

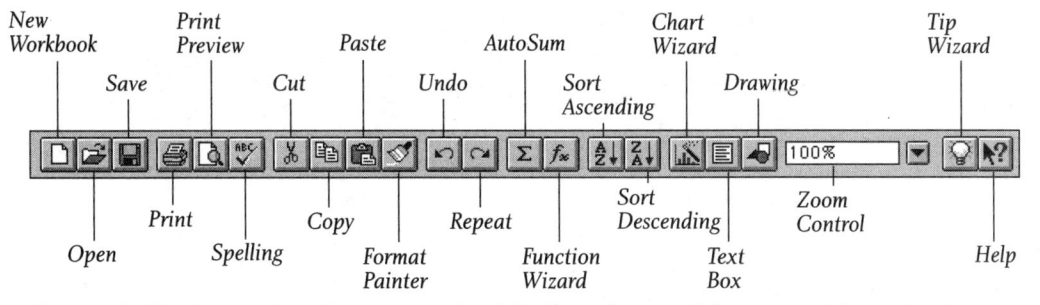

Figure 1. *The Standard toolbar appears, by default, at the top of the screen, right under the menu bar.*

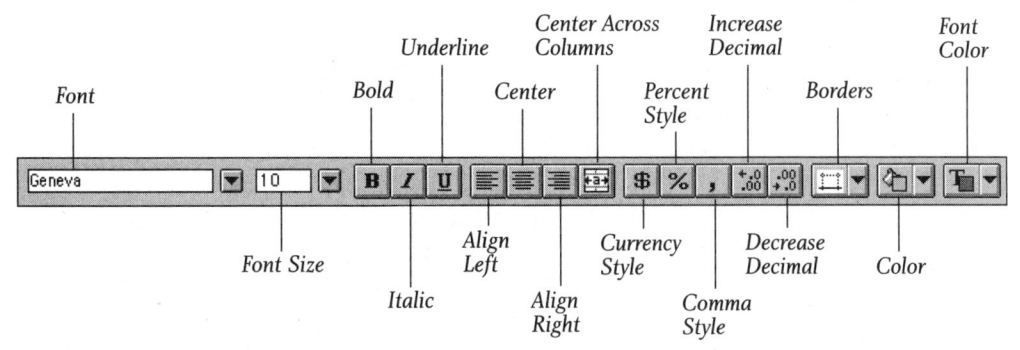

Figure 2. *The Formatting toolbar appears, by default, at the top of the screen, right under the Standard toolbar.*

Standard & Formatting Toolbars

229

Appendix B

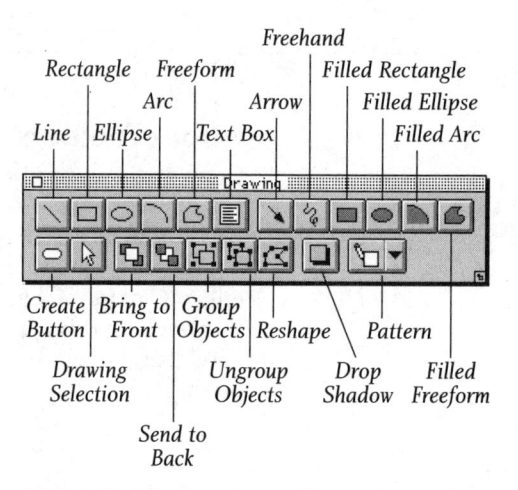

Rectangle Freeform Freehand Filled Rectangle
Arc Arrow Filled Ellipse
Line Ellipse Text Box Filled Arc

Create Button | Bring to Front | Group Objects | Reshape | Pattern
Drawing Selection | Ungroup Objects | Drop Shadow | Filled Freeform
Send to Back

Figure 3. *The Drawing toolbar appears when you click the Drawing button on the Standard toolbar. By default, it's a floating toolbar. See Chapter 7 for details.*

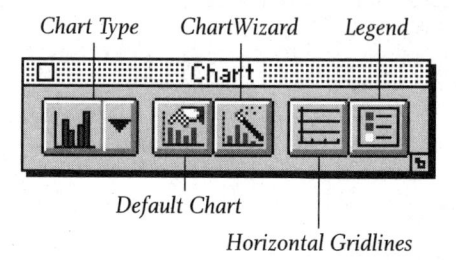

Chart Type   ChartWizard   Legend

Default Chart
Horizontal Gridlines

Figure 4. *The Chart toolbar appears when you switch to a chart sheet or click on an embedded chart. By default, it's a floating toolbar. See Chapter 9 for details.*

FUNCTIONS C

About Functions

Functions are predefined formulas for making specific kinds of calculations. Functions make it quicker and easier to write formulas. I tell you about functions in Chapter 5. In this appendix, I provide a complete list of every Excel 5 function, along with its arguments and a brief description of what it does.

Math & Trig Functions

ABS(number)	Returns the absolute value of a number.
ACOS(number)	Returns the arccosine of a number.
ACOSH(number)	Returns the inverse hyperbolic cosine of a number.
ASIN(number)	Returns the arcsine of a number.
ASINH(number)	Returns the inverse hyperbolic sine of a number.
ATAN(number)	Returns the arctangent of a number.
ATAN2(x_num,y_num)	Returns the arctangent from x- and y-coordinates.
ATANH(number)	Returns the inverse hyperbolic tangent of a number.
CEILING(number,significance)	Rounds a number to the nearest whole number or to the nearest multiple of significance.
COMBIN(number,number_chosen)	Returns the number of combinations for a given number of objects.
COS(number)	Returns the cosine of a number.
COSH(number)	Returns the hyperbolic cosine of a number.
COUNTBLANK(range)	Counts the number of blank cells within a range.
COUNTIF(range,criteria)	Counts the number of non-blank cells within a range which meet the given criteria.
DEGREES(angle)	Converts radians to degrees.
EVEN(number)	Rounds a number up to the nearest even whole number.
EXP(number)	Returns *e* raised to the power of a given number.
FACT(number)	Returns the factorial of a number.
FLOOR(number, significance)	Rounds a number down, toward 0.

Appendix C

INT(number)	Rounds a number down to the nearest whole number.
LN(number)	Returns the natural logarithm of a number.
LOG(number,base)	Returns the logarithm of a number to a specified base.
LOG10(number)	Returns the base-10 logarithm of a number.
MDETERM(array)	Returns the matrix determinant of an array.
MINVERSE(array)	Returns the matrix inverse of an array.
MMULT(array1,array2)	Returns the matrix product of two arrays.
MOD(number,divisor)	Returns the remainder from division.
ODD(number)	Rounds a number up to the nearest odd whole number.
PI()	Returns the value of pi.
POWER(number,power)	Returns the result of a number raised to a power.
PRODUCT(number 1,number2,...)	Multiplies its arguments
RADIANS(angle)	Converts degrees to radians.
RAND()	Returns a random number between 0 and 1.
ROMAN(number,form)	Converts an Arabic numeral to a Roman numeral, as text.
ROUND(number,num_digits)	Rounds a number to a specified number of digits.
ROUNDDOWN(number,num_digits)	Rounds a number down, toward 0.
ROUNDUP(number,num_digits)	Rounds a number up, away from 0.
SIGN(number)	Returns the sign of a number.
SIN(number)	Returns the sine of a number.
SINH(number)	Returns the hyperbolic sine of a number.
SQRT(number)	Returns a positive square root.
SUBTOTAL(function_num,ref1,...)	Returns a subtotal in a list or database.
SUM(number1,number2,...)	Adds its arguments.
SUMIF(range,criteria, sum_range)	Adds the cells specified by a given criteria.
SUMPRODUCT(array1,array2,array3,...)	Returns the sum of the products of corresponding array components.
SUMSQ(number1,number2,...)	Returns the sum of the squares of its arguments.
SUMX2MY2(array_x,array_y)	Returns the sum of the difference of squares of corresponding values in two arrays.
SUMX2PY2(array_x,array_y)	Returns the sum of the sum of squares of corresponding values in two arrays.
SUMXMY2(array_x,array_y)	Returns the sum of squares of differences of corresponding values in two arrays.
TAN(number)	Returns the tangent of a number.
TANH(number)	Returns the hyperbolic tangent of a number.
TRUNC(number,num_digits)	Truncates a number to a whole number.

Math & Trig Functions

Statistical Functions

Function	Description
AVEDEV(number1,number2,...)	Returns the average of the absolute deviations of data points from their mean.
AVERAGE(number1,number2,...)	Returns the average of its arguments.
BETADIST(x,alpha,beta,A,B)	Returns the cumulative beta probability density function.
BETAINV(probability,alpha,beta,A,B)	Returns the inverse of the cumulative beta probability density function.
BINOMDIST(number_s,trials,probability_s,cumulative)	Returns the individual term binomial distribution probability.
CHIDIST(x,degrees_freedom)	Returns the one-tailed probability of the chi-squared distribution.
CHIINV(probability,degrees_freedom)	Returns the inverse of the one-tailed probability of the chi-squared distribution.
CHITEST(actual_range,expected_range)	Returns the test for independence.
CONFIDENCE(alpha,standard_dev,size)	Returns the confidence interval for a population mean.
CORREL(array1,array2)	Returns the correlation coefficient between two data sets.
COUNT(value1,value2,...)	Counts how many numbers are in the list of arguments.
COUNTA(value2,value2,...)	Counts how many values are in the list of arguments.
COVAR(array1,array2)	Returns covariance, the average of the products of paired deviations.
CRITBINOM(trials,probability_s,alpha)	Returns the smallest value for which the cumulative binomial distribution is greater than or equal to a criterian value.
DEVSQ(number1,number2,...)	Returns the sum of squares of deviations.
EXPONDIST(x,lambda,cumulative)	Returns the exponential distribution.
FDIST(x,degrees_freedom1,degrees_freedom2)	Returns the F probability distribution.
FINV(probability,degrees_freedom1,degrees_freedom2)	Returns the inverse of the F probability distribution.
FISHER(x)	Returns the Fisher transformation.
FISHERINV(y)	Returns the inverse of the Fisher transformation.
FORECAST(x,known_y's,known_x's)	Returns a value along a linear trend.
FREQUENCY(data_array,bins_array)	Returns a frequency distribution as a vertical array.

Appendix C

FTEST(array1,array2)	Returns the result of an F-test.
GAMMADIST(x,alpha,beta,cumulative)	Returns the gamma distribution.
GAMMAINV(probability,alpha,beta)	Returns the inverse of the gamma cumulative distribution.
GAMMALN(x)	Returns the natural logarithm of the gamma function.
GEOMEAN(number1,number2,...)	Returns the geometric mean.
GROWTH(knowy_y's,known_x's,new_x's,const)	Returns values along an exponential trend.
HARMEAN(number1,number2,...)	Returns the harmonic mean.
HYPGEOMDIST(sample_s,number_sample,population_s,...)	Returns the hypergeometric distribution.
INTERCEPT(known_y's,known_x's)	Returns the intercept of the linear regression line.
KURT(number1,number2,...)	Returns the kurtosis of a data set.
LARGE(array,k)	Returns the k-th largest value in a data set.
LINEST(known_y's,known_x's,const,stats)	Returns the parameters of a linear trend.
LOGEST(known_y's,known_x's,const,stats)	Returns the parameters of an exponential trend.
LOGINV(probability,mean,standard_dev)	Returns the inverse of the lognormal distribution.
LOGNORMDIST(x,mean,standard_dev)	Returns the cumulative lognormal distribution.
MAX(number1,number2,...)	Returns the maximum value in a list of arguments.
MEDIAN(number1,number2,...)	Returns the median of the given numbers.
MIN(number1,number2,...)	Returns the minimum value in a list of arguments.
MODE(number1,number2,...)	Returns the most common value in a data set.
NEGBINOMDIST(number_f,number_s,probability_s)	Returns the negative binomial distribution.
NORMDIST(x,mean,standard_dev,cumulative)	Returns the normal cumulative distribution.
NORMINV(probability,mean,standard_dev)	Returns the inverse of the normal cumulative distribution.
NORMSDIST(z)	Returns the standard normal cumulative distribution.
NORSINV(probability)	Returns the inverse of the standard normal cumulative distribution.
PEARSON(array1,array2)	Returns the Pearson product moment correlation coefficient.

Statistical Functions

Statistical Functions

Function	Description
PERCENTILE(array,k)	Returns the k-th percentile of values in a range.
PERCENTRANK(array,x,significance)	Returns the percentage rank of a value in a data set.
PERMUT(number,number_chosen)	Returns the number of permutations for a given number of objects.
POISSON(x,mean,cumulative)	Returns the Poisson distribution.
PROB(x_range,prob_range,lower_limit,upper_limit)	Returns the probability that values in a range are between two limits.
QUARTILE(array,quart)	Returns the quartile of a data set.
RANK(number,ref,order)	Returns the rank of a number in a list of numbers.
RSQ(known_y's,known_x's)	Returns the square of the Pearson product moment correlation coefficient. If you know what that means, I hope you're making a lot of money.
SKEW(number1,number2,...)	Returns the skewness of a distribution.
SLOPE(known_y's,known_x's)	Returns the slope of the linear regression line.
SMALL(array,k)	Returns the k-th smallest value in a data set.
STANDARDIZE(x,mean,standard_dev)	Returns a normalized value.
STDEV(number1,number2,...)	Estimates standard deviation based on a sample.
STDEVP(number1,number2,...)	Calculates standard deviation based on the entire population.
STEYX(known_y's,known_x's)	Returns the standard error of the predicted y-value for each x in the regression.
TDIST(x,degrees_freedom,tails)	Returns the Student's t-distribution.
TINV(probability,degrees_freedom)	Returns the inverse of the Student's t-distribution.
TREND(known_y's,known_x's,new_x's,const)	Returns values along a linear trend.
TRIMMEAN(array,percent)	Returns the mean of the interior of a data set.
TTEST(array1,array2,tails,type)	Returns the probability associated with a Student's t-test.
VAR(number1,number2,...)	Estimates variance based on a sample.
VARP(number1,number2,...)	Calculates variance based on the entire population.
WEIBULL(x,alpha,beta,cumulative)	Returns the Weibull distribution.
ZTEST(array,x,sigma)	Returns the two-tailed P-value of a z-test. Really.

Appendix C

Financial Functions

DB(cost,salvage,life,period,month)	Returns the depreciation of an asset for a specified period using the fixed-declining balance method.
DDB(cost,salvage,life,period,factor)	Returns the depreciation of an asset for a specified period using the double-declining balance method of some other method you specify.
FV(rate,nper,pmt,pv,type)	Returns the future value of an investment.
IPMT(rate,per,nper,pv,fv,type)	Returns the interest payment for an investment for a given period.
IRR(values,guess)	Returns the internal rate of return for a series of cash flows.
MIRR(values,finance_rate,reinvest_rate)	Returns the internal rate of return where positive and negative cash flows are financed at different rates.
NPER(rate,pmt,pv,fv,type)	Returns the number of periods for an investment.
NPV(rate,value1,value2,...)	Returns the net present value of an investment based on a series of periodic cash flows and a discount rate.
PMT(rate,nper,pv,fv,type)	Returns the period payment for an annuity.
PPMT(rate,per,nper,pv,fv,type)	Returns the payment on the principal for an investment for a given period.
PV(rate,nper,pmt,fv,type)	Returns the present value of an investment.
RATE(nper,pmt,pv,fv,type,guess)	Returns the interest rate per period of an annuity.
SLN(cost,salvage,life)	Returns the straight-line depreciation of an asset for one period.
SYD(cost,salvage,life,per)	Returns the sum-of-years'-digits depreciation of an asset for a specified period.
VDB(cost,salvage,life,start_period,end_period,factor,...)	Returns the depreciation of an asset for a specified or partial period using a declining balance method.

Logical Functions

AND(logical1,logical2,...)	Returns TRUE if all of its arguments are TRUE.
FALSE()	Returns the logical value FALSE.
IF(logical_test,value_if_true,value_if_false)	Specifies a logical test to perform and the value to return based on a TRUE or FALSE result.
NOT(logical)	Reverses the logic of its argument.
OR(logical1,logical2,...)	Returns TRUE if any argument is TRUE.
TRUE()	Returns the logical value TRUE.

Lookup & Reference Functions

ADDRESS(row_num,column_num,abs_num,a1,sheet_text)
    Returns a reference as text to a single cell in a worksheet.

AREAS(reference)   Returns the number of areas in a reference.

CHOOSE(index_num,value1,value2,…)
    Chooses a value from a list of values.

COLUMN(reference)   Returns the column number of a reference.

COLUMNS(array)   Returns the number of columns in a reference.

HLOOKUP(lookup_value,table_array,row_index_num,…)
    Looks in the top row of a table and returns the value of the indicated cell.

INDEX(…)   Uses an index to choose a value from a reference or array.

INDIRECT(ref_text,a1)   Returns a reference indicated by a text value.

LOOKUP(…)   Looks up values in a vector or array.

MATCH(lookup_value,lookup_array,match_type)
    Looks up values in a reference or array.

OFFSET(reference,rows,cols,height,width)
    Returns a reference offset from a given reference.

ROW(reference)   Returns the row number of a reference.

ROWS(array)   Returns the number of rows in a reference.

TRANSPOSE(array)   Returns the transpose of an array.

VLOOKUP(lookup_value,table_array,col_index_num,…)
    Looks in the first column of a table and moves across the row to return the value of a cell.

Information Functions

CELL(info_type,reference)   Returns information about the formatting, location, or contents of a cell.

ERROR.TYPE(error_val)   Returns a number corresponding to an error value.

INFO(type_text)   Returns information about the current operating environment.

ISBLANK(value)   Returns TRUE if the value is blank.

ISERR(value)   Returns TRUE if the value is any error value except #N/A.

ISERROR(value)   Returns TRUE if the value is any error value.

ISLOGICAL(value)   Returns TRUE if the value is a logical value.

ISNA(value)   Returns TRUE if the value is the #N/A error value.

Appendix C

ISNONTEXT(value)	Returns TRUE if the value is not text.
ISNUMBER(value)	Returns TRUE if the value is a number.
ISREF(value)	Returns TRUE if the value is a reference.
ISTECT(value)	Returns TRUE if the value is text.
N(value)	Returns a value converted to a number.
NA()	Returns the error value #N/A.
TYPE(value)	Returns a number indicating the data type of a value.

Date & Time Functions

DATE(year,month,day)	Returns the serial number of a particular date.
DATEVALUE(date_text)	Converts a date in the form of text to a serial number.
DAY(serial_number)	Converts a serial number to a day of the month.
DAYS360(start_date,end_date,method)	Calculates the number of days between two dates based on a 360-day year.
HOUR(serial_number)	Converts a serial number to an hour.
MINUTE(serial_number)	Converts a serial number to a minute.
MONTH(serial_number)	Converts a serial number to a month.
NOW()	Returns the serial number of the current date and time.
SECOND(serial_number)	Converts a serial number to a second.
TIME(hour,minute,second)	Returns the serial number of a particular time.
TIMEVALUE(time_text)	Converts a time in the form of text to a serial number.
TODAY()	Returns the serial number of today's date.
WEEKDAY(serial_number,return_type)	Converts a serial number to a day of the week.
YEAR(serial_number)	Converts a serial number to a year.

Text Functions

CHAR(number)	Returns the character specified by the code number.
CLEAN(text)	Removes all nonprintable characters from text.
CODE(text)	Returns a numeric code for the first character in a text string.
CONCATENATE(text1,text2,...)	Joins several text items into one text item.
DOLLAR(number,decimals)	Converts a number to text, using currency format.
EXACT(text1,text2)	Checks to see if two text values are identical.

FIND(find_text,within_text,start_num)
: Finds one text value within another. This function is case-sensitive.

FIXED(number,decimals,no_commas)
: Formats a number as text with a fixed number of decimals.

LEFT(text,num_chars)
: Returns the leftmost characters from a text value.

LEN(text)
: Returns the number of characters in a text string.

LOWER(text)
: Converts text to lowercase.

MID(text,start_num,num_chars)
: Returns a specific number of characters from a text string.

PROPER(text)
: Capitalizes the first letter in each word of a text value.

REPLACE(old_text,start_num,num_chars,new_text)
: Replaces characters within text.

REPT(text,number_times)
: Repeats text a given number of times.

RIGHT(text,num_chars)
: Returns the rightmost characters from a text value.

SEARCH(find_text,within_text,start_num)
: Finds one text value within another. This function is not case-sensitive.

SUBSTITUTE(text,old_text,new_text,instance_num)
: Substitutes new text for old text in a text string.

T(value)
: Converts its arguments to text.

TEXT(value,format_text)
: Formats a number and converts it to text.

TRIM(text)
: Removes spaces from text.

UPPER(text)
: Converts text to uppercase.

VALUE(text)
: Converts a text argument to a number.

Database Functions

DAVERAGE(database,field,criteria)
: Returns the average of selected database entries.

DCOUNT(database,field,criteria)
: Counts the cells containing numbers from a specified database and criteria.

DCOUNTA(database,field,criteria)
: Counts nonblank cells from a specified database and criteria.

DGET(database,field,criteria)
: Extracts from a database a single record that matches the specified criteria.

DMAX(database,field,criteria)
: Returns the maximum value from selected database entries.

DMIN(database,field,criteria)
: Returns the minimum value from selected database entries.

DPRODUCT(database,field,criteria)
: Multiplies the values in a particular field of records that match the criteria in a database.

Appendix C

DSTDEV(database,field,criteria)	Estimates the standard deviation based on a sample of selected database entries.
DSTDEVP(database,field,criteria)	Calculates the standard deviation based on the entire population of selected database entries.
DSUM(database,field,criteria)	Adds the numbers in the field column of records in the database that match the criteria.
DVAR(database,field,criteria)	Estimates the variance based on a sample from selected database entries.
DVARP(database,field,criteria)	Calculates variance based on the entire population of selected database entries.

INDEX

Symbols & Numbers
101
#NAME? 67, 190
#NUM! 67, 69
#REF! 28, 29, 44, 193
1904 date system 80
3-D
    cell references 77, 84, 187, **193-197**, 199
    charts see *charts, 3-D*
3-D View command 152

A
ABS function 66
absolute cell reference 36, **37**, 78, 187, 191
accounting underline 93, **94**, 95
ACOS function 68
active cell 3, **16**, 17, 21
Add Report dialog box 207
Add View dialog box 205
add-ins **201-208**, 210
    installing 203
    removing 203
    using **204-208**
Add-Ins command 201, 203
Add-Ins dialog box 201, 202, 203
Advanced Filter command
    on the Filter submenu 181
Advanced Filter dialog box 181
Align Left button 7, 89
Align Right button 7, 89
alignment see *formatting, alignment*
Alignment tab
    of the Format Axis dialog box 144
    of the Format Cells dialog box 90, 91, 176
    of the Format Chart Title dialog box 141
    of the Format Data Labels dialog box 142
All command
    on Clear submenu 26, 115, 137, 139
amortization table 73
Apple menu 2, 123, 156
Application menu 14
Apply command
    on the Name submenu 191

Apply Names dialog box 191
Arc button 107, 108
argument **57**, **58**, 61
Arrange command 48
array **195**
Arrow button 107, 108
arrowheads **118**
As New Sheet command
    on Chart submenu 43, 126
ASIN function 68
ATAN function 68
AutoFill **34**
    creating custom lists 211, **217**
AutoFilter 178, **179-180**
AutoFilter command
    on the Filter submenu 179
AutoFit 102, **104**
AutoFit Selection command
    on Column submenu 104
    on Row submenu 104
AutoFormat
    for cells 85, **105**
    for charts **154**
AutoFormat command 105, 154
AutoFormat dialog box 105, 154
AutoSave 201, **204**
AutoSave command 204
AutoSave dialog boxes 204
AutoSum button 7, **63-64**
AVERAGE function **69**, 185
Axes command 139
Axes dialog box 139

B
Balloon Help 2, **12**
Balloon Help menu 10, 12
black and white printing 169
Bold button 6, 7, 93
borders see *formatting, borders*
Borders button 6, 7, 95, 96
Borders tab
    of the Format Cells dialog box 96
Bring to Front button 107, 121
Bring to Front command
    on Placement submenu 121

241

Index

button (in a dialog box) 9
buttons see *individual button names*

C

calculation 211, 214
Calculation tab
   of Options dialog box 216
Calculation tab
   of the Options dialog box 80
Cancel button
   in a dialog box 9
   in the formula bar 20, 24, 60
cell 13, **16**
   activating 16
   clearing contents 26
   copying 25, **30-33**, 35
   deleting 25, 26, 27, **29**
   deselecting 19
   editing 24, **25**, 37
   formatting see *formatting, cells*
   inserting 25, 27, **29**
   links to charts **130**
   moving 25, **38**
   names see *names*
   note 26, **106**, 169, 214
   range see *range*
   selecting 16
   selecting with names 192
   reference 3, 13, **16**, 22, 23, 24, 57, 58
cell address see *cell, reference*
cell gridlines
   displaying or hiding 211, 214
   printing 169
cell pointer **3**, 16, 32
   moving **16**
cell reference area 192
Cells command
   on Format menu 87, 90, 91, 94, 96, 98
   on Insert menu 27, 29
Center Across Columns button 7, 90
Center button 7, 89
centering a report on a page **161**
chart sheet **41**, 125
   inserting **43**
Chart submenu 43, 126
Chart tab
   of Page Setup dialog box 158, 160
Chart toolbar 7, **135**, 139, 140, 153, **230**
Chart Type button 135, 153
Chart Type command 153
Chart Type dialog box 153

charts **125**
   3-D 125, 135
   activating 131, **136**
   adding a legend **139**
   adding data **132**, **133**
   adding data labels **138**
   adding or removing axes **139**
   adding or removing data **131**
   adding or removing gridlines **140**
   adding titles **137**
   area **148**
   axes 135, **139**, 144-146
   changing type **153**
   data labels 135, **138**, 142
   data point 135, **150**
   data series 138, **150**
   deactivating **136**
   deleting 129
   editing **135-140**
   editing titles **137**
   embedded 125, 129, 131, 133, 136
   embedding in a worksheet **126**
   exploding pie **151**
   creating **125-134**
   formatting see *formatting, charts*
   gridlines 135, **140**
   legend 135, 138, 139, 142
   links to worksheets **130**
   moving items 135, **152**
   plot area **149**
   removing data **134**
   removing data labels **138**
   removing titles **137**
   rotating **152**
   scale 146
   selecting items **136**
   selection handles 129
   tick marks 135, 145
   titles 135, 137
   walls **149**
ChartWizard 43, 125
   for adding or removing chart data **131**, 133
   using **127-129**
ChartWizard button 7, 126, 135
ChartWizard dialog box 126, 127-128, 131
check box **8**
Chooser 155, **156-157**
Claris FileMaker Pro 54
Clear submenu 26, 100, 115, 134, 137, 139
clicking **4**
Clipboard 31, 123, 195
close box **3**, 55
Close command 55

Color button   7, 97
column   3, 13
    changing width   21, 85, 91, **101-104**, 171
    deleting   25, 27, **28**, 103
    hiding   101, 103
    inserting   25, **27**
    selecting   **18**, 102
    unhiding   103
Column command   27
column headings   **3**, 18, 102
    displaying or hiding   211, 214
    printing   169
Column submenu   103, 104
Column Width dialog box   103
Comma Style button   7, 86
Command key   4, 6
commands   see *individual command names*
CONCATENATE function   **83**
Consolidate command   198, 200
Consolidate dialog box   198-199, 200
consolidations   187, **198-200**
Contents command
    on Clear submenu   26
Copy button   7, 31, 100, 114, 132, 195
Copy command   30, 31, 35, 100, 114, 132, 133, 195
COS function   **68**
COUNT function   **70**, 185
COUNTA function   **70**, 185
COUNTBLANK function   58, **79**
Create Button button   107
Create command
    on the Name submenu   189
Create Names dialog box   189
Create New dialog box   124
criteria range   see *range, criteria*
Crosstab sheet function   201
Currency Style button   7, 86
Custom AutoFilter dialog box   180
customization   **211-222**
    calculation options   216
    editing options   213
    general options   212
    list options   217
    of toolbars   218-222
    view options   214-215
Customize dialog box   220, 221
Cut button   7, 38, 114
Cut command   38, 114

D

data form   176-178
    for browsing records   **177**
    for deleting data   **177**
    for editing data   **177**
    for entering data   **177**
    for finding records   **178**
Data Labels command   138
Data Labels dialog box   138
Data menu   176, 177, 178, 179, 181, 182, 184, 185, 198, 200
database   **175-186**
    field   **175**
    creating   **176**
    criteria   178, 179, 180
    record   **175**
Database functions   **186**, 239-240
Date & Time functions   **80-81**, 238
Date button   166
DATE function   58, **80**, 81
DAVERAGE function   **186**
DAY function   **81**
DB function   **71**
DCOUNT function   **186**
DCOUNTA function   **186**
DDB function   **71**
Decrease Decimal button   7, 86
default
    chart type   153
    font   **92**, 94, 100, 211, 212
Default Chart button   135, 153
Define command
    on Name submenu   188, 189
Define Name dialog box   188, 189
DEGREES function   **68**
Delete command   28, 29
Delete dialog box   28, 29
Delete Sheet command   44
dialog box   4, **8**
dialog sheet   41
DMAX function   **186**
DMIN function   **186**
DOLLAR function   **83**
double-clicking   **4**
Down command
    on Fill submenu   33
drag and drop
    enabling/disabling   213
    to add chart data   **133**
    to copy cells   **39**
    to copy objects   114

Index

to insert cells **39**
to move cells **39**
to move objects **114**
dragging **4**
Drawing button 7, 107
Drawing Selection button 107, 112, 113
Drawing toolbar **107**, 108, 109, 110, 111, 112, 113, 116, 120, 121, 122, **230**
drop shadow border 119
Drop Shadow button 107
DSUM function **186**

E

edit box **8**
Edit menu 16, 17, 26, 28, 29, 30, 31, 33, 34, 38, 40, 44, 46, 100, 114, 115, 123, 130, 132, 133, 137, 139, 183, 192, 195
Edit tab
  of Options dialog box 213
Ellipse button 107, 109
Enter button (on formula bar) 20, 21, 23, 24, 59, 63, 72, 74, 137, 190, 194, 196, 197
error values see *individual error value names*
  as function argument 58
EVEN function **66**
Excel
  application icon 14
  document icon 14
  launching 14
Excel Help see *help*

F

FALSE 76, 77
file see *workbook*
file formats **54**
File menu 10, 14, 15, 53, 55, 56, 158, 160, 161, 164, 165, 166, 167, 168, 170, 172, 173, 174, 207, 208
Filename button 166
Fill command 30, **33**, 35
fill handle 30, **32**, 35
  using to copy cells **32**
  using to create a series **34**
Fill submenu 33, 34
Filled Arc button 107, 111
Filled Ellipse button 107, 111
Filled Freeform button 107, 111
Filled Rectangle button 107, 111
filter 175, 179, 180
Filter submenu 179, 181
Financial functions 71-75, **236**

Find File command 56
Find File dialog box 56
floating text 148
Font box 7, 92
Font button 166
Font Color button 7, 94
font formatting see *formatting, fonts*
Font Size box 7, 93
Font tab
  of the Format Axis dialog box 144
  of the Format Cells dialog box 94, 96
  of the Format Chart Area dialog box 148
  of the Format Chart Title dialog box 141
  of the Format Data Labels dialog box 142
  of the Format Legend dialog box 143
footer 155, 158, **164**
  codes 166
  setting location 158, 161, **164**, 171
  specifying contents 158, **165-166**
Form command 176, 177, 178
Format 3-D View dialog box 152
Format Axis dialog box 144, 145, 146, 147
Format Axis Title dialog box 141
Format Cells dialog box 86, 87, 88, 89, 90, 91, 92, 94, 95, 96, 97, 98
Format Chart Area dialog box 148
Format Chart Title dialog box 141
Format Chart Walls dialog box 149
Format Data Labels dialog box 142
Format Data Point dialog box 150, 151
Format Data Series dialog box 150
Format Gridlines dialog box 147
Format Legend dialog box 143
Format menu 44, 45, 87, 90, 91, 94, 96, 98, 100, 101, 103, 104, 105, 117, 118, 119, 120, 121, 141, 142, 143, 144, 145, 146, 147, 148, 149, 150, 151, 152, 153, 154
Format Object dialog box 117, 118, 119, 120, 122
Format Painter button 7, 99
Format Plot Area dialog box 149
Formats command
  on Clear submenu 26, 100
formatting
  alignment 21, 85, **89-91**, 141
  arrowheads **118**
  axes **144-146**
  borders 85, 93, **95-96**
  cell color **97-98**
  cells 26, 30, 38, 80, **85-106**
  charts 129, 135, **141-154**

chart area **148**
chart walls **149**
clearing **100**
column width see *column, changing width*
copying **99-100**
databases 176
data labels **142**
data series and points **150-151**
fill color 111, **120**
fonts 85, **92-94**, 141
gridlines 140
legends **143**
lines **117**
markers **150**
numbers 20, 85, **86-88**, 101
object borders **119**
object patterns **120**
objects 111, **117-120**
patterns 85, **97-98**, 141
plot area **149**
row height see *row, changing height*
scale **146**
shading **97-98**
tick marks **145**
titles **141**
Formatting toolbar 7, 86, 89, 90, 92, 93, 94, 95, 96, 97, 141, 142, 143, 144, **229**
formula **13**, **22**
  as function argument 58
  calculating **22**
  copying 30, **35**, 187
  displaying 214
  entering **20**, **23-24**, 187
  in databases 176
  with absolute cell reference **37**, 187
  with cell references 22
  with names 190
formula bar **3**, 20, 21, 23, 24, 59, 60, 61, 62, 63, 72, 74, 102, 137, 148, 190, 192, 194, 196, 197, 214
  activating 20
  deactivating 20
Freeform button 107, 110
Freehand button 107, 108
function see also *individual function names*
  13, 22, **57**, 186
  as function argument 58
  entering **59-62**, 187
  in consolidation 198, 200
  in subtotal 184
  nested 59, 62
Function button (on Formula bar) 61, 62
Function command 61
function name 57

Function Wizard **61-62**, 72, 74, 186, **190**, 196
Function Wizard button 7, 61
Function Wizard dialog boxes 61
Function Wizard [Nested] dialog box 62
FV Function 75

G

General alignment **89**, 100
General format **86**, 100
General tab
  of the Options dialog box 53, 165, **212**
Go To command 16, 17, 192
Go To dialog box 16, 17, 192
graphics see also *objects* **123**
Gridlines command 140
Gridlines dialog box 140
Group and Outline submenu 185
Group Objects button 107, 113
Guide Help menu 10

H

header 155, 158, **164**
  codes 166
  setting location 158, 161, **164**, 171
  specifying contents 158, **165-166**
header row 182, 183
Header/Footer tab
  of Page Setup dialog box 158, 165, 166
Height command
  on Row submenu 103
help
  browsing **10**
  context-sensitive **12**, 84
  online 2
  searching **11**, 84
Help button 7, 11, 12, 84
Help button (in a dialog box) 9, 12
Help History window 10
Hide Balloons command 12
Hide command 45, 49
Hide command
  on Column submenu 103
  on Row submenu 103
  on Sheet submenu 45
HLOOKUP **77**, 78
Horizontal Gridlines button 135, 140

I

I-beam pointer 25

Index

IF function 58, **76**, 79
Increase Decimal button 7, 86
Info window 214
Information Functions 79, **237**
Insert dialog box 27, 29
Insert menu 27, 29, 43, 61, 106, 124, 126, 137, 138, 139, 140, 162, 163, 188, 189, 190, 191, 194
installation
    adding add-ins **202**
    typical 201
INT function 66
IRR Function 75
IS functions 79
ISBLANK function 79
ISERR function 79
ISERROR function 79
ISLOGICAL function 79
ISNA function 79
ISNONTEXT function 79
ISNUMBER function 79
ISREF function 79
ISTEXT function 79
Italic button 7, 93

L

large buttons 218
Left command
    on Fill submenu 33
LEFT function 82
Legend button 135, 139
Legend command 139
Line button 107, 108
links see *3-D cell references*
list see *database*
loan payments, calculating **72**
Logical Functions **76, 236**
logical values see *individual logical value names*
    as function argument 58
Lookup & Reference functions **77-78, 237**
Lotus 1-2-3 file formats 54
LOWER function 82

M

Macintosh Help menu 10, 12
Macro command 210
Macro dialog box 210
macros **209-210**
Maintenance Installation window 202

margins 155, 158
    setting **161**, 164, 171
Margins tab
    of Page Setup dialog box 158, 161, 164
marquee 31, 38, 63, 99, 126
Math & Trigonometry functions **63-68, 231-232**
MAX function **69**, 185
MEDIAN function **69**
menu bar 2
menus **4**
    using **5**
Microsoft ClipArt **124**
Microsoft Excel 4.0 international macro sheet 41
Microsoft Excel 4.0 macro sheet 41
Microsoft Excel command 14
Microsoft Excel Help command 10
Microsoft Excel Setup 201, **202**
Microsoft Excel Workbook file format 54
Microsoft Office Manager **2**, 14
Microsoft Word 54
MID function **82**
MIN function **69**, 185
mixed reference **37**
MODE function **69**
MONTH function **81**
mouse pointer **3**
mouse, using **4**
Move or Copy dialog box 46
Move or Copy Sheet 46
moveable palette **6**
MS Excel Help window 10, 11, 12

N

Name submenu 188, 189, 190, 191, 194
names 84, 187, **188**
    creating **189**
    defining **188**
    deleting **189**
    using for 3-D references 193, **194**
    using in a formula **190**, 193
networks
    and printing 157
New command 14
New Data command 133
New Window command 47
New Workbook button 7, 14
note see *cell note*
Note command 106
Note dialog box 106

Notes command
    on Clear submenu   26
NOW function   **81**
number format codes   **88**
number formatting   see *formatting, numbers*
Number tab
    of the Format Axis dialog box   144
    of the Format Cells dialog box   87, 88
    of the Format Data Labels dialog box   142

O

Object command
    on the Format menu   117, 118, 119, 120
    on the Insert menu   124
objects   **108**
    copying   **114**, 213
    cutting   213
    deleting   **115**
    display options   214
    drawing   **107-110**
    embedded   **124**
    formatting   see *formatting, objects*
    grouping   **113**, 121
    modifying   112
    moving   **114**
    reshaping   **116**
    resizing   **115**, 129
    selecting   **112-113**
    selection handles   109, **112**, 113
    sorting   213
    ungrouping   **113**
ODD function   **66**
OK button   9
On This Sheet command
    on the Chart submenu   126
Open button   7, 15
Open command   15
Open dialog box   9, **15**
operators   13, **22**, 57, **83**, **178**
Options command   53, 80, 165, 212, 213, 214, 215, 216, 217
Options dialog box   53, 80, 165, 212, 213, 214, 215, 216, 217
orientation   155, 158
    setting   **159**
orientation
    cell contents   91
outline   184, **185**, 199, 214

P

Page Break command   162

page breaks   155
    automatic   162, 214
    automatic vs. manual   **163**
    inserting   **162**
    removing   **163**
Page Number button   166
page order   155, 158, 169
Page Setup command   159, 160, 161, 164, 165, 166, 167, 168
Page Setup dialog box
    Apple standard   158, 159, 160
    Excel   155, **158**, 159, 160, 161, 162, 164, 165, 166, 167, 168, 169, 170, 171, 174, 207
Page tab
    of Page Setup dialog box   158, 159, 160, 162
pane   **51**
paper size   155, 158
    setting   **159**
Paste button   7, 31, 38, 114, 123, 132
Paste command
    on the Edit menu   30, 31, 35, 38, 114, 123, 132, 133
    on the Name submenu   190, 194
Paste Name dialog box   190
Paste Special command   30, 100, 132, 193, 195
Paste Special dialog box   99, 100, 193
Pattern button   107, 120
patterns   see *formatting, patterns*
Patterns tab
    of the Format Axis dialog box   144, 145
    of the Format Cells dialog box   98
    of the Format Chart Area dialog box   148
    of the Format Chart Title dialog box   141
    of the Format Data Labels dialog box   142
    of the Format Data Point dialog box   151
    of the Format Data Series dialog box   150
    of the Format Gridlines dialog box   147
    of the Format Legend dialog box   143
    of the Format Object dialog box   117, 118, 119, 120
Percent Style button   7, 86
PI function   **67**
pie chart   133
Placement submenu   121
Placement tab
    of the Format Legend dialog box   143
PMT function   **72**, 74
pointing   **4**
polygon   **116**

247

Index

pop-up menu 9
preview area (in a dialog box) 9
print area 167, 174
Print button 7, 174
Print command 6, 155, 167, 172, 173, 174
Print dialog box 167, 170, 172, 173, 174
    for Report Manager 208
Print Preview 155, **170**
    for changing page setup options **171**
    window 161, 170, 174
Print Preview button 7, 170
Print Preview command 170
print quality 158, 169
Print Report command 207, 208
Print Report dialog box 207, 208
print scaling 155, 158
    reducing or enlarging a report or chart **160**
print titles 168
Print Topic command 10
printer 156, 157, 164
printing **155-174**
PRODUCT function **65**, 185
PROPER function **82**
PV Function **75**

Q

QuickDraw GX **155**
    choosing a printer **157**
    printing **173**
    setting paper size **159**
Quit command 6

R

RADIANS function **68**
radio button **8**
RAM see *random access memory*
RAND function **67**
random access memory 52, 203
range **17**
    criteria 181
    deselecting **19**
    names see *names*
    reference 17, 22, 23, 24
    selecting **17**, **19**
    selecting with names **192**
Record Macro submenu 209
Record New Macro command
    on Record Macro submenu 209
Record New Macro dialog box 209
Rectangle button 107, 109

Redo command 40
relative cell reference 30, **36**, 187, 191
Remove Page Break command 163
Remove Split command 51
Rename command
    on Sheet submenu 44
Rename Sheet dialog box 44
Repeat button 7, 40
Repeat command 40
Report Manager 201, **207-208**
Reshape button 107, 116
Right command
    on Fill submenu 33
RIGHT function **82**
round corners 119
ROUND function 58, **65**, 73, 86
ROUNDDOWN function **65**
ROUNDUP function **65**
row 3, 13
    changing height 85, 91, **101-104**
    deleting 25, 27, **28**, 103
    hiding 101, 103
    inserting 25, **27**
    selecting **18**, 102
    unhiding 103
Row command 27
row headings **3**, 18, 102
    displaying or hiding 211, 214
    printing 169
Row Height dialog box 103
Row submenu 103, 104

S

Save As command 52, 54, **55**
Save As dialog box 52, 54, 55
Save button 7, 52, 54
Save command 6, 52, 54, **55**
savings contributions, calculating **74**
Scale tab
    of the Format Axis dialog box 144, 146
    of the Format Gridlines dialog box 147
Scenarios command 207
scientific notation 86
Scrapbook 123
scroll bar
    in data form **177**
    in worksheet window **3**, 16, 19, 42, 51, 214
scrolling list **8**
Search dialog box 56
Select All button 18

248

Selected Axis command 144, 145, 146
Selected Axis Title command 141
Selected Chart Area command 148
Selected Chart Title command 141
Selected Data Labels command 142
Selected Data Point command 151
Selected Data Series command 150
Selected Gridlines command 147
Selected Legend command 143
Selected Plot Area command 149
Selected Walls command 149
selection handles see *object, selection handles* or *chart, selection handles*
Send to Back button 107, 121
Send to Back command
   on Placement submenu 121
series 30, **34**
Series command
   on the Clear submenu 134
   on the Fill submenu 34, 217
Series dialog box 34
SERIES function 130
Setup window 202
sheet **41**
   changing order in a workbook 46
   copying 46
   deleting 44
   hiding 45
   moving 46
   renaming 44
   selecting multiple **42**
   switching **42**
   unhiding **45**
Sheet Name button 166
Sheet submenu 44, 45
Sheet tab
   of Page Setup dialog box 158, 167, 168, 169
sheet tabs **3**, 42, 44, 174, 214
shift-click **17**
shortcut keys 4, **6**, **223-228**
   for Application menu commands **226**
   for cell pointer movement **227**
   for cell selection **227**
   for data entry **228**
   for Data menu commands **226**
   for Edit menu commands **224**
   for File menu commands **223**
   for Format menu commands **225**
   for Help commands **226**
   for Insert menu commands **224**
   for Tools menu commands **226**

   for using dialog boxes **228**
   for using edit boxes **228**
   for View menu commands **224**
   for Window menu commands **226**
   modifier keys **223**
shortcut menu **5**, 218
Show All command
   on the Filter submenu 179
Show Balloons command 12
SIN function **68**
size box **3**
SLN function **71**
Sort Ascending button 7, 182
Sort command 182
Sort Descending button 7, 182
Sort dialog box 182, 183
sorting 175, **182**
Spelling button 7
split bar 51
Split command 51
SQRT function **67**
stacking order **121**
Standard toolbar **7**, 11, 12, 14, 15, 31, 38, 40, 50, 61, 63, 84, 99, 100, 107, 114, 122, 123, 126, 130, 132, 170, 174, 182, 183, 195, **229**
Statistical Functions **69-70**, **233-235**
status bar **3**, 12, 20, 171, 214, 216
STDEV function **70**, 185
STDEVP function **70**, 185
Stop Macro button 209
Stop toolbar 209
Style command 100
submenu **4**, 5
SUBTOTAL function **184**, 185, 186
subtotals 175, 183, **184**
Subtotals command 184
SUM function 35, 57, 58, **63**, 185, 196
Summary Info command 53
Summary Info dialog box 53
summary information **53**, 212
SYD function **71**

T

tab (in a dialog box) **8**
tab scrolling buttons (for sheet tabs) 42
tab split box (for sheet tabs) 42
TAN function **68**
Template file format 54
Text (Tab Delimited) file format 54

249

Index

text box **122**
Text Box button 7, 107, **122**
Text file format 54
Text functions **82-83, 238-239**
Time button 166
Tip Wizard button 7
title bar **3**, 62
Titles command 137
Titles dialog box 137
TODAY function **81**
toolbar 2, 7, **218**
   anchored see *toolbar, docked*
   buttons see *individual button names*
   creating **221**
   customizing 211, **220**
   deleting **222**
   docked 107, **219**
   floating 107, 218, **219**
   hiding **218**
   moving **219**
   resetting **221**
   resizing **219**
   showing **218**
   using buttons **6**
   tearing off button menus **6**
toolbars see *individual toolbar names*
Toolbars command 218, 220, 221, 222
Toolbars dialog box 218, 220, 221, 222
Toolbars shortcut menu 218
Tools menu 53, 80, 165, 201, 203, 204, 207, 209, 210, 212, 213, 214, 215, 216, 217
ToolTip **6**, 218
Total Pages button 166
TRUE 76, 77

U

Underline button 7, 93
Undo button 7, 40, 130, 183
Undo command 25, 40, 44, 130, 183
Ungroup Objects button 107, 113
Unhide command
   on Column submenu 103
   on Row submenu 103
   on Sheet submenu 45
   on Window menu 45, 49
Up command
   on Fill submenu 33
UPPER function **82**
user name 211, 212

V

value 13, **21**, 22
   entering **20-21**
VAR function 185
VARP function 185
vertices **116**
view **205**
View Manager 201, **205-206**, 207
View Manager command 205, 206
View Manager dialog box 205, 206
View menu 50, 205, 206, 218, 220, 221, 222
View tab
   of Options dialog box 214
Visual Basic module **41**, 209, 210
   inserting **43**, 210
Visual Basic toolbar 43
VLOOKUP **77-78**

W

WEEKDAY function **81**
Width command
   on Column submenu 103
wildcard characters **178**
window
   activating **47**
   arranging **48**
   closing all at once **55**
   creating **47**
   gridlines 211
   hiding **49**
   list on Window menu 47
   removing splits **51**
   resizing panes **51**
   splitting into panes **51**
   unhiding **49**
   zooming the view **50**
Window menu 45, 47, 48, 49, 51
workbook 3, **41**
   closing **55**
   creating **14**, 46, 47
   default number of sheets 41, 212
   finding **56**
   opening **15**
   recently opened 15, 211, 212
   saving **52**
   windows see *window*
   with links, opening 197
worksheet see also *sheet* 13, **41**
   basics **13-24**
   editing **25-40**
   inserting **43**

    links to charts **130**
    selecting **18**
    with links, opening 197
Worksheet command 43
worksheet window see also *window* **3**
wrap text **91**, 104

Y

YEAR function **81**

Z

zero values 214
zoom box **3**, 48
Zoom command 50
Zoom Control box **7**, 50
Zoom dialog box 50

More from Peachpit Press

Camera Ready with QuarkXPress
Cyndie Klopfenstein

A practical guide to creating direct-to-press documents using XPress. Includes a disk full of QuarkXPress templates that you can use to create postcards, brochures and other common documents.
$35 *(206 pages)*

Desktop Publisher's Survival Kit
David Blatner

Here is a book that provides insights into desktop publishing on the Macintosh: troubleshooting print jobs, working with color, scanning, and selecting fonts. A disk containing 12 top desktop publishing utilities, 400K of clip art, and two fonts is included in this package.
$22.95 *(176 pages)*

Everyone's Guide to Successful Publications
Elizabeth Adler

This comprehensive reference book pulls together all the information essential to developing and producing printed materials that will get your message across. Packed with ideas, practical advice, examples, and hundreds of photographs and illustrations, it discusses planning the printed piece, writing, design, desktop publishing, preparation for printing, and distribution.
$28 *(412 pages)*

Four Colors/One Image
Mattias Nyman

Find step-by-step procedures and detailed explanations on how to reproduce and manipulate color images using Photoshop, QuarkXPress and Cachet. A terrific, invaluable resource for those who need high-quality color output.
$18 *(84 pages)*

How to Boss Your Fonts Around
Robin Williams

Ever had a power struggle with your fonts? This book will put *you* in control and answer all your Macintosh font questions. What is a screen font, an outline font, a resident font, a downloadable font? What is ATM? How do you install fonts, use Suitcase or MasterJuggler, avoid font ID conflicts and make sure your fonts print at a service bureau? Written in a friendly style by the author of the bestselling *The Little Mac Book*.
$12.95 *(120 pages)*

The Illustrator 5.0/5.5 Book
Deke McClelland

Experienced Illustrator users and novices alike will learn many helpful tips and techniques. Very thorough and comprehensive, *The Illustrator 5.0/5.5 Book* gives in-depth coverage of Illustrator's latest features. $29.95 *(660 pages)*

More from Peachpit Press

Illustrator Illuminated, 2nd Edition

Clay Andres

Illustrator Illuminated uses full-color graphics to show how professional artists use Illustrator's tools to create a variety of styles and effects. Each chapter shows the creation of a specific illustration from concept through completion. Additionally, it covers using Illustrator in conjunction with Adobe Streamline and Photoshop. $24.95 *(200 pages)*

Jargon: An Informal Dictionary of Computer Terms

Robin Williams with Steve Cummings

Finally! A book that explains over 1,200 of the most useful computer terms in a way that readers can understand. This book is a straightforward guide that not only defines computer-related terms but also explains how and why they are used. It covers both the Macintosh and PC worlds. No need to ask embarrassing questions: Just look it up in *Jargon!* $22 *(688 pages)*

The Little Mac Book, 4th Edition

Robin Williams

Praised by scores of magazines and user group newsletters, this concise, beautifully written book covers the basics of Macintosh operation. It provides useful reference information, including charts of typefaces, special characters, and keyboard shortcuts. This fourth edition is totally updated and cooler than ever. $17.95 *(408 pages)*

The Macintosh Bible, 5th Edition

Edited by Darcy DiNucci

This classic reference book is now completely updated. *The Macintosh Bible, 5th Edition* is crammed with tips, tricks, and shortcuts that will help you to get the most out of your Mac. $30 *(1,100 pages)*

The Macintosh Bible "What Do I Do Now?" Book, 3rd Edition

Charles Rubin

Completely updated, this bestseller covers just about every sort of basic problem a Mac user can encounter. The book shows the error message exactly as it appears on screen, explains the problem (or problems) that can produce the message, and discusses what to do. This book is geared for beginners and experienced users alike. $22 *(352 pages)*

PageMaker 5 for Macintosh: Visual QuickStart Guide

Webster and Associates

Here's an ideal book for new users and for those who want to use the latest features of PageMaker 5. Learn about many powerful innovations through an easy, right-brained approach that shows you how to get the most out of PageMaker. $13.95 *(234 pages)*

More from Peachpit Press

Photoshop 3 for Macintosh: Visual QuickStart Guide

Elaine Weinmann and Peter Lourekas

Completely revised for Photoshop 3, this indispensable guide is for Mac users who want to get started in Adobe Photoshop but don't like to read long explanations. QuickStart books focus on illustrated, step-by-step examples that cover how to use masks, filters, colors, and more. $19.95 *(264 pages)*

The Photoshop 3 Wow! Book (Mac Edition)

Linnea Dayton and Jack Davis

This book is really two books in one: an easy-to-follow, step-by-step tutorial of Photoshop fundamentals and over 150 pages of tips and techniques for getting the most out of Photoshop version 3. Full color throughout, *The Photoshop Wow! Book* shows how professional artists make the best use of Photoshop. Includes a CD-ROM containing Photoshop filters and utilities. $39.95
(208 pages, includes CD-ROM, available Fall 1995)

ZAP! How your computer can hurt you—and what you can do about it

Don Sellers

This unusual resource book covers everything from eyestrain to pregnancy to carpal tunnel and back problems. *ZAP!* will help you work smarter—and healthier. $12.95 *(150 pages)*

QuarkXPress 3.3 for Macintosh: Visual QuickStart Guide

Elaine Weinmann

Winner of the 1992 Benjamin Franklin Award, this book is a terrific way to get introduced to QuarkXPress in just a couple of hours. Lots of illustrations and screen shots make each feature of the program absolutely clear. This book is helpful to both beginners and intermediate QuarkXPress users.
$15.95 *(240 pages)*

QuarkXPress Tips & Tricks, 2nd Edition

David Blatner and Eric Taub

The smartest, most useful shortcuts from *The QuarkXPress Book*—plus many more—are packed into this book. You'll find answers to common questions as well as insights on techniques that will show you how to become a QuarkXPress power user. Includes a CD-ROM with useful XTensions and demos. $21.95
(286 pages, includes CD-ROM)

Order Form

800-283-9444 • 510-548-4393 • FAX 510-548-5991 • CANADA 510-548-5991

Qty	Title	Price	Total

SUBTOTAL	
ADD APPLICABLE SALES TAX	
SHIPPING	
TOTAL	

Shipping is by UPS ground: $4 for first item, $1 each add'l.

Customer Information

NAME

COMPANY

STREET ADDRESS

CITY   STATE   ZIP

PHONE (   )   FAX (   )

Payment Method

❏ CHECK ENCLOSED   ❏ VISA   ❏ MASTERCARD

CREDIT CARD #   EXPIRATION DATE

COMPANY PURCHASE ORDER #

Tell Us What You Think

PLEASE TELL US WHAT YOU THOUGHT OF THIS BOOK:

WHAT OTHER BOOKS WOULD YOU LIKE US TO PUBLISH?

MAC   PEACHPIT PRESS • 2414 Sixth Street • Berkeley, CA 94710